There Was a Man ...

There Was a Man ...

who carried Jesus' cross
through a nine-month
cancer battle

"Finished Well"
"Found Faithful"

By Eric Heerwagen

with Sally Heerwagen

XULON PRESS

Xulon Press
2301 Lucien Way #415
Maitland, FL 32751
407.339.4217
www.xulonpress.com

Printed in the United States of America.

ISBN-13: 978-1-5456-7980-7

"There Was a Man"

The Crucifixion:

*"There was a man
walking by, coming from work,
Simon from Cyrene,
the father of Alexander and Rufus.
They made him carry Jesus' cross."*

Mark 15:21
(The Message)

"I love it when I read the Bible and new insights
pop off the page. The Word of God is like that ...
it speaks to me right where I am ... some days more
than others. Last night as I was thinking about Easter
weekend, I turned to Mark 15. Two things popped off
the page for me – encouragement to be a great father,
and perspective on my suffering.

Written by
Eric Heerwagen
seven months into the battle.

[Read full context in the entry on Good Friday, April 6, 2012.]

"There Was a Man"
includes:

JOURNAL ENTRIES – Eric wrote often, sometimes daily, in "CaringBridge" (see below) to keep family, friends, and others up to date on how God was guiding, teaching, and carrying him through this cancer battle. Occasionally entries were written by his wife Tammy.

RESPONSES – These are just a few of the messages, or excerpts from messages, written into the CaringBridge Guestbook by family members, friends, and friends of friends, from around the world. Countless others did not write in, but followed along.

~ From October 2011 through June 2012 ~
Eric's site was viewed more than 50,000 times,
and the Guestbook contained over 2,200 responses.

PHOTOS – with captions

MEDICAL NOTATIONS – (*Inserted in italics*)

FOREWORD, PULLOUTS, and **EDITOR'S NOTES**
were written by Eric's mother, Sally Heerwagen.

[Eric and Tammy's home church,
Village Baptist Church in Beaverton, Ore.,
is often written simply as "Village."]

[CaringBridge is a safe, personal, non-profit, protected
website where people can tell their health story.
It provides a simple way to connect with family and
friends, and a way for them to respond to the writer.]

Contents

(A bookmark for you.)

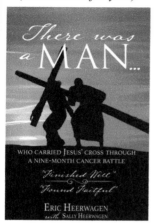

*"The righteous flourish
like the palm tree and grow
like a cedar in Lebanon.
They are planted in the
house of the Lord; they
flourish in the courts of
our God. They still bear
fruit in old age; they are
ever full of sap and green,
to declare that the Lord is
upright; he is my rock, and
there is no unrighteousness
in him."* Psalm 92:12-15

**Be encouraged,
keep trusting and loving
God — no matter what!**

(A bookmark for a friend.)

*"The righteous flourish
like the palm tree and grow
like a cedar in Lebanon.
They are planted in the
house of the Lord; they
flourish in the courts of
our God. They still bear
fruit in old age; they are
ever full of sap and green,
to declare that the Lord is
upright; he is my rock, and
there is no unrighteousness
in him."* Psalm 92:12-15

**Be encouraged,
keep trusting and loving
God — no matter what!**

To purchase additional books:

Bound book — $17.99
Available at: Amazon or Barnes and Noble Online *(search for author Eric Heerwagen)*
Contact Sally Heerwagen — *artsallyheer@gmail.com*
eBook — $8.99
Available at: Amazon.com (Kindle); BarnesandNoble.com (Nook); and Apple iBooks

"Many will see and fear the Lord and put their trust in him." Psalm 40:3b

To purchase additional books:

Bound book — $17.99
Available at: Amazon or Barnes and Noble Online *(search for author Eric Heerwagen)*
Contact Sally Heerwagen — *artsallyheer@gmail.com*
eBook — $8.99
Available at: Amazon.com (Kindle); BarnesandNoble.com (Nook); and Apple iBooks

"Many will see and fear the Lord and put their trust in him." Psalm 40:3b

Dedication

From a Mother's Heart

Dear Reader,

Thinking back over countless shared times with my younger son Eric, even from before he was born and through all the years since, I know the prayers of this mother's heart – that this precious child might become a man mightily used by God – were heard.

You'll see in the following pages that Eric was a dearly-loved baby, a tender-hearted little boy, a focused and talented teenager, an amazing college student; a good friend, a hard-working young man; a servant leader, a loving brother, son, grandson, and uncle; a cherished husband, an established and respected leader, a deeply caring father; and a man of great integrity.

He was a man who had grown up facing facts, asking for God's guidance, choosing to trust God no matter what, and being thankful.

He was a man who – above all – loved God.

*"The righteous flourish like the palm tree
and grow like a cedar in Lebanon. They are
planted in the house of the Lord; they flourish in the
courts of our God. They still bear fruit in old age;
they are ever full of sap and green, to declare
that the Lord is upright; he is my rock,
and there is no unrighteousness in him."*

Psalm 92:12-15   Eric's life verse]

Foreword
Before There Was A Man ...

By Sally Heerwagen, Eric's mother

THERE WAS A BABY:

In 1971, while living in Missouri, our family of five – dad Art, 31, mom Sally, 29, son Brian, 8, and daughters Kristi, 7, and Cyndi, 6, had each accepted Jesus Christ as Savior and Lord.

Four years later, in 1975, we relocated to Burns, Ore., a small, high-desert town in Eastern Oregon, where we owned and operated "The Burns Times-Herald," the local weekly newspaper.

That was the same year, our family received our earliest and best Christmas present ever! On Nov. 14, a precious little boy, Eric Martin Heerwagen, was born into our now-Christian family.

Times-Herald Hires New Employee

A new staff member was employed at the Times-Herald last week, publishers Mr. and Mrs. Art Heerwagen are pleased to announce.

He is Eric Martin Heerwagen, who was officially hired at 3:54 p.m., November 14, at Harney County Hospital, Burns, Oregon.

Eric first contacted the Times-Herald for employment about nine months ago. "We didn't have any openings on our staff at that time," Heerwagen said, "but felt that we could use Eric a little later in the year, so Sally and I got busy and created a new position."

The first interview with Eric actually began at 4:30 a.m. on November 14, with official employment beginning 12 hours later.

"I was convinced that we had a winner the first week we knew about Eric last spring," said Mrs. Heerwagen, "but Art wasn't convinced until Dr. Frank Sykes, who was present at the final interview, told him everything was going to work out fine."

The new employee weighs six pounds 6½ ounces and is 18½ inches tall. He has blue eyes and blonde hair. Eric is a recent graduate of Stork University located in Heaven. References furnished by Eric included Mr. and Mrs. Oscar Heerwagen of Scottsdale, Arizona and Mr. and Mrs. Jack Goldsmith of Denver, Colorado.

The new staff member can be located at P.O. Box 473, Burns, Oregon 97720. His home address is Box 333 Hines, Oregon.

Eric's birth made front page news.

As Eric's mom, I treasured the times when I held my tiny baby boy close, sitting in a rocking chair softly singing Christmas carols.

I couldn't help thinking about Mary and her tiny baby boy Jesus, and I prayed my baby boy would grow into a man used mightily by God.

From the very beginning, Eric was amazingly cheerful, always waking up with a smile, even when in pain from recurring ear infections.

Eric also was determined. Shortly after he started eating solid food, he decided he didn't want anyone to feed

Left to right: **Brian, 12, Kristi, 11, Cyndi, 10, and baby Eric.**

him; for several days all his solid-food meals were Cheerios – he could pick them up in his tiny, sticky fingers and feed himself.

Up until age 2, he barely needed to say a word. With five "moms and dads," Eric's every need was anticipated and cared for. And every correction, though lovingly given, often was made by more than one person. When he did begin communicating on his own, it was in full sentences, even paragraphs.

Left to right, front: **Eric, 2, Cyndi, 12,** (back) **Kristi, 13,** and **Brian, 14.**

THEN THERE WAS A BOY:

Frequently, upon seeing our family for the first time – two slightly older parents, three rather-grown-up-looking kids, and a cute little boy – people would ask whose baby Eric was. With a delighted look on his face, his reply was always the same – "I'm my whole 'samily's' baby."

Being independent, persevering, and keeping up with his "sibs."

From Eric's point of view, though he was so much younger than his siblings, he figured if his "sibs" could do it, he could too. But, his comprehension was way ahead of his physical abilities. He'd rush forward in anticipation of doing what he saw, understood, and wanted to do, only to be frustrated when he wasn't quite big enough, strong enough, or old enough to pull it off. Early on, Eric developed a habit of perseverance.

Then there were those times when someone would step in at just the right moment to give him a little help along the way. During the summer when Eric was 3, our family and Aunt Ruthie and her two girls from Denver shared a vacation week at the beach in Lincoln City, Ore. One evening after we'd all blown up enough balloons to fill a room, Eric, his "sibs" and cousins all decided to see who could pop the most balloons by landing on them.

2

Although Eric was as quick as all the others to land on the balloons, he didn't weigh enough to pop even one. Aunt Ruthie to the rescue! Following right behind him, so he wouldn't see her, she'd stick a pin in balloon after balloon as Eric landed on them. Those loud pops had everyone laughing until they cried.

AGE 4 WAS A LANDMARK YEAR FOR ERIC:

♦ **Salvation** – One day, my sweet, tow-headed 4-year-old stood in front of me with a concerned look on his face, and in a very serious voice asked,

> "Mommy, is it OK if I love someone more than
> I love you?"
> I answered carefully, "It depends on who that
> someone is ..."
> Quickly he answered, "It's Jesus!"
> "That's OK, then," I replied, "because I love
> Jesus even more than I love you, too."

Our following conversation made it clear that Eric had already given his life to Jesus Christ as Savior and Lord. That marked the beginning of his remarkable, lifelong journey with Jesus.

Loving Jesus, and having eye surgery.

♦ **Corrective Eye Surgery** – Eric was born with an eye condition called strabismus, or crossed eyes, so he was physically unable to see out of both eyes at the same time. From the age of 1, he spent many months wearing a patch part-time on his dominant eye to ensure he wouldn't lose vision in the passive eye.

Age 4 was the optimal age for surgery, offering the best chance that his brain might learn to use both eyes at the same time. Following the surgery, though Eric's eyes appeared "straightened," he never did develop binocular vision. His "monocular vision," meant he still could only see with one eye at a time, so he had no actual depth perception.

3

◆ **Kindergarten** – It was obvious God had gifted Eric with intelligence, tenacity, eagerness to learn, a sweet and gentle spirit, and a huge funny bone. He took great delight in telling everyone he met that his favorite word to spell and define was – a-m-p-h-i-b-i-a-n. More than

Kindergarten at age 4.

Starting school, missing his big brother, and moving.

ready for school at age 4, he could hardly wait to get to school on his first day. After insisting he didn't need my help, he climbed out of the car and ran in all by himself.

That fall, our family took Brian to Eugene, Ore., to begin his first year at the University of Oregon. We got him moved in and settled, said our "Good-byes," and headed back home to Burns. In the back seat little Eric was sobbing inconsolably. Somehow he had assumed he would never see Brian again. Thanksgiving, Brian's first visit back home from college, was a joyous celebration!

HIS GRADE SCHOOL YEARS:

By the time Eric was in first grade, we had sold the newspaper

Dad and Eric, 6, at the beach flying a kite.

in Burns and moved to Portland, Ore., where his dad worked for Portland Magazine. Vacation days spent at the beach were a family favorite.

Just before Eric started second grade, his dad accepted a position as director of communications with CBFMS (Conservative Baptist Foreign Mission Society in Illinois, now WorldVenture in Colorado).

That summer, all three older "sibs" were on different short-term ministry trips, so Dad, Mom, Eric, our yellow lab Tawny, and Eric's "little buddy," a stuffed teddy bear named "Bozzy," made the cross-country move. On the way, we stayed overnight with relatives in Denver. The next day, about two hours after leaving Denver, Eric discovered he'd left "Bozzy," at Aunt Marty's house. Happily, Bozzy rejoined us in Illinois after "bravely, flying on a plane all by himself."

4

At the end of that summer, having completed their summer ministries, Eric's siblings all came "home" to Wheaton, Ill. In the fall, Cyndi began her last year of high school in Wheaton, Kristi began college at a local community college, and Brian returned to the University of Oregon in Eugene.

♦ **At age 8** – Eric announced that he wanted to be baptized. That meant standing up in front of the entire congregation, telling why he wanted to be baptized and what baptism meant to him. So, he did. That same year, Eric was placed in the TAG (Talented and Gifted) program at school. He loved his teachers, excelled in the extra challenges, and grew in his habit of persevering in hard things.

Baptism, T.A.G., "Little Sibs Week," and suffering in silence."

The next year, Eric was like an only child much of the time. All three older kids were away in college – Brian in Oregon, Kristi in Minnesota, and Cyndi nearby in Illinois. As part of "Little Sibs Week" at Cyndi's college, Eric spent an overnight there with her. When he got home, his dad asked how he'd liked it and if he was ready to go to college.

In front of Cyndi's dorm: (left to right) **Dad, Cyndi, Mom, Kristi, Brian, and** (in front) **Eric, 8.**

Eric replied, "I can read the headlines now, 'Boy, 8, goes to college, takes teddy bear.'" (Bozzy had gone along, too.)

One day Eric and I stopped at the library. As usual, I parked, got out, locked the car, and put the keys in my purse. Coming around the back of the car, I was horrified to see that Eric's fingers were shut in the car door. It seemed to take forever to get the keys out of my purse so I could unlock the door and free his little hand. Through it all, he didn't say a word.

When I asked why he hadn't yelled, he replied through his tears, "It's the library, we're supposed to be quiet!"

5

◆ **At age 10** – Now in the fifth grade, doing hard things included delivering newspapers on his bike early every morning. While Eric didn't mind getting up early for the deliveries, he hated collecting subscription money and always put it off for as long as possible.

A newspaper boy at age 10.

Doing hard things, growing in Christ, and trips to Oregon.

One day I impatiently asked, "Why don't you stop acting like a 10-year-old and just do it." Eric's dad immediately replied, "He 'is' a 10-year-old!" Funny, how easy it was to assume Eric was older than his years.

Eric grew in his relationship with Jesus – making choices to live for Christ, not just for himself. He was becoming known for his integrity, doing things with excellence, as well as for his amazing comprehension, vocabulary, and wit.

Even though he very often found himself in a largely grown-up setting, he still exhibited signs of age-appropriate behavior ... often at my expense. One day I returned home from work, parked the car in the garage, and gathered my purse and other things. Just as I stepped out of the garage, I heard a loud popping sound. A water balloon had landed right at my feet and a geyser of water whooshed up under my dress. Eric jumped up and down with glee, laughing uproariously. He had finally mastered the science involved to make a water balloon explode exactly where and when he wanted.

In April of 1986 the five of us flew to Oregon for Brian's wedding to Lorraine Gentry. Kristi was a bridesmaid, Cyndi sang a solo, and 10-year-old Eric, looking handsome in a grey tuxedo, was an usher.

Eric, 10, at Brian's wedding.

♦ **At age 11** – By now, Eric's three older siblings were all living in the Portland, Ore., area. So, for his 11th birthday gift, we gave him a round-trip plane ticket to visit them. His dad and I really missed celebrating his birthday with him, but it was a great time of sharing for our four kids. According to Eric, the only less-than-wonderful thing was that, because he was under 12, he had to be personally escorted by a flight attendant on and off the plane.

Time with his "sibs," Boy Scout camp, and thinking ahead.

ERIC'S MIDDLE-SCHOOL YEARS:

Eric's first camping trip away from home with the Boy Scouts was a huge challenge for us; we missed him terribly. For him it was a huge success.

He thoroughly enjoyed himself and threw himself whole-heartedly into everything offered – except showering. When we picked him up at the end of the week, we laughingly considered letting him ride home tied outside on the roof rack.

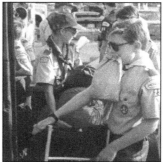

Eric was already thinking hard about his future, and wrote the following for an 8th grade assignment:

Loading all his gear onto a bus for Boy Scout camp.

"In 15 years from now I want to be settled down with a good family of at least one child and a beautiful and thoughtful wife. I also want to be in a job that helps other people, such as a missionary oriented job or work in a mission agency. I also want to be settled down in a good house somewhere in northwest Oregon with the rest of my immediate family.

Fifteen years from now, I hope to be all these things and more."

7

Over the next years, Eric maintained a straight-A grade point average and participated in every church youth group function. Together he and his dad, did red-flannel winter camping with the Boy Scouts and, with a friend and his dad, took a week-long wilderness camping trip in the Boundary Waters Wilderness Area on the Minnesota/Canada border. He and his dad also trained for and did a bike trip in Michigan's Upper Peninsula with the Scouts. In addition, Eric rock climbed, rappelled off cliffs, went white-water rafting, and attended church camp.

School, outdoor activities, and a servant's heart.

Eric and a buddy enjoy-camping in Minnesota.

Rappelling.

He attacked each activity with enthusiasm and his usual passion for excellence, and always went the extra mile if there were tasks to be done – especially the ones no one else wanted to do. He was developing a true servant's heart.

In the spring of 1989, just months before his 14th birthday, Eric's first niece was born to his brother Brian and wife Loraine. While I flew to Oregon to meet our first grandchild, Eric and his dad stayed home in Illinois. Upon my return, the first thing his dad said to me was, "I had no idea how much listening you do every day!" Eric had amazing communication skills and he always had much to share.

ERIC'S HIGH-SCHOOL YEARS:

♦ **As a freshman** – When Eric auditioned for the debate team, the school drama coach was present. She called him at home that evening and talked him into joining the Thespians instead.

Even as a little boy, costumes and acting were part of Eric's everyday fun – being Elvis, Moses, or a clown in a curly blue wig.

8

As a Thespian Eric learned and excelled. He did everything from helping out backstage, to set construction, acting, singing, and dancing. He was in several musicals like "Grease," "Cinderella," "Anything Goes," and "Godspell." For "Godspell," the cast learned to sign some songs so the hearing-impaired parents of one girl could enjoy the performance. Eric did his signing left-handed, and greatly

In the musical "Cinderella."

enjoyed telling people that, "Only left-handed people are in their right minds."

There also were comedies and dramas: "Fools," "Rumors," "Up the Down Staircase," and "The Diary of Anne Frank." In the melodrama, "The Woman in White," Eric was a most convincing villain with his menacing manner, slicked-back black hair, and curling mustache. The younger brother of a high school and youth group friend refused to believe the villain was Eric saying, "Eric could never be such a bad man!"

Playing many parts — always honoring God.

Even as his love of acting grew, he remained outspoken in his commitment to honor God in all he did. He refused roles requiring him to use foul language or to take God's name in vain. And, he wasn't afraid to take a public stand on his convictions. When a policeman visiting one of his high school classes, looked directly at Eric and asked him, "What would you do at a party where all your friends were drinking?" Eric immediately replied, "I wouldn't be there!"

Eric played several parts in "Anything Goes:" (left) **a handsome leading man, and** (right) **a very proper clergyman.**

◆ **As a sophomore** – After wearing that "handsome-leading-man" black tuxedo in "Anything Goes," in the spring of 1991, he wore it three more times in the months that followed. First, at senior prom as the guest of a senior girl student he had tutored in chemistry. Second, as a groomsman in his sister Kristi's wedding in Washington. And, third, again as as a groomsman, for his sister Cyndi's wedding in Illinois.

That winter, when Eric's high school Spanish teacher announced the need for families to host a Spanish-speaking exchange student from Costa Rica for several weeks, we volunteered.

Hosting an exchange student, snow, and hot chocolate.

The boy, who was Eric's age, spoke very little English.

On the drive home from O'Hare Airport, we could see he was becoming increasingl concerned about something. Finally, he asked if people got hurt when the snow fell on them.

What he could see, on both sides of our Chicago-area roads, were endless, huge, ugly, blackish ice-crusted piles – the result of snow plows repeatedly clearing the salted streets. Struggling to find an appropriate word he would understand, we finally told him that snow falling was light, like feathers.

Late one night, just days before he was to return to Costa Rica, it began to snow. Eric set up lawn chairs in the backyard and the two boys sat out in the dark, letting the feathery snow fall on them. When they were just about frozen, they'd come in for hot chocolate and to warm up. Then, they'd go right back out again.

◆ **As a junior** – Having started school at age 4, Eric was always a year younger than most of his class-mates. At the start of his junior year, he was still too young to drive. So, one day, I dropped him off at the back door on the lower level of the

Studying often meant sitting on the floor, whistling, and wearing his elephant cap.

10

high school and, as happened every morning, he went bounding in. I saw he'd left something he needed in the car, so, I grabbed whatever it was and went running after him.

What a surprise! As he hurried down the hall, he was greeting student after student by name. With smiling faces and waving hands, they responded, "Hi, Eric," "Hey, Eric." All were much younger than Eric, and many were in wheelchairs. For him, acknowledging each person was just "business as usual." But for each delighted student, he had started their day with the joy of being recognized, greeted, and valued. Eric lived out what he believed.

A caring heart, another niece, and taking a huge risk.

In March of 1992, Eric once again became an uncle when Brian and Lorraine, in Oregon, had their second little girl.

That summer, between his junior and senior years, Eric, his dad, and I drove to Colorado where we visited the Mesa Verde/Cortez area. Led by a guide from the local Ute tribe, a group of us hiked down narrow, rocky paths along steep canyon walls to visit ancient cliff dwellings.

After having seen all there was in one direction, our guide told us there was one more cliff dwelling to visit. It was located in the other direction, around the bend and up nearly four stories. Reaching it required climbing a 40-foot ancient wood ladder up the sheer canyon wall.

The only ones who went were a woman who identified herself as a seasoned tri-athlete, her sister, and our brave young son. We prayed until they all returned.

That night, as we ate supper at a local restaurant, Eric said that ascending and descending that ladder had been the most terrifying and dangerous thing he'd ever done. He admitted the only reason he'd done it was that he didn't want to be bested by two women.

Right then, we overheard a conversation from a nearby table: "That climb was terrifying. I never would have agreed to do it if that boy hadn't gone – I just couldn't be outdone by a boy!" That was the tri-athlete. And, her sister replied with feeling, "Me neither!"

With the "Masterpeace East Traveling Team" (back row, second from right).

A silent clown, Eric loved delighting children with a variety of balloon creations.

Later that summer Eric went on a short-term ministry trip with DELTA Ministries International. As a member of the "Masterpeace East Traveling Team," he with 11 other young people traveled from Oregon to Maine and back. They visited churches, sharing the love and joy of Jesus through singing, acting, and clowning.

Sharing Jesus, clowning, and studying in Spain.

Once again Eric's dedication to excellence came through. He had mastered the art of making balloon animals, even a tiny Jonah that rolled around in the belly of a whale. With his expertly applied clown makeup, wearing a brightly striped clown suit, huge red shoes, and a multi-colored curly wig, he ministered to countless children that summer. He continued to use balloon art and clowning as a ministry tool for years afterwards, and also taught many others how to do it, too.

♦ **As a senior –** In 1993, during his senior year of high school, Eric was privileged to be an exchange student for a couple of weeks in Santander, a port city on the northern coast of Spain. His host family's grandmother required that he speak only Spanish, so his language skills increased greatly.

Eric on an outing with his host family in Spain.

Eric loved singing. He sang bass in concert choir (left) and also had been selected to sing in the a capella choir (right).

At the very last rehearsal before the a cappella choir gave its final performance for one of the graduation ceremonies, the choir director found himself baffled and a little distressed. For the very first time, the choir had ended up a full tone flat on one of their standard pieces. As Eric told us about it, he laughed gleefully. He had caused it, just to see if he could.

In May of 1993, at age 17, Eric graduated. He received many honors, and was class valedictorian. He also had excelled in several advanced-placement courses, and had received many scholarship offers.

Eric and "sibs" right after graduation. Left to right: **Brian, 29, Kristi, 28, Cyndi, 27, and Eric, 17, the tallest one of all.**

Our whole family's dearest tiny gift had become a godly and loving young man.

13

ERIC'S COLLEGE YEARS:

That next fall, Eric began classes at Illinois State University (ISU) in Normal, Ill., on a full Presidential Scholarship. His chosen major was physics, and much to his dismay, he had to call home for parental permission to take a required class ... he wasn't yet 18.

By the end of his freshman year, Eric had decided he wanted more from life than explaining to classrooms of kids why static electricity made their hair stand on end.

Moving into the dorm at Illinois State University.

Changing majors, two new nephews and serving on the kitchen crew.

So, he changed his major to mass communications, and continued with his Spanish minor. He sang in the college choir, was very active in campus ministry, and had a growing desire to serve the Lord in full-time ministry.

In the winter of 1994, Eric's sister Kristi and her husband in Washington had a son. Then, in 1995, Eric's dad and I relocated to Oregon, to again become owner/operators of a weekly newspaper. This time it was, "The South County Spotlight," in Scappoose, a town near Portland. That same winter, Eric's sister Cyndi and her husband had a son.

For the summer of 1995, Eric had a job on the kitchen crew at The Navigators Conference Center in Colorado Springs, Colo. At the end of that summer, instead of coming home to Oregon, he flew directly to ISU to begin his junior year.

Working at the Navigator's Conference Center.

14

A HUGE INTERRUPTION:

One hot muggy afternoon, a few days later, as he was opening a window in his dorm's laundry room, he lost his footing and fell right-elbow-first through the window. After pulling himself back through the broken window, he somehow made his way upstairs to the main level where he met the ambulance as it arrived.

Eric spent a night with his sister Cyndi and family in Illinois on his way home to Oregon.

Eric underwent extensive major surgery for hours overnight, to reattach a severed ulnar nerve and to repair other resulting injuries to his right arm, wrist, hand, and some of his fingers.

God's providence in a painful trial, and a total change of plans.

Providentially, the Midwest's number one nerve specialist was at that hospital, and Eric's summer insurance and his school insurance were both in effect ... he was double-insured. What a blessing! Eric's injury was so severe, and his recovery so prolonged, he had to drop out of school for a semester, so he came home to Oregon to recover. While he did eventually regain full use of his arm, a permanent lack of feeling remained in a couple of his fingers.

Being away from school gave Eric time to re-examine what God wanted him to do with his life. Cross-cultural ministry was very appealing, so months later, when he returned to ISU, he discovered that a term of school in Mexico would enable him to complete graduation requirements early. It also would increase his fluency in the Spanish language.

Eric attended the University of Mexico in Oaxaca for a semester. While there, he spoke only Spanish and excelled. Back at ISU, that allowed him to test out and earn credits enough to graduate from college summa cum laude mid-year in 1996, just after turning 21.

15

Following graduation, Eric came home to Scappoose, Ore., to live with us and "Oma," his grandmother. That year, each of his three "sibs" had another child, so now he was "Uncle Eric" to seven kids ... four little girls and three little boys.

Still seeking God's direction for his life, Eric took some classes at Western Seminary in Portland, Ore., while working at a couple of different jobs. He also moved into an apartment with a friend he met after he began attending Village Baptist Church in Beaverton, Ore.

An uncle to seven, an amazing son, and making new friends.

ERIC'S SINGLE ADULT YEARS:

Soon after Eric had moved out on his own, the U.S. Postal Service announced new specifications required for all weekly newspapers' subscriber systems and reports. As newspaper owners, His dad and I would have had to acquire and learn to use a new, cost prohibitive computer system. When we told Eric what we needed, he said he could do it for us ... all at no cost. So, he designed a program for software we already owned, and very patiently taught me to use it!

During that time he had started to work at Intel as a temp and, a short time later, he was hired on full-time ... which was the beginning of his rapidly upward-moving career.

Eric became a member of Village Baptist Church where he was very involved with cross-cultural ministry ... being fluent in Spanish helped. And he was active in the young adult group where many long-lasting friendships were formed.

THEN HE MET TAMMY:

Tammy Morris also was active in Village's young adult church group. One of six children in her Christian family, she was a graduate of George Fox University in Newberg, Ore., and was

Something he said tickled Tammy's funnybone.

working as a CPA. As Tammy and Eric got better acquainted, they realized they had much in common.

Each had a deep love for Jesus and a commitment to serve Him.

Both were dedicated to doing every job with excellence, had quick and witty minds, great senses of humor, and loved adventure.

What began as a friendship soon blossomed into love, followed

August 18, 2001, presenting Mr. and Mrs. Eric Heerwagen

by a marriage proposal and a wedding. Eric and Tammy were married at Village Baptist Church.

Eric's eldest nephew was the ringbearer, and his two youngest nieces were the flower girls. Both the Morrises and the Heerwagens were delighted with the match, and the couple's number of shared extended family members virtually doubled.

ESTABLISHING LIFE TOGETHER:

After returning home from their honeymoon in Jamaica, it was back to work as usual for the newlyweds.

Eric continued to move up the career ladder at Intel, often making trips overseas, and Tammy remained a highly valued member of the accounting firm where she worked.

Two lives become one, loving God, and sharing many new adventures.

17

Together they stayed involved at Village, spent time with friends there, made time to celebrate birthdays and holidays with both large extended families, took vacation trips ... some overseas, and eventually bought their first house.

INCREASING THEIR SHARED LIFE:

On November 17, 2004, just three days after Eric's 29th birthday, Eliana Hope – Ellie – was born.

It's worth recalling here the essay Eric wrote as a middle school student:

> *"In 15 years from now I want to be settled down with a good family of at least one child and a beautiful and thoughtful wife. I also want to be in a job that helps other people, such as a missionary oriented job or work in a mission agency. I also want to be settled down in a good house somewhere in northwest Oregon with the rest of my immediate family.*
> *Fifteen years from now, I hope to be all these things and more."*

MAKING FAMILY TRADITIONS:

Life with their precious new baby meant major changes in lifestyle for both Eric and Tammy. And it offered them many opportunities to work out which of their own family activities would be carried on in their new family.

Loving Jesus, following Him and serving Him was of first importance in this new family. And, so was spending time in prayer together every day. Spending time with extended family on both sides was important. And, so was continuing traditions carried over from both families ... like trimming the Christmas tree and vacation days at the beach.

THEN THERE WERE FOUR:

Timothy Myeong-Bo Heerwagen was born in South Korea on October 22, 2007. On May 30, 2008, at the age of six months, he was joyously greeted at Portland International Airport by his new family, some of his new extended family, and some close family friends.

On December 31, 2008, with many of those same people present, Timmy was officially adopted in a Washington County, Ore. judge's chambers.

A LIFESTYLE OF COMMITMENT:

Over the years, Eric's tender caring heart, great sense of humor, integrity, work ethic, and passion for serving God were demonstrated in the man he had become – all because he had decided early to follow Jesus and lived out what he believed. And, like Eric, Tammy's early commitment to living a godly life, and the traits she exhibited every day, resulted in their being greatly blessed day by day.

Blessed as they walked side-by-side with the Lord.

Of course there were the usual bumps in the road, but together they faced each one, made the necessary adjustments and continued on. They were raising their young children, Ellie and Timmy, in that same joyful and committed lifestyle – daily following Jesus.

MORE THAN EVERYDAY UPS AND DOWNS:

In September of 2011, at the age of 35, Eric found himself suffering from an excruciatingly painful lower left leg. It had been diagnosed and was being treated as Achilles tendinitis.

Even while struggling to be able to walk, Eric continued to fulfill the heavy demands of his busy schedule with Intel, including several cross-country flights between Oregon and New York.

THEIR DEVASTATING CHALLENGE:

In October 2011, everything changed. Eric and Tammy began a nine-month cancer battle. Together they chose to openly share their unwavering trust in God as they traveled step by step with the Lord Jesus Christ on this journey.

In Eric's Own Words

"There have been lots of twists and turns since Oct. 1, 2011. You'll find my story to be full of the "atypical" – almost a dozen ER trips, multiple hospital stays, anaphylactic shock, a broken tooth; Hulk-like radiation treatments taking me from wheelchair, to walker, to no-help-needed; a glorious trip to Hawaii, good and bad chemo results, difficult conversations with our kids, brain surgery, depression, anxiety, and lots more.

"I hate the cancer raging inside of me, but I firmly believe God is using my short time of suffering to further change the world for His glory and His honor. I know lives are impacted through my faith story; many have written in to share how God is using this to change them.

"It is my prayer that God uses my story to change your life, too. What an awesome thing it would be to see you in eternity."

Eric Heerwagen

"In Eric's Own Words" is part of any entry written in his CaringBridge journal on June 22, 2012, after more than eight months of suffering, just four days before the Lord took him home.

With Eric's and Tammy's permission ... what follows is:

"There Was A Man"

October 2011

~ *The First Month* ~

Saturday, Oct. 15, 2011 – 1:12 p.m.

God's watchcare through a horrible October ...

(This is long ... sorry.) The last few weeks have by far been the worst health times in all my life. There's so much I don't understand and have yet to learn, but, here's what is in my mind and heart today.

I believe God loves me deeply, and He is not the one responsible for "hitting the smite button" on me. Even through really rough weeks, He is showing His watchcare.

♦ THROUGH HIS TIMING:

Multiple plane trips without complications from the DVT (*deep vein thrombosis – blood clot in the left lower leg vein*), and possibly forming pulmonary embolisms (*blood clots*) in my lungs; and our prompting to go to the ER (*emergency room*) Saturday, Oct. 1, just before I was to fly out again to do a full week on the East Coast (I can't imagine flying with massive DVTs in my left leg and embolisms in both lungs).

The next week, when I was in and out of the hospital, I was supposed to be in New York doing a major project for work. While I would have loved to have been there, I had done so much pre-work that the project was well able go forward without me. Even this week, I already had a few days marked as "out of office." So, while I hate missing work, and really hate

Timmy, 3, visits Daddy in the hospital.

not having the joy of taking some key projects across the finish line, I know the timing of my being out couldn't be better.

Thursday night, just a few nights after being released from the hospital – when I found the lump in the right side of my neck – was one of the hardest nights I've ever had. And, while

I'd rather not have my lymphatic system going wild, the lump itself made for a much easier and more reliable biopsy (*removal of tissue for diagnostic examination*). I trust the biopsy results will help shape my treatment.

Our second ER trip, while unwanted, showed that the embolisms were going down. So then, when the clots got worse, we knew the pill-form blood-thinner medicine really wasn't working. The leg ultrasound helped seal the deal. Now an injectable medicine (*twice-daily self-administered Lovenox shots in the abdomen*) is working well against the clots. And, thanks to Oxycodone 24/7 (*a narcotic pain killer*), I can walk almost without a limp. On our third and fourth ER trips we actually had the same doc .... who ever heard of continuity of care in the ER?

This week, Monday through Wednesday, were hideous days with narcotics-induced constipation and the process of fixing that. When we met with the ENT (*ear, nose and throat*) doc early this week, we pushed for the biopsy and CT scan (formerly CAT scan) to be done as early in the week as possible because we wanted answers before the weekend. Well, earliest we got was Thursday, way too late for us. (In hindsight, God knew Wednesday was going to be an ugly day for me, and there was no way I could have been on a biopsy table for any length of time ... you fill in the blanks. ☺)

On Thursday of this week, a very sweet lady at the hospital encouraged us to try and pull the Friday CT scan a day earlier. Thanks to her and a great scheduler, we got in just about an hour after the biopsy. Before my biopsy, I had spoken with a scheduler and said we'd call back later if we secured doctor approval to do the CT scan on the same day. While I was in biopsy, Tammy called scheduling again to say we had doctor approval and, guess what, she got the same scheduler.

♦ THROUGH THE GENEROSITY OF SO MANY:

Friends, neighbors, family, co-workers are delivering meals, doing our yard work for us, watching over our kids [Ellie almost 7, and Timmy almost 4], spending time with us at the hospital and ER, listening, hugging, flexing, spending the night with me at the hospital, and so much more. I especially love that our teenage neighbor, on his third year of chemo for cancer, made us a pie and a handmade card. Even people we don't know have been praying. What an amazing way to tangibly feel the love of those around us. In our independence, we often miss that blessing of receiving.

♦ THROUGH HIS BIBLE:

A verse I was told to memorize as all this health stuff was coming down, (my version from memory – I've said it a lot in the last weeks, many times through streams of tears):

> "The Lord is the one who goes before us,
> He will go with us. He will not leave us or forsake us.
> Do not be afraid or discouraged."
>
> Deut. 31:8

God is with us in this. I am convinced of that. Even if horrible things come in the next week, my God is with me, near to me, and wanting to take my anxieties (Philippians 4:5-7). He is with my family and cares for them more than I ever could. He is watching over us. He loves us deeply and grieves with us over the broken bodies we have. He will not give us more than we can handle (still learning that one – I've been at the end of myself so many times in the last few weeks).

He loves me so much He will not waste my suffering if I choose to learn in the process ... and I do think I'm learning, a lot.

He will not change even as everything around us changes. My little faith is in Him who is the Creator of everything. I am thankful that the suffering I have now is but a blip on the timeline of eternity. My weakness serves to better show His strength.

All these things above are true, not because I believe them, but because they are from the Bible, God's Word to humanity.

GOD IS GOOD: As the old call/response of the church goes.

> "God is good   –   All the time.
> All the time   –   God is good!"

Wednesday, Oct. 19, 2011 – 1:17 p.m.

Lots of tears ...

We are still very early in the diagnosis phase. We know it is cancer, but that's about it. I've spent a lot of time crying over the last few weeks, but yesterday was by far the most tears. Fortunately, there have been lots of loved ones to cry with me. We hope to have a better diagnosis and roadmap for treatment by the end of next week.

♦ WHAT WE EXPECT IN THE NEXT WEEK OR SO:

Thursday: bone marrow biopsy (*a needle is inserted into the bone to extract bone marrow for diagnostic examination*) with hematologist (*blood and bone marrow specialist*), consult with urologist (*specialist in reproduction/urination organs*), and pre-op meeting with ENT (*specialist for ear, nose, and throat*).

Friday: recover from Thursday.

Sunday: discontinue blood thinning medicine that is helping my body fight the clots (necessary so the surgery can be done safely).

Monday: 5:30 a.m., outpatient open-neck biopsy (*removal of lymph node tissue for diagnostic examination*) under general anesthesia. This will let us know more specifics about what type of lymphoma (*a type of blood cancer, often considered curable even in late stages*) I have. Once we have a name for it, we can fight it.

♦ SPECIFIC PRAISES:

I am on medical leave from work. Intel has been wonderful through all this, and thanks to short-term disability, we don't have to be concerned about finances at this time.

We are surrounded by so many who care and help. My sister-in-law is coordinating meals, a huge help; and, as I write this, my big sister is playing with Timmy upstairs.

We have neighbors who know so much about cancer ... their son is in his third and final year of treatment for Leukemia. It was a huge blessing to visit them yesterday; we cried and got some great tips. I know we'll lean on them in the days ahead.

The kids received the news fairly well. We were open about this being cancer, but we also told them we believe this to be very curable.

♦ SPECIFIC PRAYER REQUESTS:

The DVTs in my left leg really hurt; I'd love for those to reduce in size and pain soon. Unfortunately, with Monday's surgery, I have to discontinue blood-thinning doses, and I am concerned about things actually worsening.

Pray the kids will process Daddy being sick. Ellie is a bright girl and catches a lot. We pray God's protection and endurance for our children.

Pray for Tammy to have the strength she needs as she now has easily two times the load with my being sick. I am so blessed to have her as my wife, and I see the toll my poor health is taking on her. Pray that she might find the breaks she needs.

Pray for all the testing ahead, that the docs would get solid, actionable answers.

Pray for an easily-treated lymphoma, a curable cancer, even in late stages.

Pray for God's healing. We'd welcome a miracle, but recognize God may choose to take us through this the long way.

Pray for better sleep at nights; nights have been rough lately.

~ *Responses from Family and Friends* ~

Thanks for the specific information. It helps to know how to better pray for you and the family. All the best,   *Kris K., Village*

There are so many praying for you and the family. We trust God to see you through as you are overwhelmed by His grace.
Chip and Liz M., Tammy's parents

Just a quick note to give you a "hug" and let you know, we are praying. Beth said to let her know anytime if you just a need a [babysitter] break ... You are loved by many but mostly by Jesus.
Leslie E., Village

You and your family will be in my daily prayers. I want you to know that before this, I so admired your walk in faith with the Lord and how it showed at work. Rest in the Lord and in the blessings ahead. Always,
Charlie B., Intel

Tears in my eyes and no words to say ... and me a writer! Just know that we are bringing all of you before the Lord and asking for His mercy, grace and healing to rain down on you.   *Becky J., formerly at Village*

I'm so glad that God has already made your eyes open to all things positive. You will be amazed and in awe of all the wonderful blessings He will share with you through this journey, and He will share MANY! That said, when you have less than positive moments, know that Jesus can take anything you have. Anger, fear, frustration.. you name it. Here's a Halloween groaner for you —Why didn't the skeleton cross the road? He didn't have enough guts! You've got guts Eric! You'll be on the other side of this journey in no time!   *Kim S., neighbor*

We're lifting you guys up in prayer daily and trusting His plan in all of this. Please let us know if there is any way we can help beyond prayer and meals. In Him,   *Jennifer and Kevin Y., Village*

As I was praying for you, John 16:33 came to mind: "These things I have spoken to you that in me you might have peace. In the world you shall have tribulation; but be of good cheer; I have overcome the world." Did you notice that "ericheerwagen" has the word "cheer" right in the middle of it? I am praying tonight that you will be of good cheer knowing that He has overcome all that this world can throw at us!
Dawn R., Tammy's sister

Thursday, Oct. 20, 2011 – 10:03 a.m.

Best sleep in weeks ...

Last night, thanks to prayers and modern medicine, I was able to sleep like a log from 9:30 p.m. to 2:30 a.m.

What a huge blessing. So now we get ready for some nasty test procedures today. At least they get us closer to answers and treatment. Taking it one day at a time.

Second Entry Thursday – 4:41 p.m.

What a day!

First, thanks to all the visitors. We are so surrounded by love and care. What an awesome blessing.

♦ SO, TODAY ... three specialists in one day.

The hematologist: We started the morning with the bone marrow biopsy on my left lower leg. Thanks to numbing agents, it wasn't too bad. (I wouldn't watch the procedure on The Learning Channel ever, though.) The possible bad news with that visit was that there is a chance that the lymphoma has spread to the liver. NOTE: the hematologist said that even if the liver is involved, the intent would be cure and not simply palliative (*to relieve or lessen pain, not cure*). We'll get calls from the hematologist as he has results.

The urologist: By the time we got to the urologist, I was a fine mess. While I trust God to do what is best, and I know He loves me deeply, the thought of cancer spreading to my liver was a lot to take in. The "urinologist" was as invasive as one could imagine. Good news, though, is that he didn't see signs of cancer and found the source of a bleed, with no signs of infections. Wonderful news.

The ENT: From there we met with the ENT. (Had a nice lunch with Tammy just before the appointment ... she is my bride and I love her so dearly. All this seems to heighten our bond.)

The ENT doc said we needed to be off Lovenox longer, so Friday is now the last dose before the Monday procedure.

♦ SPECIFIC WAYS TO PRAY:

Peace ... I admit to fear being a strong emotion this morning. We need rest while we wait for answers that lead to a specific treatment plan. We've got lots of waiting ahead.

Going off the blood thinner is scary. I don't want the clots to worsen. Pray that we won't lose ground by skipping a few days of Lovenox.

The PET scan is now scheduled for Tuesday. Pray for a very clear readout that can further inform treatment. (Fast-growing cancer, which mine seems to be – just watching the lymph masses grow – may actually be easier to treat.) Please, God, may that be the case.

Brain MRI is Thursday. We'd love for this to just be a checkbox as the docs clear up any outstanding concerns. Ideally, they find nothing needing care.

Keep the kids and Tammy in your prayers. Timmy has his 4th birthday party this Saturday. We'd love for him to have a fun and normal party. (Thanks to the Morris clan, Tammy's extended family, for running the party.) As for Tammy she is in lockstep with me on this, and physical and emotional fatigue are sure things. As always, we'd love healing to come quickly.

Third Entry Thursday – 11:10 p.m.

This one's from Tammy ...

Thanks so much everyone for the notes you have left on Caring-Bridge. Believe it or not, we just sit and read them, cry, and feel loved. Some have asked about helping out – so many of you have helped in so many ways – thank you! Childcare, grocery shopping, lawn mowing, cleaning, just coming over to talk, meals, etc. We appreciate the love you have shown us.

We want your prayers most of all. For Eric, the next biggest help is visiting with him and helping him pass the time – he's so accustomed to always doing something that lying around in pain is driving him crazy. For me, all the other practical things are a huge help. Thanks so much.

~ *Responses from Family and Friends* ~

Thought about you and prayed often throughout the day. Glad this day is behind you and you can continue to forge ahead as you battle and win this fight! Love you guys, and as always call for anything! I'm assuming it's okay, but wanted to check. Can I ask my neighbors/friends to pray for you?   *Chick L., Village Life Group*

In my tears, I pray. I pray for peace (John 14:27) as you walk through today. Tammy and Eric, you two are beautiful examples of life on this earth.   *Dawn Denise R., friend*

Thank you for sharing the specific prayer requests. I lifted them up as soon as I read them and will continue to pray for you and your family.   *Lori H., Village*

Eric and Tammy, My heart aches for you as I have learned of your current health road-bump. You are in our prayers continuously. Hugs to all!   *Tanya P., formerly at Village*

We're praying for you, Tammy, Ellie, and Timmy! Praying for God's healing, wisdom, strength, and peace.   *Lynda F. and family, Village*

Praying for you all. Please don't hesitate to call if there's anything I can do to help   *Mythraie G. Village*

Hi Eric, A friend of mine from Mexico had posted this morning and I thought of you immediately:
> Cuando pases por las aguas, yo estaré contigo; y si por los ríos, no te anegarán". Dios estará contigo a cada paso. No hay nada que temer cuando Jesús está cerca. Él está con contigo en el valle, caminando contigo tomado de tu mano. Nunca pasarás por un valle en esta vida solo. Nunca estarás un día solo. Dios ha dicho: "Yo estaré contigo."

Loosely translated: When you pass through the waters, I am with you; And through the rivers, do not anegarán (don't know this word). God will be with you through each passing. There is nothing to fear when Jesus is near. He is with you in the valley, walking with you hand in hand. You never go through the valley in this life alone. You are never alone, even for one day. God says: "I am with you."   *Nancy O., Village*

Friday, Oct. 21, 2011 – 12:25 p.m.

Things are moving fast ...

Another good night's sleep. My leg continues to hurt, making it hard to even walk around. For pain, I'm on oxycodone. Tylenol is ruled out with increased liver enzymes showing in last blood lab. (So, we're doing everything we can to avoid the "complications" of narcotics.)

This morning, I had to apologize to Tammy for harsh words spoken. (I was trying to get to Timmy's room, a short distance down the hall, and just couldn't make it without big pain. Really torqued me!)

On the good news front, the brain MRI originally scheduled for Thursday next week is now set for today at 2:45 p.m. In a "God-wink" we got the same scheduler with whom I spoke yesterday, and there was a cancellation in the system that she could fill with my appointment. I'm very thankful to have more tests getting done sooner than later. I am eager (very understated) to name this thing and treat it to get well. (Though, if we could just skip to 100 percent well, that would make me so happy.)

Thanks again to everyone for prayers, calls, helps, and love.

It's Still Friday – 8:10 p.m.

No news is good news?

Well, the brain MRI is done ... nearly a week ahead of when we planned. It took about an hour of holding still, and my leg and bone marrow biopsy area didn't hurt too badly. The good news is they didn't admit me ... so no huge tumor found. Still don't know what they found about the "ditzel" (*a small unidentified mass seen on the X-ray*), but for now we will assume that no news is good news. The oncologist (*cancer specialist*) has been very accessible and calls when there is news to share.

So, tonight I am kicking back ... enjoying the help of pain meds, and watching all the activity around me as Tammy's brother and his wife are helping get us ready for the flurry of 3- and 4-year-olds coming tomorrow to celebrate Timmy's 4th birthday. Happy birthday early to my son.

~ *Responses from Family and Friends* ~

Your openness, honesty and faith during this time are inspirational.
You're in my prayers.   *Jeffrey McG., friend*

People that you don't even know here in Arizona prayed for you.
We'll keep praying and updating the prayer warriors here.
Sandy G., formerly at Village

Thank you for the update Eric. Glad to hear your test was earlier
than expected. Hope you have an awesome time celebrating Timmy
tomorrow. Praying for you all,   *Mythraie G., Village*

As I was reading this verse this morning, I thought of you guys and
wanted to share it:
> *"But now, this is what the LORD says— he who created
> you, Jacob, he who formed you, Israel: 'Do not fear, for I have
> redeemed you; I have summoned you by name; you are mine.
> When you pass through the waters, I will be with you; and when
> you pass through the rivers, they will not sweep over you.
> When you walk through the fire, you will not be burned; the
> flames will not set you ablaze. For I am the LORD your God,
> the Holy One of Israel, your Savior; Do not be afraid, for I am
> with you" " Isaiah 43:1-3, 5a*

Lori H., Village

Eric and Tammy, It was a privilege to pray with you and the
elders/pastors the other night. My family and I are thinking about you
and praying for you daily. Be encouraged that God is with you. He knows
your heart, mind, soul and body better than anyone. Before you were
born, He knew that you would need to paddle through this rapid (Psalm
139:16). I'm praying that His Presence would envelop you and your
family as you navigate these rough waters. Draw close to Him. Feel His
love and the love of your family and friends.   *Scott R., Village*

It is so thrilling to see His Holy Spirit invited into the events and
situations surrounding Eric and Tammy now and all the days ahead. We
are encouraged throughout God's Word by the promise of His presence,
wisdom, strength, healing, and guidance. God has truly blessed us with
an amazing family of believers. We are covering all of you with prayers
for His intervention at all times and in all ways. Love,
Bonnie and George J., Tammy's aunt and uncle in Arizona

Saturday, Oct. 22, 2011 – 7:53 p.m.

Esperando ...

I just remembered that in Spanish "to wait" and "to hope" are the same verb, "esperar." Today is a day where it is hard to hope, and it is very hard to wait.

But there are lots of pluses about today: a great party for Timmy, a great wife, unsolicited lawn mowing by a kind neighbor, delicious dinner delivered to us hot and ready, my sister making the 30-minute drive just to cheer me up. These are things that give hope (esperanza) midst the wait. That said, the wait and the unknown are proving hard to deal with.

Timmy's early morning birthday gifts.

I have real struggles today – with fear, pain, discouragement, and more. The wait to find out the specifics of this thing is hard and will remain hard. My leg keeps hurting even through the meds (though I am getting some blocks of sleep – huge blessing), and my energy level is super low. If only we could fast forward to the end of this.

Now, again, on the plus side. God is blessing even in the midst of hard times. He is giving us what we need (and more) to make it through each day. God doesn't change, and this cancer did not catch Him by surprise. So, I try to remind myself that I am not doing this alone, and I hope and wait on Him. I and my family are under His loving care. We choose to put our hope in Him. Thanks to everyone for the encouragement.

Monday, Oct. 24, 2011 – 1:29 p.m.

One lump or two?

Surgery (*open-neck biopsy on the right side of my neck*) is done and I'm just waiting to be discharged. As expected, the recovery room time took longer than average, but I think I'm feeling mostly normal now.

I've already had the first Lovenox shot so I can start fighting the blood clots/DVTs again. For the next day I get to wear a very fashionable "ascot." Once that is gone, I can show off my lovely bandage. Follow up with the ENT is in a week.

The docs said to expect daily calls ... so cool. It could be quite some time (a week plus) before we have the full picture, but thankfully they now have the lymph-node mass necessary to fully diagnose and then create a custom treatment plan.

Tomorrow is the "last" major fact-finding test ... a PET scan *(three-dimensional images with radioactive substances in the tissue)* in the afternoon.

Here's to waiting and hoping, trusting that my God is big enough for anything. Or, as Junior Asparagus from "VeggieTales" would say, "God is bigger than the Boogie Man."

Thanks and love to all.

~ *Responses from Family and Friends* ~

"Patience is waiting. Not passively waiting. That is laziness. But to keep going when the going is hard and slow – that is patience (author unknown)." I know you feel like you're not being very patient in your waiting but getting up every day and living through the questions, looking for the gifts in the difficulties, failing and trying again, shows enormous patience. Still praying for an easing of the pain, and for joy overflowing. All the best,   *Kris K., Village*

Eric , when you were a child, I did everything I could to try to keep you from hurting or feeling sad. I still never want to see you hurt, but since we've grown up, I understand that sometimes we do. I also understand how much God loves us, and that He will never forsake us or give us more than we can bear. Not only are you an amazing person, you are an amazing person with a "mustard seed!" And that faith is shared by so many of us, who love you, Tammy, Ellie, and Timmy. Tammy, I thank God for you, that He brought you and Eric together, for the godly woman you are, and the loving wife and mother you are. I'm also thanking God for your quick wit and sense of humor ... both essential to keep up with Eric, and so much fun for me!!! All our love and prayers (and Reese's Peanut Butter Cups).   *Cyndi F. and family, Eric's sister*

Praying and praising God with you. So wonderful to hear of His faithfulness in the middle of pain and wondering. Praying for God's grace as you wait, freedom from pain, rest, encouragement and healing.   *Becky J., formerly at Village*

Tuesday, Oct. 25, 2011 – 9:48 a.m.

Good news and more questions ...

I had a good night's sleep in my recliner last night. I was concerned that a full night's sleep would elude me, but thankfully, I got pretty good sleep and the neck surgery site feels like it is healing well. I believe I can take the "ascot" off today and leave just the primary set of bandages in place until next Monday when I meet again with the ENT.

♦ GOOD NEWS AND MORE TESTS:

Less than an hour ago, we got a call from my hematologist. The cancer has not yet made it to the bone marrow. Re the liver ... the high liver enzymes could be explained by Hepatitis C (the doc had some narrowing info back from initial tests), though more tests are needed. (I read up a bit on Hep C and I really don't think I want that, I also don't seem to fit the risk factors, but ... hmmmm.) It would be awesome to not have Hep C or cancer that has spread to the liver, but barring a miracle I likely have one or the other.) NOTE: I remain wide open to a miracle.

♦ FINALLY:

More looking is needed to find out what now both the CT scan and brain MRI uncovered – a 9mm "anomaly." This afternoon's PET scan may or may not help on that front, so ... likely more tests. God willing we are not adding a brain tumor to the mix. I'll admit this one has me worried some ... I didn't ask lots of follow up questions with the doc because we honestly don't know what it is yet. The unknown is hard to deal with, even knowing God is loving and in control.

In closing, we're doing our best to take it one day at a time. I'm working hard on reminding myself that I am not alone (Philippians 4:5-7), that God is able to use this to grow me personally (from James), to grow my family, and to grow His Kingdom (like Paul's struggles in Philippians.)

There is no guarantee of healing in this lifetime, but I have a promise of full healing with God in eternity because my faith is in Jesus (John 3:16, Romans 3:26, and Romans 6:23). That said, I'm in no hurry to go to Heaven.

Recently, an author I like, Randy Alcorn, posted this on Facebook:

> "Do not be impatient to go to Heaven. Hold lightly to the things of Earth, yet count it a great privilege to have a long life in which to serve the Lord on Earth. 'I desire to depart and be with Christ, which is better by far; but it is more necessary for you that I remain in the body.'" (Philippians 1:23-24)   – Charles Spurgeon

Here's to quickly finding out more of what this is I am fighting, and then fighting it. I want to see my grandchildren grow old. Pray for healing and faithfulness each day as I, Tammy, the kids, and those around us learn more about what God has for us to do each day. May He find us faithful in the tasks set before us.

Second Entry Tuesday – 5:52 p.m.

Glow in the dark ...

I had my first PET scan today. I felt a bit like Peter Parker's "Spider-Man" with the radioactive spider. My nuclear tech came in with the radioactive glucose all covered up in a fancy metal (I imagine lead-lined) cylinder. Oh, and her outfit was complete with one of those nuclear exposure badges too. The real deal.

After about two hours at the hospital, all is done and we're back home. The kids will get to hug me briefly and then keep their distance. Radiation is not a great thing for little kids. The good news ... Daddy can be their nightlight tonight. ☺

I say it often, but it is well worth saying again and again ... THANK YOU so much for all the encouragement, prayer, and love.

♦ SO ... NEXT STEPS? Mostly, we ... WAIT:

Wait on the liver enzyme tests – Hep C is still in the running; not nice, but likely better than lymphoma spread to the liver.

Wait on the results from the biopsy and PET scan – this will tell us more specifically what we're dealing with and what we'll aggressively move to cure.

Wait for next steps on the brain anomaly – not sure what the doc will need to do to figure that out.

Wait for the DVT pain to improve – still on pain meds that at least cut the pain some.

Wait for the post-op visit with our ENT on Monday – "ascot" stays on until tomorrow, then I can at least try and clean up some.

Most of all – we wait on God to provide what we need most each day, and I trust that full healing is totally possible.

~ *Responses from Family and Friends* ~

Eric, I love you and I pray for you every day, and I am so glad you are a Christian and can lean on Him through this whole journey. While family is important and I'm so glad you have Tammy, your kids, the Heerwagen side of the family, AND all of us, I'm more thankful that you have Jesus. Love you and praying always,   *Shellie M., Tammy's sister*

I just returned to the office from vacation. I was expecting to hear the good news that your clots were all behind you – half expecting to see you sitting at your normal spot, with a quick smile and dedicated focus to whatever you might be working on. I have a very heavy heart as I read through the journal updates – a sense of "how in the world could this really be happening?" Eric, thank you for making suggestions on what we can pray about. May you find rest and peace today. You are in all of our thoughts and prayers.   *Mike T., Intel*

It is beautiful to see you traveling this road; being real, yet choosing to trust God, and look to Him. You are a big light shining Him. Sending lots of love to you, Tammy, Timmy, and Ellie. Praying for all of you.
Pamela K., Ellie's school teacher

Hi Eric, I just heard about your diagnosis and I am praying for you and your beautiful family. I am hoping for the best for you. I am glad to hear the cancer has not spread into the bone marrow. Warm regards,
Bindu C., Intel

Eric, Thank you for sharing! I'm praying for you and your big day on Monday. I'll also ask my life group to pray for you tomorrow. In Christ,   *Lynda F. and family, Village*

Wednesday, Oct. 26, 2011 – 10:03 a.m.

Short night ...

Good news ... no ER trip. Good news ... only one call to on-call doc at 4 a.m. Good news ... doc will look to get more effective pain meds for my left leg.

Really good news ... I don't think my doc was too hacked off with me for calling. ☺ (Starting yesterday afternoon I just couldn't get ahead of the pain.)

Thanks for the funnies being sent my way. Laughter is truly good medicine. Speaking of medicine, I am finding food (in moderation) to be therapeutic too ... Reese's Peanut Butter Cups ... mmmmmmm; later for lunch today my parents are bringing East Indian food. Yum-O. Blessed to have a new day ahead and praying for definitive answers sooner than later.

A Little Later Wednesday – 11:54 a.m.

Urgent prayers needed ...

"Atypical" is my name I guess. Preliminary biopsy of the lymph node shows melanoma *(a different form of malignant cells)* and not lymphoma. The melanoma, if that is what they keep as the diagnosis, is showing up in my chest, abdomen, and neck. We still don't know what the liver is doing.

♦ MORE TESTS ... STAT:

MRI this afternoon on the leg since it is behaving "atypically." Meeting with Dr. Patton *(brain doc)* downtown to discuss treatment of the brain anomaly, which could easily be melanoma and would require fairly quick action to prevent a bleed in the brain. The doc mentioned something like a "gamma knife" procedure *(focused radiation, no knife)*. We likely will meet with a melanoma specialist early next week.

We've got so many more questions. From Tammy's quick Google, this sounds much worse than lymphoma. Expecting a miracle. We hope and pray that all this still remains in the curative space, but must admit that our minds quickly wander.

Much Later Wednesday – 9:02 p.m.

Ugly day ...

What should have been a quiet, restful day at home turned sour, pretty fast. Hematologist/oncologist, Dr. Andersen, called to say preliminary pathology showed melanoma. So with melanoma as a possibility, we headed off to visit a brain surgeon to see what the brain anomaly meant. Dr. Patton suggested we wait for treatment, but eventually we'll need to attack it with a gamma knife.

From the brain doc, we went to get an MRI of my leg. The leg pain is horrible and way beyond what it should be for simple DVT. We won't know the test results until tomorrow. [It's now been over a month of intense, debilitating leg pain.]

♦ DURING THE MRI:

Dr. Andersen called and updated Tammy with the latest: I believe I have "carcinoma" ... more tests are needed to figure out the source, and what type we are dealing with; it could be up to another week before we get answers and work toward a treatment plan.

Based on the PET scan results ... the cancer is in the chest, abdomen, and neck. It doesn't seem to be in the liver or bone marrow, though Hep C is a possibility to explain the high liver enzymes. And I have a newly-found kidney stone lying in wait.

I've got clearance to increase the dosing on oxycodone ... to keep the pain level down to a 3-out-of-10. So we'll be dialing in the right dosing over the next day plus. Hopefully the next posts will be cogent. ☺ [Ed. Note: Eric's posts remained amazingly clear and to the point, even as stronger and stronger pain meds were used.]

And now we wait again ... wait for final results of the biopsy, wait to determine if the medical community feels what I have is treatable or not. We trust it will be curable, but there is a chance that this will fall into the "miracle-needed-here" category.

I'm tempted to put in something theological and encouraging like, "God is grieved by this, too." Or, "We are putting our hope in a good God who can make the best out of this regardless of the outcome." Or, "We're casting our worries on God because He cares for us." These are all true, but they are hard to get behind tonight. We're in a big unknown space and it is very uncomfortable.

We'd love to fast forward to knowing the treatment and prognosis, but ... we can't. So we wait. I'm angry, sad, discouraged, but also trying to hold on to hope. Thanks for your prayers and love.

~ *Responses from Family and Friends* ~

I continue to be amazed by the widening circle of praying people for you ... God is using even this to His glory! I want to post this prayer for you by someone you do not know, after he read your Oct. 25 morning journal entry:

"Father, thank you for faith such as this. Please take this example and blend it with my thoughts and thinking about you. Teach us Lord to hold lightly to things of this earth yet understanding that our work here is for you and your plan. We humbly accept this task because you are God. Bring an amazing miracle for Eric to see. Bless his socks off, Lord! We bow before you in awe when we ask this in the name of your Son, Jesus Christ, amen."

Chip M., Tammy's dad

The ladies in our Bible Study Fellowship group are praying for you and asking for God's great mercies through all the testing and for His healing grace and miraculous touch. The Lord brings you to mind continually throughout the day. *Mary Ann B., Tammy's friend*

You have an ARMY of prayer warriors with you on this. There are people all around who are lifting you up, holding your arms up and commanding a miracle telling this mountain to move from your life with our little mustard seed, mountain-moving faiths. *Kris K., Village*

Eric, you've got a lot of family, loved ones and co-workers behind you. You'll continue to be in our prayers as you work to identify this and then what can be done to treat it. Stay strong! *Adam M., Intel*

Eric, Your faith is an inspiration and I believe in the power of prayer and will be continually praying for you and your family. One thing that comes to mind is, "they shall mount up with wings like eagles run and not grow weary, for the Lord renews their strength, even youths grow tired and weary, young men may stumble and fall, but those who put their trust in the Lord will rise above it all."

Rich C., Eric's high school friend

Thursday, Oct. 27, 2011 – 6:03 p.m.

Still waiting ...

In case you were wondering, we're still waiting. Hopefully, the doc will call before the day is done, but we don't even really know what data he'll have to share. Maybe he'll at least have insight on yesterday's leg MRI. Best case is, he will tell us with which type of cancer we're dealing.

Overall today I am feeling wiped out and more sick than usual. That said, with a higher dose of pain meds, the leg pain is under better control. I suspect a large portion of my challenge is nerves. Sitting tight for now.

ONE HOUR LATER – 7:06 p.m.

Pathology is back ...

I'll keep this short. Please don't go wild with Google. Our consult with our hematologist/oncologist is tomorrow at 4:30 p.m.

Pathology shows adenocarcinoma of the lung (source), with secondary cancers in the left fibula (I've been having much more than DVT pain), and brain (the 9mm anomaly). The chest, neck, and abdomen also are involved.

More tests will be done to make certain the exact cancer type we're dealing with, but Tammy and I, along with our doctor, may choose to pursue treatment sooner than later given the best available data. Other needed tests are: more stains – 3-plus days out; and genetic testing – 7 to 10 days out. Still a lot unknown. Please continue to keep us in your prayers.

VERY MUCH LATER – 11:19 p.m.

A work-in-process entry ...

OK, so for a few days now I've been trying to think through an entry that explains my world view through the cancer process. At this stage it seems almost presumptuous to post any "theological dissertations," but here's the outline going through my head.

"Why me God?" – *changing to,*

> "What do you have for me today God? I know you have plans for me, to prosper and not to harm. To give a hope and a future. You love me more than I will ever know."

"I'm in control and know the best for me." – *changing to,*

> "God is in control and wants me to follow Him daily through the good and bad times."

"It's all about me." – *changing to,*

> "It's all about God who loves me deeply and grieves as I go through this. He will be (and already is) using this to touch so many lives."

"I am strong and can will myself through this." – *changing to,*

> "I am weak and must depend on God for all I need, trusting for healing, but knowing His plan is ultimately the best."

"I can't do this!" – *changing to,*

> "With the help of God and so many who love me, I will fight this daily with faith that healing can come – either in this life or in eternity with Him."

"I must be healed in this life, because who else will care for my family?" – *changing to,*

> "He is able to care for my wife and kids."

I've not had enough time to make the impact I want."
> – *changing to,*

> "What if God gets more glory through my losing the cancer battle?"

Healing from the consequences of sin is the hugest miracle ever – and it's open to everyone who accepts it. For those of you who don't share my Bible-centered world view, I'd welcome questions. Might give me a good diversion from the cancer battle to come.

I'm sure there's a ton more to write, but I think I'll stop. Today has rocked our world. If only we could just edit out October 2011.

That said, in the midst of a really horrible situation, we put our faith in God and hope to keep growing each day.

Please pray that we'd see God at work each day. Specifically pray for wisdom as we consult with our hematologist tomorrow at 4:30 p.m. This should kick off the long process of treatment and, God-willing, full remission.

~ *Responses from Family and Friends* ~

I know it's been a long time since we've been in touch. I am saddened to hear about what you are going through. You and your family are in my thoughts and prayers; I sympathize with the agony of waiting. Would that I could do aught else. Blessings to you and to your family.
Sara P., Eric's college friend

Your words are true. God is grieved. He can bring the best out of this no matter what, and He does care for you. But you are also right in that they are not words easily spoken. Remember Christ was in such agony in the garden that He sweat drops of blood. Thank you for your honesty. I pray you will continue to bring all of your emotions, as well as pleas for healing, before the Lord. We are not in your shoes, but we are crying and pleading [along] with you. Hold on to Jesus. He will walk with you through this. *Becky J., formerly at Village*

So concerned for what you are facing right now. Though I don't know you, Eric, you have my prayers! *Nancy P., mom of Tammy's friend*

Our hearts break for you during this difficult time filled with unknowns. Please know that you have an East Coast family lifting you up daily for healing and restoration. Our God is still sovereign and He WILL be glorified throughout this ordeal.
Dan and Lisa B., friends in Boston

Just read through your guest book. Man, you have a lot of great friends and family! Praise God! You're not going through this alone. I was thinking of the Psalm 23 passage. God does not always deliver us from the valley of death, but He is there with us. My prayers are not only for your healing but for strength for your family as they are trying to deal with this. Lord bless. *James J., friend*

Friday, Oct. 28, 2011 – 4:58 p.m.

Expect delays: tonight's meeting ...

Just a short note to say that it will likely take more time than normal for us to absorb what Dr. Andersen shares tonight.

In the past few weeks, I have tried to be a timely journalist and let all of you know developments as they happen. We, as praying people who have lived on the other side of times like this, know that specific updates and prayer requests are great to get. However, tonight, I'm going to force space.

Our parents will get updates (our dads will be in the room at the meeting with us) and they can update our siblings. Updates beyond that will likely be done tomorrow via CaringBridge.

Here's to the fight ahead! Thanks again for covering us in so much love, care, and prayer.

"The biopsy came back consistent with Stage IV adenocarcinoma lung cancer. It clearly fits into a lung panel.

"Any cancer that has left home base *(in this case the lung)* is Stage IV. You can have just one spot in a bone or brain, or multiple spots; it's still Stage IV.

"The PET scan showed enlarged hot nodes in the neck and in the chest, and in the abdomen you have a consolidation abnormality 4.7 centimeter – *(atypical)*.

"The brain MRI showed a 9 mm nodule in the frontal parietal region.

"The left lower extremity (leg) MRI showed what could be a primary bone tumor. That means there are two uncommon tumors at the same time … making it even more atypical.

"More specific lab tests are in process. We could wait for those results to come in, but that will take from 7-10 days. What we can do is treat using standard lung chemotherapy, and then tweak the therapy once the results are in. That would be my preference, because things are growing in front of us.

"With reference to the grade of a tumor under the microscope – how aggressive the cells are – grade 1 is not very aggressive; grade 3 is very aggressive; and grade 2 is somewhere in between. Yours is grade 3.

"Radiation on the leg, can be done now, but is merely palliative *(only relieving pain, not curing)*, so for pain, take 3 oxycodone pills every 3 hours as needed. Clearly you have DVTs and PE clots, so you'll continue with the twice-daily Lovenox shots. And, if needed later on, the brain nodule can be treated with a gamma knife. And, we'll treat with two 3-week cycles of standard chemotherapy and then regroup.

"For Monday's chemo – Expect fatigue the first week; the second and third weeks should be better. You'll have no resistance to infection, and, since it's flu season, call if you have fever, etc.

"We'll monitor blood counts, red and white; and give you anti-nausea meds. A nurse will check your veins because there's no port, and treatment on Monday will be by IV, if your veins are good. You can expect hair thinning, and hair loss is a guarantee after cycle 2 or 3.

"You may have an allergic reaction to the chemo [this first time], so you'll take steroid pills before treatment. Odds of a reaction are less than 5 percent. Of that 5 percent, a reaction tends to be a mild, flushing sensation, change in heart rate, and blood pressure.

"We will start very slowly, I guess theoretically someone could be exquisitely sensitive and have a more severe reaction, but I haven't seen one of those in years. Treatment takes about three hours.

"Outcomes: what to expect – You're very atypical; you don't fit into the averages. Within the patient population, the average person with this type of cancer is 70 years old, has a heavy-smoking history, heart disease, diabetes, and may not be able to tolerate therapy. One would look at you and say, "young, healthy, and able to tolerate treatment." So you're very odd; I can't quote data that fits a demographic like you. It just doesn't exist.

"Stage IV adenocarcinoma lung cancer is not curable. It is not in an area of curability, but in an area of treatability. The average outcome, on the average population with Stage IV lung cancer, is 8-14 months. Really critical is the response to chemo.

"Our goal is to treat it, knock it down, and control it for as long as we can."

Questions asked
by Eric, Tammy, or their fathers:

Q: Are there experimental treatments to consider?

Dr. Andersen: "What's probably going to confound your eligibility is your odd presentation, because in trials they want a very clean-cut demographic. We can't even consider it right now; we don't have all the answers back yet. But let's say we get test results back and have more information, at every step along the way there are always options for other therapies. We could have second or third line options – after information is clearer and after the first chemo."

Q: There must be something positive you can leave us with …

Dr. Anderson: "It is hard, I agree, when you're talking to a 35-year-old, and you're talking about Stage IV cancer. Where is the silver lining? There may not be a silver lining."

Q: At what point do conversations change from treatment to palliative?

Dr. Anderson: "That happens when I feel we've run out of options for treatment, and/or the patient tells me otherwise."

Time to fight ...

We have a plan of attack. Chemo starts Monday.

Our prayer is that the cancer in my body will react really well to the cocktail of meds delivered. We'll go two rounds and test just before the third round. We will also hope that the sub-type of cancer I have will have specific traits (determined by ongoing tests) that will allow us to layer on even more cancer-destroying meds.

The best plan the doc can offer is treatment with remission as the intent. We will continue to ask God for full healing.

♦ PLEASE PRAY FOR:

Hope for us – we don't want to be discouraged by "averages;" my case is not average.

Endurance through the chemo, etc.; I am scared of what chemo could bring.

Truth to invade our minds day and night; there are lots of lies and discouragements there right now.

My body to respond really well to the chemo treatments in the coming weeks, and for a good response from my body to the pain killers over the weekend.

Wisdom to know whether to pursue radiation and possibly even a biopsy of the cancer in the leg that is causing so much pain.

God's protection over the kids – we want them to know what they need to, but we also want to protect some of their innocence.

~ *Responses from Family and Friends* ~

Just read your most recent update ... Wow! Thank you so much for letting all of us share in the unknown with you. I'm learning much and so appreciate the wisdom and perspective you are able to give. Praying for your strength of heart, mind and spirit, constantly!

JerriLyn K., friend

Thanks so much for sharing your heart Eric. Though I've never met you, I feel like I know you. Thanks for keeping us updated and suggesting ways to pray. May you see the Holy Spirit move in everyone you meet through this battle.   *Nancy K. W., Tammy's college friend*

Like so many others here I really wish I had some divine revelation on what to say to you, but your post says more than I could. We have been praying for you since we first heard, even the boys pray daily for you (though Zac keeps forgetting your last name, and you end up being Mr. Wheel ... I'm not certain but I think he is connecting HeerWAGEN to wagon wheel – just a guess). We love you all very much and are asking all the people we know to be praying for you! God Bless,

Keith K., friend

Eric, I agree with your "world view." Only God and with God can we do anything in this world. God loves you more than you will ever know. Julie [her daughter who had cancer and is now with the Lord] said that we live in a fallen and sick world, and some of the stuff just gets on us, even as God's children. Through it all, you will give God the glory and we are praying that will mean a complete healing that will give Him just that. I am enlisting as many praying Christians around the world as I can. We prayed for you at church last night as well. May God give you the strength for each day as you take this one day at a time.

Kathy B, Village

"A work in process ..." Eric this entry is so powerful! I am so touched by your faith and how you are looking at the situation! God is working through you immensely! Many prayers and love from us! Love you guys!

Ashley M., Tammy's sister-in-law

Eric, I am so sorry to hear this news. We hope and pray that God will continue to bless you and keep you safe, and strengthen you as you go through this very difficult chapter in your life, and bring you more blessings in the days to come. We know God can do anything and are expecting miracles. God bless you my friend,

Kyle R., best man at Eric's and Tammy's wedding

Saturday, Oct. 29, 2011 – 6:34 p.m.

Good grief!

Denial, anger, bargaining, depression, or acceptance? Not sure where I land in the grief spectrum. Mostly, I've been super tired today.

Had a few visitors. Beat the neighbor at Scrabble while his mom and sister helped spruce up our house. Unfortunately I drained myself dry of energy in doing so (insert nap). Saw my sister, mom, and nephews, too, nice visit. While I know fighting is what we must do, the weariness and pain pushes for the opposite – fear and resignation. My sister encouraged me to find my fight (insert another nap).

Thanks also to Ellie's school bus buddy's family who took Timmy and Ellie to the zoo. Huge help to have had the noise out of the house for a few hours this morning. (NOTE – even as I type this, Timmy is running loops through the downstairs with Ellie's pink stroller, making copious amounts of noise.)

Now I work to keep my head screwed on straight. We won't really know how effective chemo is until nearly nine weeks out. Just thinking about what is ahead of us is enough to get me short of breath and sick all over.

Hopefully tomorrow can bring enough distraction/non-cancer focus/rest that I won't borrow too much trouble from Monday's upcoming chemo.

~ Responses from Family and Friends ~

Thank you for the latest information, Eric. You are a wonderful young man. When we don't understand, we pray. When we weep and are sad over this, we pray. When we get mad at God over the seemingly unfairness of it all, we still pray. AND we'll continue to pray for you in these coming days.   *Terri B., Village*

Reading through your story here, I've been flooded with memories of you at Walker Hall [Illinois State University]. So many prayers and petitions for you and your family, I pray God protects and guards your hearts and minds on this journey, wherever it leads.
Bethany P., Eric's college friend

Praying for you and Tammy, Eric, and especially for your sweet children. Love in Christ,   *Laurie and Jim G., Village*

Sunday, Oct. 30, 2011 – 10:48 p.m.

Bring on the chemo ...

So it is the night before chemo. I've spent much of today sleeping and resting and working unsuccessfully to get the leg pain under control – a pretty ugly day (except for some awesome loving from my family and church family). This is somewhat disheartening since today could arguably be the "high" point going into the week of chemo. I am frustrated, confused, worn out, and at times wishing I could just hit the reset button.

♦ SO WHY FIGHT?

Here are some thoughts to bolster my resolve going into tomorrow:

> I love my wife and kids and I want to be around to grow old with them. I love the idea of eternity with God, but I am not in a rush to step into eternity.

> I am young and have lots of life ahead of me by most standard measures. Suffering can lead to maturity; I want to see the harvest of this suffering.

> The Bible encourages me (us) to ask, seek, and knock, trusting that God will provide and open doors. As such, I press forward asking for a miracle of physical healing. I am bolstered by so many praying for me and my family (many of whom I don't even know). We continue to petition God for healing. Time and time again we see God move in response to the prayers of His people.

♦ SO I FIGHT

I fight knowing the following:

> It's all about God and His glory ... not mine. I'm not saying this as an easy out, in case I don't beat this cancer, nor do I say this as if to suggest that God doesn't care or love me. He deeply loves me, and because of that I don't get to choose how this ends.

> God, in His perfect wisdom and goodness, will bring about the best possible outcome from a really lousy season in my life. This month of October, more so than any other month in my life, has shown me I am not in control. That's very scary to

say, but I believe it can also be very freeing as I fall back on who the God of the Bible is.

He is: I AM, Gracious, Compassionate, Slow to Anger, Loving, Faithful, Forgiving, and Just (Exodus 34).

I am beyond tired and often borrowing trouble from tomorrow (like I know I shouldn't). With God's help though, I will push forward one day at a time (one hour at a time) surrounded by so many who love me, trusting Him for a miracle.

Thanks for your continued prayers and love.

~ *Responses from Family and Friends* ~

Hi, Eric and Tammy, Good to see you and your kiddos today [at church]. We are praying for you as you start chemo tomorrow. "The Lord is the everlasting God, the Creator of the ends of the earth. He does not faint or grow weary; his understanding is unsearchable. He gives power to the faint, and to him who has no might he increases strength. Even youths shall faint and be weary, and young men fall exhausted; but they who wait for the Lord shall renew their strength; they shall mount up with wings like eagles; they shall run and not be weary; they shall walk and not faint" (Isa. 40: 28-31). Much love,
Brian and Melissa L., close friends

It is late on Sunday. I am thinking about you. Praying for you and amazed by the manner and reflection with which you are writing. The good Lord has blessed you richly, with family, children, a loving wife and extended family and friends. He has much in store for you. We are all anxious to have Him reveal His plans – but as you said, it is on His time and His schedule – may the good Lord's will be done! Continue to be strong Eric.   *Mike T., Intel*

"For what we proclaim is not ourselves, but Jesus Christ as Lord, with ourselves as your servants for Jesus' sake. For God, who said, 'Let light shine out of darkness,' has shone in our hearts to give the light of the knowledge of the glory of God in the face of Jesus Christ. But we have this treasure in jars of clay, to show that the surpassing power belongs to God and not to us. We are afflicted in every way, but not crushed; perplexed, but not driven to despair; persecuted, but not forsaken; struck down, but not destroyed; always carrying in the body the death of Jesus, so that the life of Jesus may also be manifested in our bodies" (2 Cor. 4:5-10 ESV). Thinking of you tonight and praying for peace and perseverance.   *Tracy D., formerly at Village*

Monday, Oct. 31, 2011, 6:30 p.m.

One down ...

Chemo – Round 1 – went fine today. I'm tired and more crabby than normal (especially given that I tried to update my iPhone OS and had stuff blow up on me), but we have the right medicine in my body to kill off the cursed cancer. Whoo hoo.

~ *Responses from Family and Friends* ~

I'm amazed at your ability to write so well in the midst of all the pain and stress you are going through. What a gift! It's often difficult for me to write when I'm going through tough times. I really appreciate your perspective and your openness.   *Mythraie G., Village*

We pray not just for healing, but that in your suffering you will experience fellowship with Christ and obtain a greater knowledge of Him. Thank you for sharing your experience walking in the path of suffering. We are praying for your entire family.
John and Sarah S., missionary friends in India

I just found out about this web page and your condition this morning. You said, "I love the idea of eternity with God, but I am not in a rush to step in to eternity." Through this and the rest of your commentary I believe you are in a great spiritual state. Now we need your physical state to catch up. I will join others in that prayer. May God bless you in this time of tribulation.   *Hector L., Intel*

Hey, Buddy! Glad the first one is done. Since you mentioned, it I did the iPhone update too and thought I lost stuff due to the scary messages it was giving me. Butcher had the same experience. But eventually it all transferred and loaded fine. Maybe that will happen for you. You need to be here in the office so we can be comparing iPhone notes! Get back in here!! Stay strong ... we are missing you here big time.
Mike L., Intel

Whoo hoo, indeed!!! Did Chip give you the verse I came across last night? Rom 15:13 - my heart echoed Paul's words as I prayed for you and Tammy: "May the God of hope fill you with all joy and peace in believing, so that by the power of the Holy Spirit you may abound in hope." Rest well tonight.   *Natalie H., Village*

[There were 225 responses in the guestbook
from October 19-31, 2011.]

November 2011

~ *The Second Month* ~

Tuesday, Nov. 1, 2011 – 3:13 p.m.

ER number 6

Off to the ER … again. Higher fever than is good post chemo. More when we know more. We're confused and frustrated for sure. Hopefully this is the cancer cells burning up. We'll see what the ER doc says.

LATER – 6:12 p.m.

Heading back home

[From Tammy] Eric's getting discharged soon. Fever is down and counts look OK. Glad about that and hoping not to need the ER again! Eric is still very tired. Please pray for good sleep tonight, and that the chemo meds will be fighting all the cancer cells super effectively – and not causing too much havoc with the "good" cells.

EVEN LATER – 8:51 p.m.

Rough day … again

[From Eric] Hard to stay positive today. No two ways about it, chemo sucks! And from everything we're told, tomorrow is likely to be even worse. I should expect to feel like I got hit by a bus. Can't say I'm looking forward to that in any way, shape or form. At least tomorrow afternoon we figure out a radiation treatment for my left leg. That could get me to walking reasonably again.

I am thankful for the huge outpouring of support for me and my family as we go through this. People around the world – many of whom we don't even know – are praying. So amazing and humbling.

I know the worst thing for me now is to grow discouraged and not fight; but it is hard to keep up the battle. One of the guestbook entries reminded me of the time when Moses had to keep his arms aloft for the Israelite armies to win. If his arms drooped, the Israelite army started to lose. Fortunately Moses' men came alongside him and held his arms up for him, and the Israelite nation won (Exodus 17:12-13). Thanks for "supporting our arms" and helping us "win the battle." We are so very weary ... so, so weary.

Blessed to not be doing this alone. Thanks again for the help with meals, chores, kid care, and so much more.

♦ PLEASE PRAY:

That tomorrow's "hit-by-a-bus" feeling will be bearable;

That the fever would subside;

That we'd connect with a Christian counselor who can help us process this last month and a bit. So much to absorb. (I've got the name of a good counselor from my church.)

That the kids would keep adjusting ... this grows harder by the day for them, things are not normal and they know it;

That Tammy would find times of refreshing ... she is having to be the strong back for the family right now.

~ *Responses from Family and Friends* ~

Hi Eric, I'm thinking of your and your family. Keep your spirits up during the chemo. I'm glad you were able to get started right away!! Hugs to you and your family!!! *Tania F., Intel*

I'm offering up prayers for you. I am so impressed by your attitude in the face of such uncertainty. God certainly has already blessed you with strength. *Lorri S., friend of Eric's Aunt Ruthie in Colorado*

We are continually lifting you and your family up in prayer. The God of the universe has you and your family in His hands.
Rich C., Eric's high school friend

Eric, we are so praying for you! God is the great physician and he knows every cancer cell that needs to be eradicated! Blessings,
Jane E., Village

Yes, let us hold up your arms Eric and Tammy. There are many of us and we all can take turns! We will not grow tired of praying for you, of holding you up however you need. Love you. *JerriLyn K., friend*

Wednesday, Nov. 2, 2011 – 8:04 p.m.

Blessed ...

In the news today … The "bus" that was supposed to hit me was smaller than expected. Thanks for your prayers! The fever is mostly under control and sleep was pretty good last night.

I now have impressive "tats" [tattoos] on my left leg – very fashionable dots that will help with the radiation therapy on my left leg fibula (*outer, thinner bone from knee to ankle*). Treatments start tomorrow and will likely run daily for two to three weeks. I'm looking forward to much less pain in the left leg. And I can use a handicap parking card, too, for the few times we actually head out and about.

I think I've found a counselor who can give me and the rest of the family some tools to help us through the recent cancer trauma. And, we still have a lot of people helping us out – my brother spent the night at our home last night. Friends of ours are taking the kids to AWANA. Other friends sent us some Jeff Allen funny DVDs, and the list goes on. What a huge blessing.

◆ SPEAKING OF BLESSINGS:

"Blessings" have been on my mind. Even midst the hideous cancer, we are very blessed. But what does it really mean to be blessed as a follower of Christ?

The book of Hebrews, chapter 11 (especially toward the end), doesn't necessarily paint a picture of Paradise-like blessings. Then, looking to the book of James, I see that suffering/testing brings perseverance, which ultimately produces maturity. I have to admit I really don't like the idea that God uses lousy times in our lives to bring about eternal blessings. I'd much rather take the blessings the easy way. ☺

That said, I know this short lifetime we're given is but a blip against eternity and we will be held responsible for how we invest what God has given us each day. I want to be one who stores treasure in Heaven. I want to daily be found faithful and thankful amidst the suffering. I know God is good and big. He has a plan for the redemption of His creation, and He has a specific plan for my life (that I know), and He has promised to bring it to completion.

So what does this mean to me today? Well, how about the great words of another "inspired writer," Cole Porter, as sung by Bing Crosby:

"When I'm worried and I can't sleep, I count my blessings instead of sheep, And I fall asleep counting my blessings;

"When my bankroll is getting small, I think of when I had none at all, And I fall asleep counting my blessings

"I think about a nursery and I picture curly heads, And one by one I count them as they slumber in their beds;

"If you're worried and you can't sleep, Just count your blessings instead of sheep, And you'll fall asleep counting your blessings."

Sweet dreams to all!

~ *Responses from Family and Friends* ~

We are praying continually for you! My Bible study up here in Ridgefield, Wash., is also on their knees for you. Prayers for peace, comfort and wisdom are at the top of the list, but especially for a miracle! Hugs to all!
Tanya P., formerly at Village

I'm so glad to hear sleep was attainable last night. Just as I plumped my pillow for the night, you came to mind. In fact, praying for you has become part of my bedtime ritual – as I look forward to a peaceful rest, I pray the same for you and more. Love you guys.   *Leslie E., Village*

Thanking the Lord for His many answers to specific prayers that you had today. Thank you for sharing from your heart – it is inspiring, and your words are faith building. Continuing to pray for you and Tammy, Timmy, and Ellie.   *Melissa and Brian L., close friends*

What an encouraging post from you today! SO glad the chemo today came in the small bus today. We are hanging in there with you in thoughts and prayers all throughout the day (and lots during the night too:). Continue to hang on tight to the Lord. You are a huge blessing to so many. Hugs and love to you, Tammy, Ellie and Timmy. Love you,
Chick and Scott L., Village Life Group

Thursday, Nov. 3, 2011 – 7:18 p.m.

The bus does laps

[From Tammy] Well, Eric is back in the hospital.

Had his first radiation session, then a quick visit to the ENT. Our last stop for the day was a chemo class – a little out of order, chemo class usually takes place BEFORE chemo begins at all. The nurse didn't like the way he looked during class, so sent him downstairs to see his doctor. We're so thankful we were there so they could see how he was doing. He could be released tomorrow but they're playing it by ear. Glad to have extra monitoring.

Friday, Nov. 4, 2011 – 10:44 a.m.

In the hospital

[From Tammy again] The doctor says Eric's here at least until tomorrow. All the labs and counts look fine, but he still feels awful. Hoping they can find where the "disconnect" is so he can start feeling better SOON! Thanks for the notes and prayers. In the sleepless times we pull up the [CaringBridge] guestbook and feel encouraged.

Saturday, Nov. 5, 2011 – 3:45 p.m.

Still in the hospital ...

[From Tammy again] Eric's still in the hospital. Today the infectious disease doctor came to look him over and see if there's anything that might have been missed in all the testing. They'll do a few more tests, but it doesn't sound like they're expecting anything. So our best guess is that he'll be discharged tomorrow – but we'll wait and see.

Thanks for your continued prayers. Eric's still in pain, although the doctor found some meds that seem to work better and that's good. The physical therapist got him a walker so we're working on building muscles and stamina after over a month of only being able to sit or lie down [because of intense leg pain]. That's a lot of work to build back up!

Please pray for the doctors as they continue to look at Eric's data. I love that he is different from any one else in the world, but his "atypical" responses are sure making this more complicated! I'm just hoping the cancer is being obliterated in a way that is also "atypical." We're still waiting on the genetic-level testing of the cancer – my prayer is that the tests will show something that allows the doctors to combat the cancer even more effectively.

And finally, thanks so much for the notes here, the visits to the hospital, and the other encouragements. We have the BEST family and friends, and we know it!

~ *Responses from Family and Friends* ~

Glad you were at the right place at the right time yesterday, yet sorry to know that it involves another hospital stay. Praying for you and your lovely family and the wonderful, skilled doctors caring for you!

Colleen H., Tammy's friend

May His healing hand surround Eric, His wisdom guide the doctors and nurses, and His protection envelop all of you. Prayers continue. We love you so much!

Bonnie and George J., Tammy's aunt and uncle in Arizona

We serve an amazing God who loves you and your family irrespective of current circumstances! I am praying to Our Lord, the One who heals, who provides, and who knows how many hairs are on your head as well as the cells in your body that are healthy or not. I am praying that he heals you completely and that in the process you and your family know and sense his presence deeply! Anxiously waiting for your return to Intel! Keep your eyes focused on Him.

Fred J., Intel

Praying the doctors will work quickly to figure everything out. Have shared with many others, so you have tons of prayers/petitions going to God. Blessings to all!

Nancy O., Village

Eric, Tammy, Ellie, and Timmy, We are praying for you daily. Remember the footprint in the sand. God is carrying you through this time. We can't do anything, but God can. Pray for comfort, peace, strength, wisdom, miracles, healing, and a good sleep tonight. Pray for God's protection over your family. Thank you for your journals and insights! We are in this journey and battle with you. Love you all.

Lynda F. and family, Village

Sunday, Nov. 6, 2011 – 11:01 a.m.

Get to go home today

[From Eric] The last few days in the hospital are pretty much a blur – thanks to my not feeling well and strong meds from the docs. ☺ Later today I should be released with yet more prescriptions, a very stylin' walker (sans tennis balls) and the hope of a few weeks of feeling better before the next chemo round. As Tammy noted in earlier posts, I am far from typical in cancer/chemo responses (something Dr. Andersen repeated this morning), but I'm hoping for the "expected" break from the harsh chemo side effects before we dive into Round 2 on November 21.

Last night's CT scan of my chest didn't raise any flags, but it didn't confirm much either. Overall, the chest lymph nodes are still swollen, the pulmonary embolisms are getting smaller, and no new masses. We were hoping to see chemo impact in the scans, but it is too early to see progress (radiography lags clinical by quite a bit). Bottom line is ... nobody quite understands why I got the fevers I got, but they are discontinuing the antibiotic and letting me go home. We'll keep watch from home.

I am SO blessed with great family (both sides) and friends. As an example, my brother, father-in-law, and dad each spent a night with me at the hospital. (Nights seem to be the hardest for me – my spirits get down all too easily, especially when I'm left alone.)

As much as I'd love to turn to the last few pages of the book they call my life and read how this all ends, I don't have that ability. In fact, I don't even know what later today holds. So, I find myself needing to rest in God's love for me and His plan to take all the bad things and work them for good. I don't like going through cancer one bit, but I am learning to actively look for God at work in the midst of the cancer.

If I allow myself to borrow trouble from tomorrow, it becomes all too overwhelming and I can't do it. However, I can do this – one day at a time – with so much help from family, friends, and my God who loves me ... even more than anyone else does.

◆ PLEASE PRAY FOR:

Full healing;

Rest for Tammy – this has been a long haul for her as well;

My pessimistic side to take a back seat to hope;

God to be glorified, and for us to see some of the goodness coming from this horrible time;

Ellie and Timmy to flex with us as we go through the cancer fight.

~ *Responses from Family and Friends* ~

Thank you for trusting us enough to share your journey so openly. Know that we are praying for you in a mighty way, for the effectiveness of treatment, for healing, for wisdom for the doctors, for the full range of emotions that you must be experiencing ... that HE will be your strength each day, hour, minute ... each step of the way. Much love to your family from ours. *Jamie M., formerly at Village*

We actually met years ago at a picnic in Allison's back yard. Ellie and Avree were "only" children then, no brothers in the picture yet. I was so impressed with your family cohesiveness and the caring you radiated to all of us during that summer gathering. As a grandmother, I have really enjoyed watching Avree's devotion to her best friend, Ellie, and have been so impressed with Ellie's ongoing kindness to Avree. I pray that you continue to feel the Lord's presence with you every step of the way; we know that He is always with us and comforts us and loves us through every situation we face. May God's blessing continue to rain down upon you and your family as you continue to serve Him. *Pamela Z., grandma of Ellie's friend*

This is Hannah, from Tammy's work. We met at the Pittock Mansion. I have to tell you that God is really using you in my life. Reading your journal has kept my thoughts turned toward God, and keeps me asking: how am I glorifying Him in this moment? What you said in your last post really hit me between the eyes, "I want to daily be found faithful and thankful amidst the suffering." I think God is teaching me how to be thankful in my life right now (you'd think that'd be an easy lesson, but not so much). So thank you for being an instrument of God in my life. I'm praying for you. *Hannah C., Tammy's coworker*

Tuesday, Nov. 8, 2011 – 11:55 a.m.

Improvement?

Well ... two relatively uneventful nights at home. Sleep is going okay and pain is better managed. The doc has me on a "happy pill" that should help even out my emotions as I process through the huge life changes.

In just a matter of weeks, I went from healthy to Stage IV lung cancer. (The doc called yesterday and said that genetic testing confirmed lung cancer – despite the "atypical" presentation.)

While in the hospital I got coaching on using a walker. At the start, I could barely get out of the room. Yesterday, I walked from the parking lot all the way in to my radiation appointment. Once at the reception desk, I was torn between celebrating and swearing (to be honest). The radiation is to reduce the pain from the cancer in my left leg. My world has been made so much smaller since the cancer. (More on that later.)

On the good news front, I am feeling more myself today. Treatments are underway and I hope to have more good days before Round 2 of chemo on November 21. So, again, I remind myself as I type to: Celebrate the little things, appreciate how big my world is (with all the love and prayers on my behalf around the world), and simply look to God to be who we know He is. He is good and big and can take something as horrible as cancer and use it for good – not just in my life, but in the lives of so many.

♦ PRAYERS:

Complete healing ... and soon please. ☺

Strength for Tammy ... this has been super hard on the kids too, their behaviors are definitely showing the stress they are under.

We want to see God glorified today in what we do or don't do. It is hard to keep a thankful heart when pain and sickness are constant companions. So please pray that we would choose thankfulness.

(As the flurry of news slows, I may not journal each day, but rather journal as there is news to share. If you get curious, give a call or email us in between journal posts.)

Thursday, Nov. 10, 2011, 8:33p.m.

Quick update ...

As of today, I'm half-way through radiation on my leg. I am walking better and the pain is under better control. Tomorrow we do another radiation dose on the leg and then head to St. Vincent's to have a "port" (*a small appliance connected to a vein beneath the skin for injections and blood draws*) installed in my chest. This should save me a lot of IV pokes in the coming weeks and months. We won't know the extent of the good being done by the chemo until we do more tests mid-December. More waiting – which I do oh so well.

We've got lots of help from those around us and continue to be so appreciative. Thanks to everyone!

Friday, Nov. 11, 2011, 8:02 p.m.

Port install done

After radiation today, I headed to St. Vincent's for outpatient surgery to install my port [in preparation for chemo]. Nurses now can access the port on my chest vs. having to hunt down a good IV vein in my arm. The port should minimize damage to my veins in the coming months.

The leg pain is still present, but on the whole I am feeling pretty good. For the moment, I think we've found the new norm. I know we'll regress with the next chemo, but for now I'll try to focus on the good things each day brings.

Beyond healing, please continue to lift up my family. They are enduring the stress of cancer right along with me.

Daddy and Timmy napping?

This weekend, my side of the family is going to deck our halls for Christmas ... I know it is early, but we love the Christmas season, and their decorating will be my early birthday present.

Saturday, Nov. 12, 2011 – 6:36 p.m.

Random updates

Today has been mostly a drowsy day, but the pain has been under much better control, thankfully. The port surgery seems to be healing well. We continue to receive so much love and care. Tammy got a gift from the neighborhood women, one of our pastors just stopped by to pray with me, another family is bringing us dinner tonight. We are very blessed. Thanks again (can't say it enough).

Tomorrow my side of the family descends on our home and will "Christmas-ize" it. (Early yes, but this way we can get family pictures in our own home with all the decorations. Photos are generous gift from another friend.)

I'm ready for cancer to be done, but likely this is just the beginning. (Note – totally open to a miracle.) November 21 is Round 2 of chemo. I don't quite know what side effects to anticipate. Hopefully we can avoid the hospital. The testing to find out if the chemo is working comes the week before Round 3 – figure mid-December. So for now we just wait and pray.

Here are some questions and answers I don't think I've addressed yet on the site, but I know some are wondering.

Q. Do you still have your hair?
A. Yes, but I expect it to fall out in about a month, in Round 2 of chemo.

Q. How are your spirits?
A. Depends on the time of day you ask. The leg pain is getting under better control, and that does wonders for my mood. Overall though, I am still really struggling with the lung cancer diagnosis – lots to process.

Q. How's Tammy doing?
A. She's a trooper. Thankfully she has good friends with whom she can cry. This is a huge change for her as well. We both are growing through this.

Q. What about the kids?
A. They are stretched thin; their behavior shows it at times. They are trying hard, but they are still kids.

Q. Has your doctor mentioned a prognosis?

63

A. Yes, but as someone once said, there is no expiration date stamped on my forehead. It is our prayer and hope that I am in the healing phase and we'll see the cancer go to full remission.

Q. Do you blame God for this?

A. I know God is good, and this cancer is simply the result of living in a broken world with broken bodies. God is saddened over my sickness, and as a believer in Jesus, I know I am promised healing ... it may be healing in Heaven or it may be healing in this life. God is good and will do what is best for me. Hard to get my head around that, and I doubt I'll ever fully understand, but I know it to be true.

Thanks again to everyone for their loving support!

~ *Responses from Family and Friends* ~

Eric, Thank you for your transparency in sharing your heart. As far as I am concerned, you are right on track. Only God knows and only God is Love and totally good. We can't go wrong with that. Prayers, tears and love go up to our Father and out to you. Trusting in the waiting and in the dark is hard to do, but God certainly rewards faith, here or there. I continue to lift up your family as well – all of them. God has called you all to a very hard thing, but He will not fail you. God's best Dear Ones!

Kathy B., Village

Many, many good and healthy thoughts your way. We're really missing you around the office – and saving your corner office for you when you're ready to return to our little zoo. Hope you have a wonderful birthday with your family and are looking forward to your daughter's birthday on Thursday. Stay strong, friend – we're all sending good vibes your way. *David Y., Intel*

Glad to hear that the pain has lessened in your leg and you've been able to get up and around better. I bet that helps to lift your emotions a bit too. Did it hurt to get the Picc line placed? I always thought that would be hard to have done, even if they do numb you up for it. I guess one must be brave when you have no choice in the matter. We continue to pray for you, Tammy, Ellie and Timmy. Look forward to see your family pic....with hair! *JerriLyn K. and family, friend*

Monday, Nov. 14, 2011, 11:35 p.m.

Happy birthday, Eric!

[From Tammy] Well, today was Eric's 36th birthday! The kids woke up excited to give him their presents and we had some good family time, as well as some fun visits from family and friends. This week should be a pretty good one as most of the chemo effects have lessened and mobility is improving. Monday, Nov. 21, is the next chemo. We'll see how it impacts him this time.

Yesterday Eric's extended family came over and decorated our home for Christmas, and it looks fabulous. We are enjoying the lights and happy decorations. Ellie's 7th birthday is this Thursday, so that will be a fun time too. Then her party with her friends is on Saturday. Please pray for Eric to have the stamina to participate in and enjoy these special times with us. The kids adore their daddy, and when he's able to be a part of things it just makes everything so much more fun.

Thanks once again to each of you for praying for Eric (and for the rest of us), for your encouraging notes, and the visits, meals, shopping, yard work, etc. We truly appreciate each act of kindness.

~ *Responses from Family and Friends* ~

Happy Birthday! I'd rather it was some cake and silly presents in an Intel conference room. I imagine you'd rather it was that, too. Please stay strong and hopeful. We need you back at the Farm. It's funny, one of the things I remember most about the grueling march that was the vPro launch was working with you on the messages down in that fishbowl conference room off the JF4 lobby. What an annoying pain that was, but I appreciate the high standard you held us all to. What came out of that was work that still endures with the product line today, almost six years later (that is the Intel equivalent of eternity). I'll catch you after Thanksgiving. ... I hope you have lots of family around for Thanksgiving. Good luck on chemo Round 2. I hope it goes smoothly and gets you on the road to healing. Take care, my friend! *Mike F., Intel*

I'm so glad they are giving you the birthday present of an early Christmas. Praying for your family. It's hard enough to have a parent sick for the short run, I cannot fathom the strain on your family during this battle. You are in our prayers. *Kristina W., Eric's college friend*

Tuesday, Nov. 15, 2011, 5:23 p.m.

A new norm?

♦ ON THE GOOD NEW FRONT TODAY:

I had a nice birthday yesterday. I really felt loved on. Thanks to everyone for the birthday wishes.

The port incisions on my chest are healing really well just in time for use with my Monday chemo. Now, instead of lots of needles and hunting for good veins, the nurses just insert a special needle into the port.

I walked in and out, unassisted, for my radiation appointment. The left leg is feeling much better. I'm using less oxycodone and using the walker way less. The last few days have been relatively good health days (using the new norm as the measure).

The kids are out of the house today! It is nice to have extra quiet for a few hours. ☺

My hair hasn't fallen out yet, despite my "nightmares" last night. With family pictures tonight, I was convinced that my hair would fall out before the photographer arrived. Pretty funny what little things become stressors.

Big picture, I'm still processing what it means to have cancer, and we won't know how effective chemo is until mid-December. Just a lot to absorb and so few answers. So ... I remind myself to take things one day at a time, and to watch for what God is doing around me and through me. God is good ... all the time.

Please continue to lift us up in prayer: healing, endurance, hope, stamina with the kids ... Thanks!

Wednesday, Nov. 16, 2011, 10:21 p.m.

"Hair" today, gone tomorrow

Well, we completed the family photos last night, and today my hair started to fall out. I'm somewhat surprised at how bothered I am by the hair loss. Now I just need to decide how long I'll "shed" hair before I just go after my head with clippers. The good news in all this is … with the hair loss, I know my body is reacting as planned to the chemo.

After my second-to-last radiation treatment today, Tammy and I headed out to meet with Dr. Andersen, lead doc on the cancer treatment. He was pleased with my progress and set dates for follow up exams, tests, and chemo. It will likely be December 8 when we do another PET scan and brain MRI. The following week, we'll have results and be able to set the treatment plan beyond December. Please pray for the chemo to stop the cancer growth and to actually reduce the cancer in the body. Here's to healing!

~ Responses from Family and Friends ~

Understand that you are adjusting to a new normal. That is good, but remember there are plenty of us praying that God will restore the "old" normal. Praying for physical rest, spiritual peace, physical healing, and God's grace to carry all of you through the coming days.
Becky J., formerly at Village

Eric. We continue to follow your journal and admire your strength to capture your thoughts for others. As always, you and your family remain in our prayers. One day at a time, one hour at a time, one minute at a time. Continue to treasure what you are thankful for. We Love You
Dave and Ginny H., Eric's dad's cousins and wife Hawaii

Eric, You were prayed for at worship band practice again tonight. People you don't even know here in Arizona are praying for you!
Sandy G., formerly at Village

God's timing is perfect. Glad you were able to get the photos done without concern for your hair. Who knows, perhaps you will like the new look. Kaara and I continue to pray for you each night. She always remembers if I forget. Hope you have a great day celebrating Ellie's birthday. Glad your pain is reduced enough for you to walk better and find some new routine. All the best,
Kris K., Village

Thursday, Nov. 17, 2011, 8:15 p.m.

A day of change

Well my hair has been shaved off ... down to a number-two clipper length. Now the rest can fall out nicely on its own. The Bible says, "... even the very hairs on your head are all numbered," (Matthew 10:30).

It made me laugh to think of God yesterday as my hair was falling out.

> God: "1201, 1202, 1203 ..."
> (a clump of my hair falls out)
> (pause)
> God: "Oh man! ... 1, 2, 3 ..."

Granted, I know God doesn't have to count, but it made me laugh all the same. The passage I used above goes on to say, " ... so don't be afraid; you are worth more than many sparrows" (Luke 12:7). A good reminder as I go through cancer. I don't have to be afraid because I know God cares for me. He knows me so well that He knows the number of hairs on my head. I keep my faith that He will bring full healing to me (hopefully in this life, but for sure in Heaven).

In other news today ... I had my last radiation appointment for my leg. Now we let the chemo do the rest of the work. Thankfully I am now getting around without a walker or any assistance of any kind. I'm still on meds to manage pain, but the pain in my leg is far less than it was.

We don't have anything medical planned between now and Monday's chemo. I just have to work on not being afraid, trusting God, and enjoying each day for what it brings – rather than borrowing trouble from tomorrow.

Thanks again for so many following my CaringBridge posts. We are so richly blessed with the prayers and help from so many. (One example: some ladies from our church make prayer quilts, and I now have a quilt from them. It's gorgeous, and I know that as they stitched it they were praying for me.) Thank you!!!

One specific prayer request for the upcoming weekend – Ellie has her 7th birthday party at Oregon Gymnastics Academy on Saturday. Please pray that I will have the stamina needed to be a part of her special party.

Saturday, Nov 19, 2011, 7:33 p.m.

Birthday success

Just a short note to say I weathered Ellie's party well enough. I was able to be present the whole time. I know Ellie had a blast. Hard to believe she is 7 now.

Monday is coming faster than I want. I am "done" with having cancer, but unfortunately I don't get to choose when I am done.

Here's to a good Sunday with limited worries about Monday. (As usual thanks for the notes, meals, visits, etc. I couldn't make it through all this, were I alone.)

Sunday, Nov. 20, 2011, 8:55 p.m.

Port time

It is chemo-eve, and I'm mostly okay with tomorrow. Since the port is new, I am actually curious how it is going to work. Here's to lots of dead cancer cells with minimal other side effects. It would be nice to avoid a hospital stay the week of Thanksgiving.

This week I am reminded that despite what I may think at times, I am not the only one with problems. A woman in our church went in for heart surgery. The surgeons couldn't restart her heart. She's been in a coma for days and just had to have part of her leg amputated. I know of others going through serious marital challenges, and others who struggle financially. And the list goes on. All that to say – this is a broken world and life can be hard, not just for me with my Stage IV lung cancer.

I am glad that I and my family have Jesus to help us through the difficult times. We are holding on to the promise of better times to come, if not in this life, for sure in Heaven. And even while I'm this side of eternity, I am trusting God to bring something of His eternal Kingdom into this world.

We ask for His healing hand in my life – complete healing now. Regardless of the situation, we look for His grace (unmerited favor), forgiveness, hope, and joy ... to be seen in our lives and understood by those who don't yet count themselves as part of God's family of believers. Thanks for keeping us in your prayers.

Monday, Nov. 21, 2011, 4:48 p.m.

Nothing is easy

[From Tammy]Well, we are back in the ER.

Eric had an anaphylactic *(severe allergic, potentially fatal form of shock affecting respiration, blood pressure and heart rate)* reaction to the chemo meds. Apparently this is rare on the "second" chemo. They were watching for the possibility on the first chemo, but not expecting it today. So, Eric got to ride in an ambulance from the chemo clinic to the ER. We would appreciate prayers for endurance. This feels like being hit when you're already down. Will need to reschedule the chemo, but we don't know when.

A LITTLE LATER – 8:22 p.m.

Home safe

[Eric here] Thanks for the prayers. We got home safely around 6 p.m. Thanks to Tammy's mom (who had the kids all day), and to a friend who gave us a freezer lasagna, we all had a nice dinner when we got home.

For those medical types out there ... my reaction to Taxol (*a chemo drug*) was severe – BP 70/40; pulse 150; red, tingly, and hot, head to toe; then ashen white; put on oxygen immediately; etc. I am thankful for knowledgeable medical staff who were able to help me when the symptoms showed up. I also am thankful for a good ER super close to the cancer treatment offices.

On the plus side – the port was great. Just a little sting when they first accessed it, but great other than that. Now we wait for tomorrow to figure out what the plan is with respect to chemo. It is likely they will continue chemo but buttress against allergic reaction.

Please pray for endurance. I think I should tattoo "atypical" across my forehead. We can't seem to catch a break. Today was discouraging and very scary. I know God is in control and He loves me more than I know, but today it seems more like He is like the "Far Side" comic ... God with His finger poised over the "Smite" button. Here's to a resetting night's sleep for all of us ... the cancer impacts so many more than just me.

Tuesday, Nov. 22, 2011, 2:44 p.m.

Pressing the pause button

Happy Thanksgiving week! This morning I got in touch with my doctor's office. With Dr. Andersen, my lead doc, being on vacation, we are pressing the pause button until he gets back. I've got a 1:30 p.m. appointment with him on Monday next week [after Thanksgiving]. The nurse I spoke with this morning said there are two options for Dr. Andersen – discontinue Taxol altogether ... and pursue a different chemo drug combo, or continue with Taxol ... but do a super slow drip (5-6 hours just to deliver it) and protect against allergic reaction with copious amounts of other meds before and during the chemo. We're disappointed by the delay – for this chemo, and for a cascading failure on the future dates for scan and chemo.

That said, we're trusting God's timing. He was not caught off guard by yesterday's brush with death. The silver lining on this delay is that I should feel really good for Thanksgiving Day. I'm still not at 100 percent, but I am doing better than I have in weeks.

Please keep the notes, visits, and prayers coming. We so appreciate the many people that are on this ride with us. It is humbling to know that you are all supporting us through this cancer. We are truly blessed.

~ *Responses from Family and Friends* ~

Eric, One of the things I am enjoying about this guestbook (although I would have rather been able to learn it another way) is that I am learning so much about your life outside of you being my brother-in-law. You are humble about your achievements, so I am learning a LOT about the Eric that is seen by those who work with you. I have also gotten to read some family stories from the years way before we knew you. There was one weeks ago by your sister and one yesterday from your mom ... what a gift to get these glimpses into who you are. You keep fighting and we will keep praying! We are all in this fight with you! Love,
Dawn R., Tammy's sister

Hi Eric: I used to work with your brother Brian. Heard of your struggle with this cancer thing and wanted to let you know we will be praying for you and your entire family. May God continue to support you with His peace.   *Wanda K., former co-worker of Eric's brother*

71

Wednesday, Nov. 23, 2011, 9:49 p.m.

Giving thanks

Thanks to our unplanned respite from chemo, we are able to host the [Heerwagen family] Thanksgiving meal at our home. They will do all the work, and we get all the fun of Turkey Day, especially the smell of turkey in the oven.

♦ A FEW CANCER-RELATED THANKS:

My leg is so much better ... the radiation and right meds have helped a ton. I even made it to the mall tonight with the family. At home I'm not even using the walker. I'm thankful that I didn't "buy the farm" earlier this week ... that allergic reaction was way too close a brush with death.

So many prayers, helps, and visits ... we definitely feel loved and cared for these days. Thanks to all who are with us on this hard journey. Hope is a wonderful thing ... we keep our hope for the doctor to say some day, "NED" (the lung cancer equivalent of remission, it stands for "no evidence of disease"). Our trust is in God whom we know can heal.

I am way thankful for my lovely wife ... Tammy has been such a huge help in all this. My love for her only grows as we laugh and cry our way through the battle with cancer.

Happy Thanksgiving!!!

~ *Responses from Family and Friends* ~

Glad you were able to get home after all the excitement ... good grief, enough already! You do have an amazing sense of humor through all of this, Eric, and for that alone I think you indeed are very A-typical! We are praying all the time for you. Hugs.   *JerriLyn K., friend*

Eric, you continue to be in our prayers. I hope you do feel better for Thanksgiving. Take care,   *Mike and Lisa T., Intel*

Hang in there, Eric. I wish I had something better to say than that, but I'm praying for you every day. Thanks for the updates. You are loved.
                    Jeff H., Village

Sunday, Nov. 27, 2011, 2:56 p.m.

Two months – already

Hard to believe that it is almost December, and Christmas is just around the corner. It has been well over a month now since getting the "cancer" diagnosis. While we celebrate the victories, such as my leg doing so much better, it is altogether too easy to grow discouraged. So, I try to take it one day at a time and keep trusting God to answer the prayers of so many.

We are so thankful for friends and family to support us through this dark valley. Most of all, I am especially appreciative of Tammy who is shouldering a heavy load.

Yesterday our neighbors put up our outdoor Christmas lights for us. No sooner had Tammy set foot outside to try and put the lights up by herself, than she was surrounded by multiple neighbors all ready to put the lights up for us. We've got great neighbors. When I started in on the lights, I was told politely to go inside and rest. ☺

Fortunately, my cancer buddy (teenager from across the street who is surviving Leukemia) came in to keep me company. He kept me from stewing too much about what I can't do these days.

Tomorrow we head to the doctor, 1:30 p.m. appointment, and find out what the next steps are for cancer treatment. It could be more of the same chemo or a complete switch. I'll post more when we know more. We are blessed by so many caring for us. Thank you!

Monday, Nov. 28, 2011, 5:28 p.m.

A good doc visit

Thanks to everyone for praying us through today's doctor's visit. As the doc walked in for today's appointment, he remarked at how "odd" my reaction had been. If someone is allergic to Taxol, they react on the first dose … not the second. At least he didn't say I'm "atypical" again. ☺

Dr. Andersen proceeded to say that he wanted chemo to start up again ASAP but with a small modification. The Taxol, which caused that severe reaction, will be replaced with a "cousin" – Taxotere. I get tons of steroids today, tomorrow, and Wednesday. With that mix, we should be able to have a "normal" chemo tomorrow. (Not that I would know what that looks like.)

As Tammy and I left the office, we set the schedule for the next two chemos and the follow-up testing. When we gave our name, the scheduler "knew" us. I guess having a chemo patient "code" *(requiring resuscitation efforts)*, and being taken out by paramedics on a stretcher, is not a common thing for the chemo office. Hopefully tomorrow's chemo won't be the subject of water cooler conversations. ☺ So, chemo is booked for tomorrow and then for December 19. A PET scan and a brain MRI will be on December 15.

♦ PRAYER REQUESTS:

Sleep tonight ... with the amount of steroids I have in my system, sleep may be elusive tonight. It would be great to have some rest before chemo.

A normal chemo ... no allergic reactions, no high fevers, no hospitalization/ER, etc.

Endurance … for me, Tammy, and the kids.

Complete healing ... we know God can do it, and keep asking Him to rid my body of all cancer.

Wisdom … with respect to going back to work in some limited capacity, I'm having a hard time figuring out what that will look like. We still haven't hit "stable" in the treatment process, and my brain focus is only good for short bursts during the day

---

~ *Responses from Family and Friends* ~

Sending energy your way. Keep up as best you can. The prayers of many are in your corner.   *Frank P., Intel*

Prayers and thoughts from my entire family to yours, Eric, glad to see that you are home. Hang in there we're thinking about you here back at Intel!   *Tim T., Intel*

So nice to see your smiling face today. Glad to hear you will be celebrating Thanksgiving with your family. I so admire your strength, endurance and honesty. Thanks for openly sharing your journey with us. Lots of love to all of you.   *Laura and Garth D., neighbors*

Tuesday, Nov. 29, 2011, 4:57 p.m.

Thank God for boring

Despite chemo staff being ready for the unexpected, today's chemo went just as planned – boring. I was even able to read a bit of a fiction book (more slowly than normal and for shorter sessions, but far better than in weeks prior), and I (just barely) lost a game of Bananagrams with my lovely wife. Thanks to God for answered prayer, and thanks to everyone on CaringBridge for the ongoing support.

On the random news front ... I still have some hair (I'd guess about 50 percent the normal density). I'd expect to see it all go this round. Just think of the all the money being saved on shampoo and barbers. ☺

Wednesday, Nov. 30, 2011, 6:06 p.m.

So, this is what it should be like

I think I am having a very "normal" Day-2 after chemo. No fever (like the first time that landed me in the hospital for days), and I feel pretty good. Based on what "normal" is, tomorrow should be a down day, but I am okay with that.

On the hair front, I've watched my hair thin by the hour. Its end is likely near. I may give the kids duct tape to wrap on their hands and set them free on top of my head. They should make short order of any clumps of hair waiting to fall. ☺ (Timmy will play; but, Ellie looked at me weird when I suggested what she could do.)

Blessed by so many caring and helping. Feel free to post on our guestbook, email, call, or even consider visiting. Thanks for keeping us in your prayers and thoughts.

~ *Responses from Family and Friends* ~

I think everyone I know is praying for you. "Eric and his family" is always the first part of any conversation. "Many" is way too small a term for the number of prayers being lifted to the Lord for you.

Chip M., Tammy's dad

Happy belated Thanksgiving, Eric, Tammy and kids! Praying for your continued journey. Thank you for your updates, they make it easier to know how to pray for you and your precious family.

Colleen H., Tammy's friend

So sorry to hear of your medical issues. I saw that you were on medical leave about a month ago, and was hoping for this to be short, but ... All the hopes and prayers of the Midwest ESS team (including mine) go out to you in your fight against cancer. May your friends and family and faith be your strength in this fight. Blessings to you, Eric.

Jim T., Intel

Just learning of your [cancer] journey and wanted to let you know that your extended Intel Family in Massachusetts will be praying for health and comfort for both you and your family. Sending you peace, prayer and hope and blessing during this Thanksgiving season and always.

Laura B., Intel

Our whole family will be praying for you. Your courage is an inspiration. Yes, it is very easy to say we have to live by His plan ... but easier said than done. I do hope the fact that your friends at Intel are praying for you and recognize your positive impact to us, helps you deal with this challenge. God bless you and your family! Happy Thanksgiving. *Rick E., Intel*

I have been praying for you on Monday and Thursday nights with my two prayer partners. I will continue to do so, until you tell me to stop. I appreciate your guidance for prayers. I have primarily been praying for complete and miraculous healing which will bring glory to God. I also pray for God's care and comfort for Tammy and your two little ones. You are certainly loved and cared for by many Christian brothers and sisters.

Jayne L., Tammy's friend

[There were 303 responses in the guestbook
from November 1-30, 2011.]

December 2011

~ *The Third Month* ~

Thursday, Dec. 1, 2011 – 6:44 p.m.

Tired

Good news for today is I am just really tired ... the steroids have worn off. So the plan is just to lie low tonight. This morning I actually spent a bit of time cruising around Costco in a motorized cart – thanks to my sister for shadowing me.

Friday, Dec. 2, 2011, 11:28 a.m.

Duct tape ☺

Based on popular demand ... here's the shot of my sweet kids helping me to "molt." Fun times. We pray these will be more fun memories as we push toward "NED" (no evidence of disease).

~ *Responses from Family and Friends* ~

Oh my goodness that is a super cute picture. I love how you have maintained your humor through all of this Eric. You are doing great and God is taking amazing care of you. Know we are still praying up here in Wisconsin!
Kristina W., Eric's college friend

Love seeing your kid's smiles as they stick/unstick you! Continuing to pray for full recovery and many more smiles along the way!
Fred J., Intel

We were acquaintances at Village. I used to teach your daughter occasionally in the 2-year-old class. I just heard of your illness tonight. Please know that my prayers are with you and your family this very minute. I also have a prayer group that meets in our home that will be lifting you up in prayer tomorrow. Praying for miraculous healing.
Dorothy G., formerly at Village

Saturday, Dec. 3, 2011, 5:59 p.m.

Chemo still hits hard

Yesterday started out decently, but by the afternoon I was hit hard – very hard. The horrible feeling I had until about 10 p.m. last night was reminiscent of the way I felt right before I was admitted to the hospital with the fever. Fortunately, no substantive fever developed and with prayer, time, and lots of meds, the major feeling of illness passed.

Today is better, but not great. I'm pretty tired, but trying to be "active" – moving off the couch every few hours – since the chemo folks say that is the best way to get through the side effects. Unfortunately, Tammy has a migraine this afternoon. We're thankful she hasn't had migraines much in the last few months of my cancer, but this afternoon we have the fun of me and Tammy both being down. So, it's movie night for the kids and a huge thanks to our friends for bringing dinner over.

All the above reflects the physical reality. The emotional/mental reality is rocky, too. While we are so very blessed (I've posted about so many of the blessings), we are weary. So I'll break the "stay-positive" mode for a bit and highlight ...

♦ A FEW SPECIFIC MENTAL/EMOTIONAL CHALLENGES

Tammy is having to be caregiver for the kids and for me. My going down hard yesterday, impacted her harder than normal, too. It has been a very long two months for her.

I'm "done" being sick , although there is a long road ahead – miracle not included. With the latest round of chemo I am "enjoying" constipation, nausea, aching joints, fatigue, etc. It is hard to think about repeating the chemo process over and over.

My hair continues to thin and disappear; that is bugging me more than normal today – despite all the nice posts about how sexy bald can be, I'm not ready to look like Kojak.

I'm noticing the simple things I can't do ... eating out, taking Ellie caroling, carrying Timmy around, going shopping, etc.

We know God remains in control and will give us what we need to get through each day. We will continue to count our blessings, too – there are many. My brother Brian has a long list already going for us. ☺

Thanks for the nearly 10,000 views on CaringBridge ... and thanks for the notes, prayers, visits, etc. We are so encouraged by so many being with us through this cancer journey. May you each have a blessed weekend.

~ *Responses from Family and Friends* ~

Please let me know if there's anything I can do. I've been reading all of your posts and praying for you every day. I'm sorry I haven't responded in your guestbook as much as I've thought about it ... I'm just not sure what to say that someone hasn't already said. I want you to know that you're on my heart and in my prayers. My brother is going thru cancer and reading your notes is a bit like talking with him. If you ever want to chat or want a visitor, you know the email to reach me at! Don't hesitate!!!

Laurie K., Intel

Sunday, Dec. 4, 2011, 10:35 p.m.

Lapse in judgment

A relatively uneventful day. Tammy and the kids were able to attend both services at church this morning, and my parents were able to take me to just the second service. It would have worked great had I not let my anti-nausea medicine lapse ... I'm told the service was really a good one. ☺

After a good nap and slamming in the right meds, thankfully I was feeling mostly better. Hopefully, the week ahead will be easier. Tammy is actually hoping to get in to work all day Tuesday ... a very welcome "break" for her. Keep the notes coming. Thanks!

p.s. Christmas cards will have to wait some ... we want the test results in. So watch for the "just-in-time" delivery of our Christmas letter/cards. That said, we do have a wonderful family photo in our possession now ... thanks to friends of friends who set up the photo shoot in our home.

Monday, Dec 5, 2011, 6:05 p.m.

A thankful heart

For those who are dutifully following my posts, you might be wondering what atypical malady I've encountered today. It seems like most days in the last two months, there has been significant news … usually not good news.

Fortunately, it seems like we are settling more into a routine cancer treatment schedule and flow. Unfortunately, the mental battle is becoming all the more difficult. I find myself in a strange limbo with my health – not good enough to get off the couch much, and not bad enough to medicate myself into oblivion. I'm finding this to be a great recipe for a bad attitude. It is altogether too easy to forget to give thanks.

A teachable moment for me came this afternoon.

Ellie's school bus was due to return, and I volunteered to meet her at the stop. While it is amazing that I could meet her without a wheelchair or walker, I instead focused on how out-of-breath the walk made me and how limited life is now. Even the small talk at the bus stop was about how cold it was, rather than how beautifully sunny it was. I was heading into a great pity party when my conscience spoke up and reminded me of the need to give thanks. "Sorry God," I said quietly.

As the bus pulled up, I watched as Ellie charged off the bus and ran to give me a huge hug. Ellie wasn't confused at all about how cool it was that her daddy would meet her at the bus stop. She gave me a great reminder of what it means to be truly, unabashedly thankful, and not distracted by the nasty situations that surround us.

Now, I know as someone with Stage IV lung cancer, I have a certain permission to complain and get grumpy. But, I have to remind myself that there is always much to be thankful for … and especially so as a follower of Christ. So here's to doing "everything without grumbling or arguing" ... "not being anxious about anything, but in every situation, by prayer and petition, with thanksgiving, presenting my requests to God," so that I will have, "the peace of God, which transcends all understanding" (Philippians).

Here's to seeing what God has in store for me and my family each day. Thanks to everyone for helping me stay positive and thankful. I so value our support network. I couldn't imagine going through this without the support of so many.

~ *Responses from Family and Friends* ~

I think it speaks volumes about you and your family that you have such an active and interested social media practice. Trending like yours would be enviable for any of our Intel business topics. I admire how well you continue to connect. I know I speak for many who appreciate the effort! Hope you'll trend toward feeling better as well.

Kathleen M., Intel

I so appreciate your journal postings! God is giving you so much wisdom and your sharing it with us is such a blessing. I am truly sorry you have to go through this pain. I do see Jesus shining through you to others on this journey. We love you all and are praying.

Lori O., Village

Thank you for your encouraging post and reminder to be thankful in all circumstances. You do have every right to be grumpy. But that is not what God calls us to! He calls us to give thanks! Praise Him in everything. Trust. Hope. I have been whining. Over nothing really. I forgot about the lovely sun during the freezing cold. I forgot about the many blessings around me that should bring me to my knees in praise. Reading your post today encouraged me. Thank you. I just read this quote: "To bring the sacrifice of thanksgiving is to sacrifice our understanding of what's beneficial and thank God for everything – because HE is benevolent. A sacrifice of thanks lays down our perspective and raises hands in praise anyway – always." My family continues to lift you all in prayer. Trusting and knowing Him to work out all things for good. We may not know what that really looks like right now but ... it is all good because HE is all good!

Anne B., Tammy's friend

Thanks for teaching us all to be thankful in all things! You are amazing and a gift to all of us. We are praying!!!!   *Dan and Jane E, Village*

Wow Eric...this sounds like chemical, biological and spiritual warfare all rolled up into an epic battle. Keep fighting the good fight.

Hector L., Intel

Tuesday, Dec. 6, 2011, 9:31 p.m.

"Chemo 101," and "Why I write" ...

♦ FIRST:

For those who haven't had to be close to the chemo process, here's my layman's version of how it works. Imagine all the cells in our body, each with their own rhythm for sleeping, eating, and reproducing ... some fast and some slow. Even grossly mutated cancer cells go through this cycle.

Chemo takes advantage of the cells' need for nutrients (the eating phase). It acts like a Trojan horse by wrapping hideous poison in something that looks like yummy food. Cancer cells, which are fast-reproducing, are among the first cells to consume the sneaky poison. Unfortunately for us chemo patients, other fast-reproducing cells in the body get hit too ... hair, mouth, stomach, bowels, and parts of the blood. As an aside, cancer meds are very targeted ... once the docs know the source of the cancer (lung in my case) they can dial in the right recipe of "poison" to deliver maximum damage to the cancer cells. (That's why we had to wait until final needle biopsy results came back before we started chemo.) So ... regarding the limited hairs I have left on my head, one might think of them as "dead men walk-ing." It's just a matter of time. ☺ [Ed. Note: From early on, Eric always learned everything he could about whatever crossed his path. And, even as a child, he was gifted in explaining it to others in understandable ways.]

♦ SECOND:

I wanted to briefly state the "why" for my writing. My top reason is that writing here [on CaringBridge] helps me to process what is happening. Writing it all "out loud – with an audience," forces me to embrace the whole truth, and to maintain what I hope is a healthier perspective, as I face down this cancer. Tongue-in-cheek ... this is cheaper than counseling. ☺

A very close second reason is this site, CaringBridge, of course. It is an amazing catalyst for focusing the prayers of God's people toward the daily needs that I and my family have. We so treasure the support we are now getting from around the world. As for those of you who have shared how blessed you have been through the site,

I praise God for His using the site to work in your lives, and I pray you'll continue to be blessed and challenged as God guides us through this journey. May God receive the praise and glory for the good He works.

p.s. One specific prayer request to add ... with chemo, my taste buds are "confused" and I'm having a challenge finding foods to enjoy. In particular, salty comes across extra salty. I'd love to find good foods I can enjoy, and focus on the good, rather than getting frustrated over what doesn't taste good. This morning's bagel and cream cheese, an old favorite, tasted OK.

~ Responses from Family and Friends ~

I just heard. Wow! What a tough road. What a beautiful witness of faith. Thank you for your thankfulness; it is a huge inspiration to me. May the peace and love of God fill your heart and those of your family and friends around you. With tears in my eyes, prayers on my lips, and love in my heart.   *Fran B., friend*

We just heard about your cancer. We are stunned and so saddened that you're having to go through this. We will be very glad to be counted among those who are praying for you. We are praying for you and will continue to watch for your updates. All our best.
                    Krista S. and family, missionary friends in Belgium

I'm extremely glad that we are able to walk with you on this journey ahead. I think this is a wonderful website and even more happy that you decided to use it sharing your most difficult stories and feelings. Praying, supporting, and a lot of listening is being done [because of your writing on] this website! Glad to see your head held high.
                                                    Sara E., Tammy's friend

Hi Eric, I was called on to help for a half hour in Preschool today while the teacher took her husband to the airport. After school Timmy and I hung the next day's coat tags on the hooks and said crazy rhymes etc. about monkeys. How fun he is and what a sweet boy. You have two very special kids that bring such joy. I know that you know this, but thought that you might like to hear it from someone else too. Thinking of you and praying for you and the family daily.   *Donna T., Village*

Wednesday, Dec. 7, 2011, 6:27 p.m.

Duh!

As of 4 p.m. today I was a bit disheartened because I just wasn't feeling great – not horrible, but not great. And then I realized my error ... I had forgotten my anti-nausea medicine this morning. Oops. In fact, I had awakened this morning convinced it was Friday. So I took Friday morning's pills from my 7"x4" compartment pill box that we pre-fill each week. Why does that matter? We're stopping the anti-nausea meds on Thursday (tomorrow) just as an experiment. Guess I need to stay on the meds for a while longer. ☺   Yes, for those counting – this is twice in one week that I've missed the anti-nausea meds.

On the good news front, my health and mobility are such that I don't require a babysitter. [Up to this time, someone had always been on hand to help Eric as needed.] Yesterday Tammy was at work, the kids were out all day, and I was okay alone at home. I'll get more alone time tonight too; the kids have AWANA, and Tammy will be at church brushing up on child safety. With anti-nausea meds on board, I think I might watch a movie while they are out. I might even pop up some popcorn ... that tastes good even with my broken taster.

~ *Responses from Family and Friends* ~

You and your family are never far from my thoughts or prayers. I am so grateful you're willing to share this with us. I pray you know how loved and cherished your entire family is. I do enjoy the updates, the specifics for knowing HOW to pray are very helpful. Again, thank you for your willingness to share and allowing us to support you. Hugs, prayers, loves, and constant support for ALL of you.   *Holly B., Village*

Thank you for your inspiration through the blogs. I wish you the best through all your treatments and I will keep you and your family in my thoughts and prayers.   *John K., Intel*

Keep writing, keep fighting! God is good and he will always be your comfort. Take care and know that your Intel family is supporting your from afar.   *Pam M., Intel*

Your words have profound impact on me as well. Please keep writing, I love the spirit and will you pour into your messages. Stay strong! My prayers are with you!   *Tim W., Intel*

Thursday, Dec. 8, 2011, 10:45 a.m.

Prayer meeting tonight

There is a prayer meeting tonight at our church for healing for me and others who are seriously ill. I plan to be present if my strength holds up well through the day.

Today, I thought I'd write down my thoughts regarding prayer for healing. I know there is a huge diversity of thoughts/beliefs among those of you reading this, so it might be of interest to some of you to read what I believe to be true ...

♦ ACCORDING TO THE BIBLE:

God has already healed me in the most meaningful way possible. Through my faith in Jesus' death and resurrection, I have forgiveness of my sin, life in God now, and the promise of eternity with Him. (John 3:16)

God will bring ultimate healing in eternity for those who put their faith in Jesus. So I know, at a minimum, God will heal my cancer when I die and join Him in His presence. Eternity will be free of sin, lung cancer ... and I hope, spiders. ☺

God can and does heal people through miracles. We see Jesus and his Apostles doing amazing miracles of healing; blind men receive sight, the lame walk, the dead are raised. Today we still see miracles of healing. I'm reminded of an arthritic woman in rural Mexico years ago who asked me to pray for her healing. The next day, to my surprise, she came to me and said she felt much better.

God gives good gifts. "... if your son asks for bread, will you give him a stone ... how much more will your Father in heaven give good gifts to those who ask ..." (Matthew 7:9-11). And, often we have not, because we ask not, ..."Ask and it will be given you;" (Matthew 7:7). So we ask for the good gift of my healing.

The Bible gives me confidence that God's plan is ultimately the best. He is the Creator and we are the created ... for His purposes. So, if in God's big plan, He decides to use my lung cancer for His glory, and somehow I am called to suffer longer, perhaps even to the point of losing my life to the cancer ... I can still be confident in God's goodness, love, and wisdom. He will carry me through each day. The truth of God's Word does not hinge on my being healed.

If God doesn't heal my cancer, my faith is not shipwrecked. My not being healed in this life is not a sign of anyone's lack of faith. I know many are faithfully praying for my healing. If I'm not healed in this life, I believe it shows that God has bigger plans to use my cancer for His good, and I know He will. (Note: I'm not a fan of the "name it and claim it" position that says we should have all sorts of health and wealth if we follow Jesus, and if we don't get it, our faith is too small. Rather I choose to put my little faith in my good God who gives good gifts and hope for Him to grant healing ... if it brings Him glory and is part of His big plan.)

I trust that the above makes some sense. There are whole books written on this, and I don't pretend to completely understand, but I think this is a good starting point.

Here's to complete healing! We'll keep praying for it.

~ *Responses from Family and Friends* ~

Your post touched me today Eric. I know it can't be easy to wrap your head around what is happening to you, but God is pleased that you are trusting him, no matter how hard it is some days. Your family is lifted up in prayer daily for your complete healing. Sending you love from Southern California.   *Dorothy G., formerly at Village*

I stand in agreement with you and your prayer team. I continue to ask God to completely heal your body and that His miraculous healing will bring glory and honor to the name of the Lord. I also really enjoy your writing. Thank you for being so open in sharing your journey with us all.   *Jayne L., Tammy's friend*

God is doing a great work in you Eric. And in your family. Very, very well written! We are praying for all of you (and your taste buds).
    Lori H., Village

Well said, Eric. Praying with you for healing ... as well as for God's strength, comfort, hope, peace and joy for you and your family ... and for Him to be glorified.   *Teckla A., Village*

Friday, Dec. 9, 2011, 10:45 a.m.

To God be the glory

Last night, many people showed up at the prayer event at our church [an occasion initiated by the Village Women's Ministry Prayer Team to pray for those in the church who are critically ill]. I know many of them came to specifically pray for me. And I know there were more at home, work, or wherever, at that same time praying for my healing as well. Many are praying daily for us. THANK YOU!!! I am humbled by the outpouring of love for me and my family. While I didn't experience an immediate healing last night, we trust God is working to bring about a full healing in His time.

As we left the prayer meeting, Tammy asked me what it felt like to have so many fervently praying to God for my healing. My first answer might surprise … it felt uncomfortable. I'd have been much more comfortable being the person praying aloud for someone else's healing. … I don't receive gifts well.

Moving beyond the amazing outpouring of love and the feeling of discomfort, let me explain what I think is the real beauty of last night. … I'll take the long way around, so hang with me please.

Do any of you remember the magnet experiments from science class? One in particular is coming to mind – the experiment with metal filings and a magnet.

The magnet comes along and all the filings line up with the magnetic field. The magnet is the agent that aligns the filings toward one force. If I can stretch that example to my situation, I think of myself as the chunk of metal God is using to focus so many people toward Himself.

The prayer last night was not focused on me or the other people who are ill, but rather it was focused on God … His power, His promises, and His goodness. We all came before the throne of the King of Kings. We believed what He says in His Bible, and we acted as He tells us to act. He says pray boldly, ask-seek-knock. He tells us to pray one for another and bear each other's burdens. That is exactly what happened last night. Praise God for drawing us to Himself!

In the days ahead, it is my prayer that God will continue to use my life to draw people to focus on Him. If He does that through a miraculous healing, I'd be good with that. ☺ If He heals me more slowly through conventional medicine, I'm good with that too. And, even if he chooses to not heal this body, I know He will work it all out for good.

I hope God uses this to draw you closer to Him. May God be honored through this cancer journey.

~ *Responses from Family and Friends* ~

Eric, we're standing with you in prayer, daring to believe, daring to ask God to heal you in this life. May the God of all peace and comfort strengthen you as you walk this road, for his grace and power are for you.
Jeff and Celeste H., Village

THANKS for sharing Eric. May God bless you as you continue in your daily walk. While it is hard to "receive" prayer/ gifts, we need to remember that if we don't receive well, we rob others of the joy of giving. Thanks again for sharing and we are praising God with you.
Wanda and Dave K., former coworker of Eric's brother and husband

Brian and I have been praying for you and Tammy and the kiddos, and were with you in spirit during the corporate prayer time. We're sorry our work schedules prevented us from being there. Thank you very much for sharing your thoughts on healing ... I totally agree and forwarded your thoughts to a good friend of mine (We just had been talking about what the Bible says about healing.). *Melissa L., close friend*

Today's post was so beautiful. Thank you. Thank you also for the privilege of praying for you and Tammy tonight. We are all so blessed to be able to go to God in prayer. *Candace L., Village*

Wow, Eric. I am proud to be your sister. You have articulated this very well. I prayed for your healing tonight even though wasn't there in person. I know that our God can hear the prayers of His people from everywhere! We love you! *Dawn R., Tammy's sister*

I was there in spirit at the prayer meeting at Village tonight. Thanks again for your updates, sharing your heart and your latest very well done post on healing. *Sandy G., formerly at Village*

Sunday, Dec. 11, 2011, 8:49 p.m.

On tap this week

It's almost Monday, a day that had a different meaning several months ago. This Monday will be much like every other day … sleep, eat, rest more, and try to do one or two things of import. Slowly, I am getting more and more stamina. I've been able to head to the mall … four stores, walking unaided ... leg hurting only at the end.

And, I even spent a few hours at our life group [one of many small groups from Village that meets for fellowship, Bible study, and prayer] Christmas party without completely crashing. Things are improving little by little. This last round of chemo, thankfully, has been more "typical."

Thanks to Dave in my life group for this great shirt. I'll wear it proudly to my next chemo! ☺

♦ OVER THE NEXT WEEK PLUS,
THERE ARE A FEW KEY MILESTONES:

Tuesday and Wednesday: I start back to work from home for a few hours each day. I am trusting Tammy's instinct on this more than my own. I am somewhat apprehensive about dipping my toes back in the work pond.

Thursday: PET scan from ankle to neck. Success would be no new growths and reduction of the existing growths. We'd accept a "no-evidence-of-disease" finding as well. ☺ We're looking forward to great results that help us continue our fight against cancer.

Friday: brain MRI. Success would be no growth. The chemo is unlikely to impact the cancer in the brain as the body is amazingly made to protect the brain from drugs like those given during chemo.

Next Monday, December19: chemo. We go back for Round 3 of the chemo and will likely get the test [PET scan] results in our consult with the doctor just before the chemo drugs get administered. There's a remote chance we'd get test results Friday, but we aren't making plans.

Once we have the test results in hand, we'll print up our Christmas letter and send out cards. We figure it best to wait to write our 2011 summary until we have results in hand, even if we are later than normal with our cards.

Thanks again to everyone who is giving so generously of their time, love, meals, prayers, etc. We are humbled by how much support we've received from friends, family, and even complete strangers.

As for prayer requests, I think the main "addition" would be a request for stamina. Tammy and I both need an extra measure of endurance as we run this cancer race. Fatigue is fast setting in.

p.s. Congrats to our neighbor who is just days away from saying he is a [Leukemia] cancer survivor. You rock, Levi!

Monday, Dec. 12, 2011, 4:40 p.m.

The way to a man's heart

For those of you who have stated a continued desire to help out however needed, we've added January and February to the meal website. The meals have been so very helpful, especially to Tammy who has had to care for three kids – Ellie, Timmy, and me. ☺ As always, thank you!!! While I hate that I have cancer, and I loathe all the trouble it brings for me, Tammy, the kids, my extended family, and beyond, we have been abundantly blessed to receive so much help and love from everyone. Now I think it is time for a nap. I'm getting quite skilled at napping. ☺

Tuesday, Dec. 13, 2011, 5:54 p.m.

Back to work ... kind of

Just a quick note to say I made it "back to work" for a few hours today [working from home]. I'm grateful to my boss, coworkers, and the agency who have kept things moving along well while I've been out. There's plenty of work to be done, but I'm not coming back to a big mess. Tomorrow, I'll try for another few hours of being "back to work."

Wednesday, Dec 14, 2011, 8:17 p.m.

Another work day

One more short day of work done. I'll now wait until after the New Year to hold regular "office hours," ... Tuesdays and Thursdays, 8 a.m. to noon-ish. Getting back to the familiar work is fun in some ways. I am really proud of how the prep work I did before leaving, paid off in a great finished product while I was out. For example, I set a strategy for hitting a certain number of test completions by year end for our training site. I found out this morning, we've already surpassed the year-end target. Huge thanks to the team ... coworkers, boss, and agency ... who all made sure it worked while I've been out.

On a side note, I have found that using the mental energy during the day leaves me with less mental/emotional reserve at night. Hopefully stamina will build so I'm not a wreck each night after I work. ☺

In other happenings, Tammy's mom and a friend of ours came over today to help Tammy deep clean all through the house. What a huge blessing; when cancer hits a household, cleaning is pretty low on the list of "to dos."

Finally, tomorrow is the PET scan. We're praying for really great results. I'm mostly eager to get the testing done and to know where we stand.

~ *Responses from Family and Friends* ~

Great work, friend ... probably the hardest work you've ever done, huh? You're amazing! We'll be glad to have you back even for a few minutes or hours this week.   *Carissa H., Intel*

Our thoughts and prayers are with you. Whenever you feel pain, know that it is shared. Whenever you feel lonely, know that there are many with you. Whenever you feel tired, borrow our strength
David and Raechel F., Intel

Yea for being able to work a few hours! Yea for a clean house! (Did you hear the jealousy in that second "yea?") Praying for increased stamina. Praying for good test results. Praying for healing. And, praying for peace of heart and mind.   *Dawn R., Tammy's sister*

Thursday, Dec. 15, 2011, 7:11 p.m.

MacGyver and chemo brain

One down, one to go. With a "stat" rush order, the PET scan results should be done in time for my Monday, December 19, appointment with Dr. Andersen. Tomorrow, bright and early, we get the brain MRI done.

Tonight Timmy has his preschool Christmas program. Thankfully I have enough energy to attend. I'm even going to drive there and back. I've been careful about driving, given the meds I'm on. My doc did say he has patients on way more of the same meds who are highly functional and drive all the time.

For fun ... If you ever find yourself in a radioactive situation and forget your lead-lined jacket ... I found out today you could use tungsten to shield yourself. I just wish "MacGyver" were still on, I'm sure he could have fun with tungsten, a Swiss Army knife, and bubble gum. I learned about tungsten from the PET scan today. The radioactive, glucose-filled syringe is enclosed within a tungsten canister. And to think ... they put that stuff inside of me. Hmmm.

Now, to tell on myself ... I have "chemo brain" today. Here are a few phrases I read/heard that got lost in translation. The right version is followed by what I thought I saw:

Caution Workers Overhead ...
   "Caution Workers Overheard"

Baby - Cribs - Mattresses ...
   "Baby - Cries – Mattresses"

Have you had tandoori chicken? ...
   "Have you had cranberry chicken?"

Christmastime blessings to all!

~ *Responses from Family and Friends* ~

I hope it will be comforting to know that your "brain on drugs" is still likely better than my regular brain – not a surprise to many who know both of us, I'm sure. If you've ever seen Quantum Leap, you may be familiar with "Swiss Cheese brain." Enjoy your son's Christmas program tonight and DRIVE CAREFULLY!   *Carissa H., Intel*

Friday, Dec. 16, 2011, 4:57 p.m.

Mixed news

Thanks for continued prayers. We were hoping for results before the weekend. The triage nurse from the clinic called this afternoon with mixed news. Apparently the chemo is working on some of the cancer, but not all. We meet with the doctor on Monday, and the nurse prepared us for a "complicated" conversation then. Unfortunately we don't know anything more than that.

At this point, we're planning on chemo for Monday, but even that may change. I'm growing weary of being "atypical." I'm glad that some of the cancer is impacted through the chemo, but I am saddened that there are parts of my body that still have actively growing cancer.

♦ PLEASE PRAY FOR THE FOLLOWING:

Wisdom for Dr. Andersen as he considers the results and what that means for my treatment plan.

Good listening ears and wisdom for us Monday as we meet with Dr. Andersen.

Complete healing ... we know that many are asking God for a miracle, and we know that God is more than able.

Peace over the weekend as we wait for more details. It is difficult to not jump to worst case scenarios.

For Ellie to handle the new news well. We plan to tell Ellie (and Timmy) about the test results. Recently, Ellie has been praying for a Christmas miracle ... total healing for me. We love her childlike faith and hope that God answers her prayers in the affirmative. If God chooses to say "not now," we pray that Ellie's faith and love for God will still remain strong.

In all of this, I know that God is with us. Even if the worst happens, I know I will step into eternity with Jesus, and God will watch over my family for me. Hopefully though, I will have many decades ahead of me to watch my family grow.

Saturday, Dec. 17, 2011, 2:07 p.m.

One day at a time

Did you know that heart disease is the leading cause of death in the U.S.? The number five killer is accidental deaths. Traffic accidents lead that list, followed by poisoning, and falls. Cancer ranks number two in the U.S. Cheery, right? ☺

Now that I've encouraged everyone with such happy figures, I will tell you why I started out with such grim statistics. With Friday's news that my cancer is still growing in areas of my body – despite two rounds of chemo – my mind is prone to jump to worst case scenarios … "Oh no! I'm going to die!"

Thankfully, with a night's sleep, I have a bit more perspective. Death, unfortunately, is a sure thing in this life. If not cancer, then something else will end my years here … like a car accident or heart disease. Interestingly enough, I don't fret each day about whether I will die by falling to my death or accidentally ingesting fatal poison. While my cancer, is a bit different and more of a real and present threat, it shouldn't be all that different.

Each day is a gift from God. I hope and pray that my life is long and that I get to see my children's children grow old; however, there is really no guarantee of that. The best I can do is to embrace each day for what it is. I can rejoice in what God has given us. He is always near, and I know I will spend eternity with Him. Those truths are great reasons for hope and joy each new day.

We don't know what Monday's conversation with Dr. Andersen will bring, but God already knows. Nothing will surprise Him, and He will be with us. He will uphold us, sustain us, embrace us, and provide for our needs each day. I don't need to worry.

Now ... I'd be dishonest if what I wrote above suggests that I live each day to the fullest – without worries and praising God all the time. … Tammy would be the first to correct that misunderstanding. ☺ On the other hand, Tammy and I try to embrace each day with thanksgiving and hope. And when the feelings of gloom and doom come … and they do … we remind ourselves of the bigger truths … Our God is big and good and He loves us deeply.

Thanks for the calls, visits, meals, helps, etc. I especially enjoy the comments on CaringBridge. They are a huge encouragement to me. I find myself even reading them in the middle of the night when sleep is elusive. We'll post more after Monday's meeting. Merry almost Christmas to all!

p.s. Tammy and I did a short video interview sharing a bit of our journey through the last few months and our conviction that, "God is with us." Our church may use it as part of the Christmas Eve services.

[Ed. note: The church did use it at all four Christmas Eve services.]

~ *Responses from Family and Friends* ~

Thanks much for the update and new prayer requests, Eric. We're praying and trust that He will be your peace over this weekend of waiting. Wonderful to be able to spend time with you and Tammy this past week!
Melissa and Brian L., close friends

This will be a long weekend for you and your families. Treasure each moment. You have a wonderful family filled with love and belief in God. Hold all those who are close to you even closer to gain strength from them as well as from your continued faith in God to get through this weekend. Love,   *Dave and Ginny H., Eric's dad's cousin and wife in Hawaii*

Last night at 2 a.m. CST, I woke up and you were on my mind and I was praying for you. The strange thing is, I never wake up in the middle of the night (I sleep like a brick). Continually praying for you brother.
Rich C., Eric's high school friend

I continue to pray and believe God for your healing, Eric. I'd like to share with you some words from Sarah Young's "Jesus Calling" devotional. "Rest with me a while. You have journeyed up a steep, rugged path in recent days. The way ahead is shrouded in uncertainty. Look neither behind you nor before you. Instead, focus your attention on Me, your constant Companion. Trust that I will equip you fully for whatever awaits you on your journey." He's equipping you every day for whatever is ahead, Eric, and only asks you, and us, to give Him the Glory and Praise. May He bless you today.   *Terri B., Village*

Prayers are still being lifted up for you and your family daily here in Arizona. I'm sorry for the mixed news, but continuing to pray for a healing miracle!   *Sandy G., formerly at Village*

Sunday, Dec. 18, 2011, 8:44 p.m.

Tomorrow …

First, congrats to Levi, our neighbor, on now officially being a chemo survivor. Also, please pray for peace for us tonight and tomorrow morning. The doctor's appointment is 10:45 a.m. We're trusting God to give wisdom … for Dr. Andersen and for us. It is hard to not let our minds jump to worst case scenarios, but we also know we are still in the 2nd Inning (so to speak), not the bottom of the 9th. The "fat lady" is nowhere to be seen yet, thankfully. (Side note: I don't think death itself is scary for me, but I get scared of the long process associated with a cancer death. Here's to trusting God for full healing instead.)

I made a quick call this weekend to determine if chemo was on or off. The doctor's answer was essentially a 50/50 chance … we'll talk on Monday.

Also, I've been having difficulty with breathing ... deep breaths make me cough and I get winded now way too easily. Doc wasn't all that concerned, but will keep a watchful eye. Hopefully, I'll post the outcome of our appointment by the end of the day tomorrow. I know you all will want to know. Please have patience though as it may take me some time before I actually post. A lot depends on what Dr. Andersen wants us to do. As always ... thank you!!!

~ *Responses from Family and Friends* ~

Thank you for your honest faith. You are in a place you probably never imagined yourself to be in (fighting cancer), and how many of us will one day (maybe soon) find ourselves in an unimaginable situation. You may never know how your words of honest faith have affected the lives around you, but I am sure God will use them to remind others facing uncertainty. Thank you for showing what honest faith looks like – not being oblivious to reality, but assured beyond circumstances that God is fully in control, that He is good and giving, and that our hope in Him is not wishful thinking but solid footing. You and Tammy have seen and embraced the Light that God sent into the world, and your reflection of His light is reaching into the world, and all of our lives. May this week bring new depths of grace and peace as you face tomorrow's news and look forward to celebrating Christmas.

Mary Ann B., Tammy's friend

Monday, Dec. 19, 2011, 4:32 p.m.

Looking for a miracle

Writing to you all from a recliner chair in the chemo room ... Dr. Andersen gave us a very detailed run down of what "mixed

response" means. We are so appreciative of a good doctor and great clinic staff. The doc spent a good portion of his weekend working on my case.

The chemo cocktail has been changed since the last two rounds didn't have the optimal result. So we drop Carboplatin/ Taxotere and switch to Cisplatin, a not-so-nice cousin to Carboplatin, and Alimta. We expect about the same side effects, except we are planning for worse nausea. Thankfully I get stronger anti-nausea meds. To the IV (*intravenous*) chemo meds, we add a daily oral med, Tarceva. Chemo will still be every three weeks. We'll get another round of tests in about eight weeks; then we'll know if the change is positive or negative.

♦ A SUMMARY OF SCAN RESULTS:

In the neck there is growth/acceleration of known nodes, a new node on the right, and some reduction of other nodes; overall increase in the abdomen; lungs seem overall worse, but some victory in the right lobe; and, we can't tell what the left leg is doing ... improving from wheelchair to walking is a good sign, but the scans couldn't say one way or the other.

The brain lesion is to be removed before the next chemo. The lesion has grown some ... from 9mm to 13mm. That's enough change to warrant Dr. Patton, radiologist, to say we need to do the gamma knife. It is an outpatient, very targeted radiologic assault, no incisions needed ... just a few screws for the halo to keep my head locked in position during the procedure. We should go in prior to the next chemo appointment ... in two-plus weeks.

The breathing/swallowing difficulties are troublesome … only if symptoms worsen. They did a measurement of oxygen saturation at rest and after a few laps around the room. The numbers did show a drop … down to 89 at the end of the walk. But we will watch and see. Hopefully this chemo round will shrink whatever is leaving me so winded.

Our good friend Dave was with us as another set of ears during the meeting with Dr. Andersen. He asked what the difference is between "curable" and "treatable." Lymphoma is "curable." They can eliminate the disease and it more than likely won't come back. Stage IV lung cancer, large cell (or non-small cell) adenocarcinoma, is "treatable … not curable." That means the goal is to slow or stop growth. The doctor's best outcome is to see "no evidence of disease" – NED – meaning the cancer is likely still there, but the treatment reduced it so far and slowed activity to a point where it can't be found. Clinically it is likely to reappear.

Each chemo cocktail combo hits a point of diminishing return. The last mix had a max of 6 Rounds. So … Dr. Andersen's goal is to stave off the cancer and extend my life beyond the average prognosis. Sadly, lung cancer is a life-limiting diagnosis. It is more likely than not that cancer is what will end my life. We've discussed the prognosis and averages with Dr. Andersen. He couched his answer with lots of caveats … I am young, a non-smoker, otherwise healthy, etc. As another cancer patient said, "there is no expiration date stamped on my forehead." I'll not post numbers here, but if you want to know, ask.

All this to say … we are in need of a miracle. We remain convinced that God can heal. We will continue to ask for complete healing while being aware that God may choose to allow cancer to take me Home. So … we press on one day at time. Hopefully the worst chemo effects will have passed before Christmas. Thanks to everyone who is standing with us. We so value the support.

This weekend was rough – filled with lots of tears. Please pray that my pessimism would be held at bay and that Tammy can hold on to her optimism. We want to plan ahead appropriately and still have the right balance of faith and action.

~ *Responses from Family and Friends* ~

You don't know us, but your brother shared of your illness. Many of us at our church have been holding you all up in prayer and will continue to do so, joining with all of Village asking our dear Lord Jesus to guide you and strengthen you with hope and His peace that passes all understanding. In Him,   *Bev M., friend of Eric's brother*

Thanks for the update and guidance on how to pray. I am blessed by your faithfulness and openness. You and your precious family are in my prayers. We are all truly "In His Grip." Merry Christmas!!!
                    Nancy K.W., Tammy's college friend

We are joining the thousands of others who are praying. We know that God is faithful even when we don't understand what He is doing. We are praying that you feel His presence tonight and in the coming days. I love all four of you so much.   *Dawn R., Tammy's sister*

Other than "you are in my thoughts and my prayers," words ... even those of Scripture ... seem far too easy and too pat, no matter which language. My heart aches for you.   *Sara P., Eric's college friend*

Thank you for the updates, I'm sure writing them helps you process the info you receive, and they help us 'praying' to focus on the immediate needs you and your family have. Praying for NED! Hugs to you, Tammy and the kids!   *Colleen H., Tammy's friend*

Hey Eric. I didn't realize how easy it is to communicate back with you right here! We are praying for your miracle here, full of faith.

> "Holy Spirit, I pray that you will so fill Tammy and Eric and with your presence and peace that they will know it. In Jesus' name, bind despair and release hope, faith, and peace into their hearts, minds, and home. Thank you for the faith of little Ellie. Hear her and all the other prayers lifted on Eric's behalf and heal his entire body of the cancer. Take every bit and cast it out of his body. In Jesus' name, I bind the cancer and loose perfect health to Eric's body. For the glory of your name, God, bring complete healing and health. Amen."

While it's tempting to throw my own "wisdom" at you or quote Scripture, I've asked God to let me know anything he wants me to tell you. Nothing yet, but when it comes, I'll pass it on. So, I'll just leave it at that for now. Peace, faith, hope.   *Rachel W., friend*

Tuesday, Dec. 20, 2011, 6:11 p.m.

Keeping faith, and preparing for "what if"

Quick update for today ... chemo side effects are coming through. Thankfully it is just the steroids, leaving me flushed off and on through the day, and fatigued. I'm not feeling the intense nausea that can come. Tammy got a half day of work in. I got a great visit with my parents ... and even lunch out at "Old Spaghetti Factory." The lunch ... timed out between steroid-flush episodes ... worked great.

Among extended family, we're having the "what if God chooses not to heal me" conversations. Hard, but necessary. We fully believe God to be capable to heal now, but we also know that there are times when God, for whatever reason(s), chooses to heal through taking the person Home. If you know us at all ... you know we like to be prepared. So, we are trying to be as ready as possible for either outcome.

On a much lighter note, "Santa" is wrapping gifts today. We're pretty much ready for a fun family Christmas. I hope those of you reading this have a blessed Christmas with family and friends.

◆ AS ALWAYS, KEEP PRAYING FOR:

Hard conversations we are having;

Total healing now;

Reduced chemo side effects in time for a great Christmas Eve and Christmas Day;

Breathing/swallowing issues to not worsen, and actually improve;

A successful gamma knife procedure (scheduled for the first week of January);

Wisdom about what to share with the kids and when. They know I have cancer and that we've changed chemo recipes. The more dire elements are saved for us adults at this point. It is still relatively early;

A good visit with the naturopathic doc next week Thursday. We'll see if there are other things we can do to help the traditional treatments be more successful.

May you find continued strength and optimism that many more good days are ahead. Know that some of your Intel colleagues out here in the Field miss you and think of you often.
Jon O., Intel

Though I have never met you Eric, and I know Tammy only a little, my thoughts and prayers are with you both. I get excited when I see Tammy at work; she has such a beautiful smile. I know what she is going through, and she stays strong at work. She is a very brave lady. You have a beautiful family, and I hope and pray you have a long happy lifetime with them. I wish you both a very Merry Christmas. God Bless!
Karen B., Tammy's co-worker

Thank you for your continued writing during this process. Your strength through this fight is an inspiration. My thoughts and prayers are with you and your family during this tough time and I'm praying for a Christmas miracle for you guys this year!
John K., Intel

Wednesday, Dec. 21, 2011, 4:09 p.m.

We believe

Today is going okay. I started out rocky – more emotional than physical, but I got a solid nap in this morning and have some good food in my stomach. The kids are at gymnastics camp all day ... Tammy is brilliant. Tammy and I remain wholly convinced that God can heal. We just don't know if and when. So we are doing our best to take things one day at a time; still eyes wide open to both possibilities.

~ Responses from Family and Friends ~

Thinking of you and your family. Your strength and faith are inspiring during your trials. Wishing you and your family a happy Christmas.
Frank P., Intel

You have friends all over the world praying for you. We check your site regularly thanks to the updates. Sending all of our very best to each of you.
Krista and Jim S. and family, missionary friends in Belgium

Thursday, Dec. 22, 2011, 3:13 a.m.

Being admitted

Went to the ER feeling short of breath around 10 p.m. Doc says either pneumonia or blood clots in lungs. Treating for pneumonia now and will do more tests tomorrow. Perhaps another CT scan. Glad there is something clinical to treat – had wondered if it was all in my head. Will update as we know more tomorrow. For now we are just waiting for a room to open up. Thank God for competent medical staff. Merry almost Christmas.

A SHORT TIME LATER – 3:42 p.m.

Test results in

Doc just called with CT scan results. Not pneumonia. New blood clot in right lung … will test anti-clot med strength. If ultrasound of legs shows more clots, they will likely install a filter in the abdomen to guard against more clots making their way to the lungs. Also found additional fluid buildup around heart that may require a procedure to relieve pressure. More tests later today. Thanks as always for prayers. Please pray in particular for endurance in the next couple days.

IT'S EVENING NOW – 11:06 p.m.

Quick update

[Tammy, here, Eric's still in the hospital] – Eric's legs apparently looked fine so no big clots there. A cardiologist needs to look over the echo cardiogram to determine next steps. Please pray for answers soon, and for the most non-invasive but effective treatment possible that will allow him to breathe more easily.

Please also pray for all of our spirits; this is hard. And especially for Ellie – she is absolutely devastated that Daddy may not be home for Christmas. Many tears tonight about that. Please pray with us that this can be taken care of and Eric can be home and mostly functioning on Christmas. And please PRAY that God would choose to HEAL Eric of this cancer NOW!!! That is our dearest desire and we would love to see God glorify Himself through showing His power in this way.

Thanks so much for the notes, visits, and practical helps. I truly don't know how people go through things like this alone. We are so blessed by all of you – not many people get the chance to see how very much they are cared for, and we are so thankful for you!

~ *Responses from Family and Friends* ~

It's daytime here in India, so we're praying right now for you.
Leah K., and family, missionary friends in India

I'm up really late tonight and I'm praying for you right now. God is with you and we trust in Him for your healing and all that is good.
Karen R., mother of Eric's best man

Eric, you and your family are not alone going through this. As you know, many, many people are praying for you on a regular basis. I just wanted to let you know that there are a large number of people (of many nationalities) here in China praying for you, as well. Blessings on each step of your journey!
Bonnie H., Village

Good morning Eric. I continue to be so amazed at your strength and faith. You have been a blessing to me. I pray daily for your healing and blessings for you and your family. In God's love.
Lorri S., friend of Eric's aunt Ruthie in Colorado

God bless you guys. Your courage and honesty is very encouraging. I prayed all through my workout today for you. As I was winded from the cardio, I thought of you and your breathing trouble and asked God for His breath of life for you. Know you are loved and surrounded by prayer.
Chick L., Village Life Group

Eric, We are thinking of you and praying/pulling for you. I agree with the other comments that your courage and I am quite sure the courage of your family, inspire and touch us all very deeply. You are all in our thoughts and prayers.
Greg B., Intel

Tammy you are heard. A great host of His people binds discouragement and asks his power to be alive in your family. And that you get Eric at home for Christmas just for Ellie.
Libby S., Village

Thanks for taking the time to write. We are so sorry you are back in the hospital and will be praying you can get home soon.
Melissa L., close friend

Friday, Dec. 23, 2011, 9:58 a.m.

I'll be home for Christmas

[From Eric] Thank God! Looking to be discharged later today! As of last night, I had visions of multiple surgeries ... like filters in the abdomen for blood clots and/or major heart surgery for the fluid buildup around the heart, but thankfully, no surgeries are needed.

♦ THE BOTTOM LINE DIAGNOSIS
IS THE FOLLOWING:

Possible pneumonia in the left lung ... oral antibiotics for a week since they are seeing "haziness" on the scans;

New blood clot, pulmonary embolism, in the right lung ... managed through increasing blood-thinner dosage;

Oh ... and the doc used the term "atypical" again, but said the clots have cleared in the legs. (As Tammy said in last night's post – "my legs look good" – ☺)

The fluid buildup around the heart is not a concern ... heart function is good and the limited fluid built up is not enough to worry the doctors. It is likely all reactionary to the stress in my chest from the clot and pneumonia.

My brother stayed here [at the hospital] last night. Tammy was home giving the kids some much needed centering. For now, I am hanging out at the hospital until they can get a few things squared away, such as oxygen (*an oxygen concentrator – a non-portable device that runs continuously on electricity, and provides higher concentrations of oxygen via a nasal cannula*) and a wheelchair to have at home (available for only as long as I have shortness of breath). I am so thankful for a good outcome, and so blessed ... to be close to great medical care and to be surrounded by so many people, literally around the world, who are loving me and my family through all this. Thank you!

Expect the next post tomorrow. I think I'll either write about "The Worst Disease Ever" ... inspired from my very sad/scared little girl's questions for Tammy last night, as Ellie realized how very serious my cancer is. Or I'll write about, "Please Lord, let me be shallow again." Feel free to vote. ☺

Loads of Christmastime blessings to you and yours!

~ *Responses from Family and Friends* ~

Just read your recent updates. Praying for healing and comfort for you and your family. Also praying for incredible wisdom for the doctors. Praying for a special peace for Ellie through all of this. Love to you all.
Mythraie G., Village

Just a quick note to let you know that our whole family is praying for you right now! I have to tell you that right before Christmas break I read one of [our daughter] Kira's writing assignments. It was entitled, "What is the nicest thing you've ever done for someone?" She answered that one of the nicest things was praying for a grown-up named Eric who has cancer. May God hear the prayers of little ones and us grown-ups too as we pray for healing! Also praying you and your family will all have a peaceful and joyful Christmas celebration.
Veronica P. and family, Village

Saturday, Dec. 24, 2011, 10:49 a.m.

"Worst Disease Ever"

Our 7-year-old is a very smart little girl, and she catches a lot more than we think. Thursday night, December 22, after visiting with me in the hospital, Tammy and the kids went home and headed up to bed. While getting a big dose of cuddles, Tammy and Ellie had a heart-wrenching conversation.

Ellie was so sad at the possibility that I'd not be home for Christmas … to her, it was as if I were dead already. She found a modicum of solace in the fact that I didn't have "lung cancer." … Last serious conversation we had in October, we thought I had a curable lymphoma. Tammy corrected her gently.

Then Ellie said, "Well, at least Daddy doesn't have the really bad kind of lung cancer." (One of her best friend's grandparents has lung cancer … we imagine Ellie picks up tidbits from her best bud Kyle.)

Tammy didn't correct Ellie, but moved the conversation along.

> "Mom, what would be the worst disease ever?" asked Ellie.
>
> "I imagine a bunch of diseases that the doctors couldn't figure out how to fix." Tammy carefully replied.
>
> "But even if we get sick and die, what happens?"
>
> With the faith of a child, Ellie said, "We get to go to Heaven and spend forever with God."

Not a bad deal, all in all.

After the kids were down, Tammy and I talked (and cried) over the phone. As Tammy relayed the conversation to me, I thought about the worst disease ever. Terminal lung cancer is pretty bad, but what is worse? The answer sprang to mind – sin.

If you don't believe as I do, please keep reading … what I am about to write is core to understanding who I am. I wholeheartedly believe it to be truth.

Ellie says sin is, "the bad things we think, say, and do." … I just asked her. ☺ Romans tells us that because of sin, humanity … all of us … are under a death sentence – forever separated from God, apart from eternal glory and ultimately condemned to hell. Totally grim.

But here's the good news – especially as I connect all this back to my cancer battle and Christmas.

Roughly 32 years ago, I believe that through a prayer of faith, I crossed from death to life – eternal life in Christ Jesus. I was forgiven my sin and promised life eternal with God. So now, as I face the possibility of dying from lung cancer, I realize that the "worst disease ever" was healed in my life decades ago, and I need not fear death. I'm already a citizen of Heaven, and stepping into eternity is the best thing that will ever happen to me. Romans 6:23 says, "For the wages of sin is death, but the gift of God is eternal life in Christ Jesus our Lord."

This is the core of the Christmas story. God stepped into our world, took the punishment for our sins, conquered the grave, and gave us life, if we just openly receive the gift of life He has given. Merry Christmas indeed!

We'll tell Ellie (and Timmy) more after the holidays. A great counselor at the hospital coached us on the next conversation – what cancer is; what cancer does; that if the doctors can't slow the cancer, my body will die; no, it's not your fault; no, you can't catch it …

For now though, we are going to enjoy the Christmas celebration and keep our hopes and prayers focused on a miracle … healing this side of Heaven. I want to celebrate many more Christmases with my family.

~ *Responses from Family and Friends* ~

Thank you for your courage and your shining example of living "God with us" daily. Praying that your Christmas is truly blessed, filled with laughter and joy. We're also praying for your little ones and the conversation you have coming up. Noah and Nate have been praying too – their prayers are often so much more direct and God-focused than ours. We love you guys. See you at the service tonight!   *Jennifer Y., Village*

Eric, you are truly amazing. While my cancer is "curable" as Dr. Anderson would put it, I share your beliefs. I, too, do not have a crystal ball on when or if this will be what takes me but I relish and live in the gift each day I am given. That is not to live as it is my last, but to be in the moment. I know you understand when you are faced by a terminal illness. We are blessed in being able to recognize the gifts we have now and to not rely on the future of possibilities. That being said, I thank God every day and ask him to guide me in my tomorrows. I am still praying for your miracle but also for eternal greatness which will be yours no matter the outcome. Love and hugs!   *Wendy W., Intel*

Wow. I am fighting the tears. I love you both with my whole heart. Thank you for the hug yesterday. I wanted to show you my support, but I think I needed the hug too. Our friendship all of these years with the both of you is beyond words. We appreciate you and Tammy so much. We hurt for you beyond words as well. We are all (the girls too) praying for a miracle. We are so glad that you get to spend Christmas at home. Christmas is about the birth of Christ, but it has an extra special meaning this year and that is love and family. Thank you for your example of your strong faith. Merry Christmas and hugs from the five of us!

Pat and Melanie D., close friends

Sunday, Dec. 25, 2011, 2:37 p.m.

Merry Christmas

Merry Christmas! The kids are having a blast. We enjoyed Christmas Eve services last night and a special Christmas Day service. I am so thankful that I've had the strength and enough health to be home for Christmas. We are cherishing the memories being made.

No complete healing miracle as yet ... as far as I can feel, but we keep trusting God to heal. In the meantime, I am celebrating small victories ... like not being on oxygen 24/7, and being able to tolerate salty foods again. Thank you!!!

Tuesday, Dec. 27, 2011, 12:33 p.m.

Marking time

I trust everyone had a wonderful Christmas. We were blessed to have many of our extended family members take turns coming to our home to celebrate Christmas with us. Going to the big family shindigs was just not an option this year. The kids made off with quite a haul. All in all we were able to keep the Christmas weekend upbeat and happy. I'm very thankful for that.

Slowly but surely my breathing is getting better. I used the oxygen concentrator last night for a bit, but am essentially going without now. Unfortunately, walking around ... even just simple trips inside the house ... leaves me winded and cranks the heart rate up fast; but things are improving.

While we were hoping for a Christmas miracle, we know God can act to heal at any time. In the meantime, I'm working to use what energy I do have to seize each day and make fun memories. I'd welcome prayer for me and Tammy as we together figure out how to "carpe diem" rather than giving in to the bad feelings and having a "crappy diem." ☺

One idea that is gaining speed is a trip to Hawaii ... I'm hoping we can make it work. It would be so much fun for the whole family to go and make wonderful memories to last a lifetime. Another project I'm working on is a DVD for each kid and Tammy. There are lots of things I'd love to say to each of them. Now, I just need to organize my thoughts and put them on paper so video production goes easier.

Wednesday, Dec. 28, 2011, 8:11 p.m.

Nobody likes bad news

We told the kids tonight that unless God heals, there will come a time where the doctors can no longer stop the growth of the bad cancer cells inside of me and my body will die. Timmy appears to have missed the whole point of the conversation (though he said he was sad about the dead fish from the fish tank). Ellie caught it all. She asked that we stop talking about it and held back her tears. Oddly, she also asked if Tammy would remarry. ...I get the impression she was already way ahead of us on this and didn't want us to confirm what she already knew to be true. Ellie is now playing computer games, and Timmy is playing happily on the floor with his toys.

On other fronts ... my health is improving, though I felt almost narcoleptic (*experiencing periods of uncontrollable deep sleep*) today. And, we are making plans to fly to Hawaii in January. I'm not sure if Ellie will swim with the dolphins or not ... she wasn't quite sure when I asked her today. ☺

Thanks for your continued prayers.

We will keep asking for a miracle and concurrently pursue the medical help available. (Tomorrow is the naturopathic doc, and next week we go after the brain lesion.)

~ *Responses from Family and Friends* ~

Having been in the house when you talked to the kids about lymphoma, I am certain that you two did an amazing job. I am also certain that you are emotionally drained. It sounds as if the kids are "reacting" typically. I am sure there will be many more conversations to come. If time with an aunt would help either of them please do not hesitate to call. I am THRILLED that you are making plans for Hawaii. What a fun trip that will be. And I am so glad that Eric is feeling better. Know that our prayers will continue: for healing, health, stamina, peace, and joy. Love,

Dawn R., Tammy's sister

Praying for all of you, and sending lots of love! That is AWESOME that you guys are making plans to go to Hawaii!! With love.

Pamela K., Ellie's school teacher

Thursday, Dec. 29, 2011, 4:02 p.m.

Making memories

I awoke early this morning, as did Ellie. I got a good chunk of time with her before the rest of the house stirred. We played and talked about this, that, and the other. We have a very sweet girl who is doing her best to process the cancer blight. (Ellie said that sometimes she would draw cancer cells and then crumple them up. Maybe I should try that.)

The naturopath visit went well. Tammy is right about foods ... avoid the processed/refined foods as much as possible. The doctor gave us some supplements to help with nausea and my messed up taste buds. If I can even get some help for my mouth, I'd be pleased. Oh ... and now I have doctor's order to soak in the tub each day ... Bummer. ☺

On the good news front, the whole family has a nice distraction ... Hawaii. I booked airfare and hotel last night (and paid for travel insurance). The kids are giddy, and I think I may be even giddier. Special thanks to my brother for volunteering to come with us and help as needed on the trip. Way to take one for the team Brian. ☺ ☺

As always, we are praying with you that God will heal miraculously. In the meantime, we are asking for stamina and minimal

110

chemo side effects. Next week, January 4, is the outpatient radiation "surgery" for the brain lesion. Hopefully that will be super easy, and after an afternoon nap I will feel right as rain. Then, January 9 is the next chemo hit.

"This is the day the LORD has made; let us rejoice and be glad in it." (Psalm 118:24)

~ Responses from Family and Friends ~

Eric, you are nothing short of an inspiration as you face whatever is to come. I wish you strength and peace as you move forward in this journey. You are never far from my thoughts and always in my prayers.

Sue B., friend

Yeah for Hawaii! Today I was praying that you would have a companion (nanny) who could either watch kiddos while you two rest, regroup or go out, or could hang with you (Eric) while Tammy is with the kids. Not sure your brother wants to be called a nanny, but I am sure glad he is going along for the ride! God probably had this one answered long before I started praying. Excellent plan! Have fun in the planning!

Kim S., formerly at Village

Friday, Dec. 30, 2011, 10:29 p.m.

Ups and Downs

Today was a mixed day. It started out not so good. Unfortunately for Tammy, my sleep last night was horrible ... fraught with all kinds of bad dreams. The worst part came in the early morning when, in my dream I reached out to catch Timmy from falling. In reality, I reached across the bed and yanked on Tammy's hair. (Ooops ... sorry, Honey.) Needless to say, both Tammy and I were quite tired this morning.

During the day, things perked up. My brother spent a few hours here, and my parents joined us for dinner. I'm "enjoying" my naturopathic remedies ... probiotic mouth rinse, egg for breakfast, and an Epsom salt bath. I'm working hard to enjoy each day for what it is. It doesn't hurt to look forward to five nights in Hawaii ... we're all quite excited. Luau and dolphin swim are now booked!

We did a construction paper loop chain to help the kids with the countdown to our trip. First loop came off tonight.

I got a little emotional earlier tonight. Listening to the radio, a series of songs hit home. One by Superchick called "We Live" especially resonated (lyrics below). It is a challenge living with a very real possibility of the cancer winning. Note: I am still wanting/expecting/hoping for a miracle. Happy almost New Year!

> "We live, we love, we forgive and never give up
> Cuz the days we are given are gifts from above
> And today we remember to live and to love
> We live, we love, we forgive and never give up
> Cuz the days we are given are gifts from above
> And today we remember to live and to love
>
> "There's a man who waits for the tests to
> See if the cancer had spread yet
> And now he asks why did I wait to live
>   'til it was time to die
> If I could have the time back, how I'd live
> Life is such a gift
> So how does the story end?
> Well, this is your story and it all depends
> So don't let it become true
> Get out and do what we were meant to do."
>
> *Chorus and 2nd verse from "We live."*

~ *Responses from Family and Friends* ~

So excited for you and the family. Sounds like you're going to have a wonderful time. Glad to hear your brother will be joining you. Get a good night's sleep ... you need to ring in the New Year tomorrow!

Laura D., neighbor

Hawaii! How exciting! Love that Super Chick song ... Here's to remembering that each day is a gift from above, each day starts new, and [our job is] living each day to the absolute fullest! Happy New Year, Eric!

Fred J., Intel

[There were 335 responses in the guestbook
from December 1-30, 2011.]

January 2012

~ *The Fourth Month* ~

Sunday, Jan. 1, 2012 – 3:34 p.m.

Firsts and lasts

FIRSTS … the first day of the New Year, a baby's first step, first time riding a bike. We love to celebrate firsts. Upstairs we have scrapbook upon scrapbook of firsts. Every year we celebrate birthdays and anniversaries. I have special memories of meeting my kids for the first time … one at the hospital and one at the airport [Timmy was born in South Korea]. Just about four months ago, Tammy and I celebrated our 10th anniversary; I still remember the first time seeing my beautiful bride in her wedding gown. It seems to me that life is full of firsts that we love to celebrate. Lasts, on the other hand, are often bittersweet or simply pass by unnoticed. (Maybe the exception is the last diaper ☺.)

LASTS ... Lately, I've been thinking in terms of lasts … last Christmas, last New Year's, last words. … While I'm still hoping for, praying for, and expecting a miracle, I also know that a real possibility is this cancer could be the thing that brings death to my body.

Thinking in terms of lasts, has added a focus to life. Quality time with my family counts all the more. Facebook posts and all the virtual games seem exceptionally empty. Laughter is all the more fun. Cuddles with my kids and an embrace from my wife are all the more sweet. Lasts make me very sad at times, but I am trying to see them as the gifts that they are.

This focus and appreciation for lasts, I believe, is something from which all of us can gain. None of us knows the time of our death. Cancer could claim my life or something completely different … heart failure, a bus. I could live to be an old man or I could be called Home before the next New Year. As such, let's, "eat, drink, and be merry," for today could be our last. Let us glorify God by enjoying what He gives us each day.

I really don't claim to have it all figured out, but the gift from cancer is a stronger awareness of how fragile life is and how precious each day is. King Solomon, who wrote Ecclesiastes, understood how fleeting life is and how "lasts" can bring needed focus. The following is what he wrote:

> "A good name is better than fine perfume, and the day of death better than the day of birth. It is better to go to a house of mourning than to go to a house of feasting, for death is the destiny of everyone; the living should take this to heart. Frustration is better than laughter, because a sad face is good for the heart. The heart of the wise is in the house of mourning but the heart of fools is in the house of pleasure"
>
> (Ecclesiastes 7:1-4).

In the days ahead, please pray that I would find a good balance between hopeful expectation of a miracle and a healthy awareness of lasts. I don't want to be morbid and morose all the time … I do want to savor what days I am given.

After the outpatient gamma-knife procedure for the brain lesion on January 4, and chemo on January 9, our family will prepare to head to Hawaii. We'll be there January 18 to 23. I'm looking forward to celebrating life and family while we're there. Here's to creating wonderful memories in one of the more beautiful places God has created.

Happy New Year!

~ *Responses from Family and Friends* ~

Appreciate you sharing your perspective. I'm always asking God to help me develop an eternal perspective and your recent posts have helped me with just that.   *Mythraie G., Village*

You are so right Eric, none of us knows the day nor the hour. May each day we have count for eternity, and may we enter eternity by God's grace and the blood of Jesus that paid our admission price. May we enter in and hear the words, "Well done thou good and faithful servant." You are for sure one of God's faithful servants. Much love, prayer and blessings for each of you,   *Kathy B., Village*

Tuesday, Jan. 3, 2012, 8:30 p.m.

If I only had a brain ...

Yesterday we met with the neurosurgeon who will participate in tomorrow's gamma-knife procedure. It was a refreshingly uneventful meeting. We're all ready for an early start ... 6 a.m. The good news is the procedure is outpatient, and I'll only have a few marks on my head from the halo they'll use to lock my head in place during the MRI and focused radiation to zap the brain lesion into oblivion. If all goes well, I will be headed home by noon.

All in all, the week is feeling uneventful (minus the brain surgery ... ☺). Next week, Monday, we start the cycle over with chemo again. I'm looking forward to getting past the chemo week and all the side effects.

Each day we are reminded of how loved and supported we are ... meals, visits, gifts, acts of service, notes, etc. Thank you!!!

~ *Responses from Family and Friends* ~

"Let us glorify God by enjoying what He gives us each day." Well said, our brave friend that we've never met! Also remember that LASTS are also often the beginnings. We continue to pray for you in the upcoming procedures and look forward with you to the wonderful times in Hawaii. Your words are such a reminder to take NOTHING for granted but be thankful for each thought, feeling, word and action of those around us.
Karen and Mike R., friends of friends

Wanted to let you know, we're praying for you. Thank you for sharing your heart with us. I don't think there's been a day where I've read your post and my heart didn't cry out to God for you and your family. May God's perspective continue to strengthen you and give you peace. I also love your picture with the shirt on that says "atypical". Cracked me up. Love,
Esther D., and family, Village

Aloha Dear Ones, Continued prayers for each of you. Just because you receive a "halo" tomorrow; don't get used to it just yet, it's only on loan to you for the procedure! You have a wonderful trip with your family to look forward to! We're here for you. With much Aloha,
Dave and Ginny H., Eric's dad's cousin and wife in Hawaii

Wednesday, Jan. 4, 2012, 6:18 p.m.

Success

The gamma-knife procedure went great. I fell asleep for most of it. It's amazing what one little pill will do. Fortunately, they still only found the one lesion. There will be a follow-up MRI in six weeks just to make sure everything was zapped like the docs intended. By tomorrow I should be back to "normal." I'll have a few days of feeling good before chemo on Monday. Here's to a normal chemo without ER or hospital this round. ☺   Thanks to all!

~ *Responses from Family and Friends* ~

What? You had a procedure go as planned?? No one had to label you "atypical" today??? HOORAY!!!! We are rejoicing with all of you that there was still just one lesion and that the procedure went so well. Hugs,
Dawn R., Tammy's sister

I'm so relieved to hear the procedure went well today. I've been following all the posts and have been amazed at your positive outlook. It is truly inspiring. Still praying for that miracle.
Liza B., Tammy's friend from middle school

Saturday, Jan. 7, 2012, 11:14 a.m.

Endurance needed

Saturday morning ... Tammy made French toast for all of us ... mmmm. I ate breakfast and thumbed through Hawaii brochures. We're all having fun dreaming about Hawaii. (Although I think Tammy is stressed with packing and planning for the trip. Unfortunately, I am not pulling my weight around the house.) Only 11 more days before we fly.

Yesterday, I was hoping for more energy. My brother Brian came to visit for a few hours. We talked website strategy; then it was time for a nap. After the nap, the family and I hit Sweet Tomatoes. I did okay until the end of the meal when my health took a turn for the worse. Back home, after a rough few hours, I was better and opted to head to bed early.

Chemo is this Monday. Hopefully I can record my video messages to my family on Saturday, January 14. (Huge thanks to a few of my friends ... they have worked with me on Intel productions ... who are taking their Saturday to help me record.) Then ... on Wednesday, January 18, we are off to Hawaii. ☺

(Note to neighbors: Please keep an eye on our place. Note to thieves reading this: Do you really want to steal from a cancer patient? ☺)

♦ FOR MY PRAYING FRIENDS/FAMILY, PLEASE PRAY FOR:

Endurance for me and my family ... Tammy gets weary with being responsible for so many things. Since I can't help much, she is in some ways like a single parent.

An uneventful chemo ... I'd love to be feeling much better by Friday and not have any complications (like all the other times). That the dosing of my Lovenox injections would be set right ... ideally, I'd drop down to one injection a day.

Both kids to process what it means for Dad to have cancer ... Pray that Ellie would talk about it when she needs to. (Special thanks to Ellie's school for all the extra care she is getting.)

Great health for the video shoot next Saturday ... I'm excited (if that is the right word) to produce great messages for each of the kids and Tammy. (God willing, I'll watch the videos with them in the years to come.)

Pray also for a smooth production. The friends helping me are volunteering their time ... so I'd love for the video gremlins to stay far away.

An awesome, memory-making trip to Hawaii ... I'm especially desiring to have extra energy in Hawaii so we can do the things we want to do.

As always ... thanks! You all have been an amazing encouragement to us. It is altogether too easy to get grumpy and/or sad with all that is happening, but with so many around us, it is hard to stay down for long. Mahalo!

Wishing you strength and energy to keep up the fight ... you have incredible faith and are amazing, staying so positive through this time. Your trip to Hawaii will be incredible for you and your family ... so glad you are doing that for yourselves!   *Lissa F., Intel*

I will be praying for all of those things for you guys. You are such an amazing light for Him in all of this. It is such an inspiration. I praise God for the voice He has given you, and I pray for your complete healing. Love you guys!   *Brian L., close friend*

Praying for you, Eric, and your family. Just finished reading your entire journal – it has been such a blessing to me to read your thoughtful courageous Christian approach to your illness. I will be praying for a memorable family time in Hawaii and of course God seeing fit for complete healing. God bless you and may He pick you all up in His loving arms and carry you a while.   *Rex B., friend of a friend*

We are praying for you and have been reading your journal entries since the beginning. Today we heard a young girl sing this song ["Blessings" by Laura Story], and immediately thought of you. God's ways are not our ways, and sometimes it's hard to see His plan. We love you both and continue to lift you up often. Your journey will affect many people, Eric, and your faith will continue to inspire.

Dan and Lisa B., friends in Boston

Monday, Jan. 9, 2012, 6:44 p.m.

The lumps feel smaller

We spent much of today at the oncology clinic – five hours just for chemo alone. Thankfully it went smoothly. In the exam, Dr. Andersen felt the lymph nodes in my neck and said he felt a good difference. Hopefully the reduction in size of the lymph nodes is a great sign of cancer being zapped throughout my body. We'll test toward the end of this month.

Once we got home, I took a good nap. I already see the "raccoon" eyes ... a telltale look from the steroids I'll be on for the next three days. Hopefully ... and prayerfully... this cycle will be kind to me and my family, especially as the countdown to Hawaii gets shorter and shorter. I can almost hear the ukuleles and feel the warm breeze on my face ... even as I sit bundled under blankets in my La-Z-Boy recliner ... ☺.

As a side note, while at church yesterday, I met a lady who is on her own cancer journey. She went through all the chemo and then back in June had a bone-marrow transplant. It will take a full year before she even knows if it worked. Apparently the whole bone-marrow transplant process is far worse than chemo. Yikes. ... It is good to have perspective.

Thanks for joining with us on our journey. May your week be blessed.

~ *Responses from Family and Friends* ~

Eric, I absolutely commend you and Tammy for being honest and up front with your kids. I believe it is very important to share with them what is going on, even at their young age. Adults don't give children enough credit for seeing reality and recognizing truths, and by excluding them from the conversation and denying it to them, we are disrespecting them. When I was young and my mother was very ill, my family did NOT include me in the conversations and this affected me greatly at the time and in later years. So, good for you and Tammy for treating your kids with such love AND respect.   *Janet G., Intel*

Just want to let you know we read every update, and pray for you daily. We're pulling for you, and hoping for and counting on the best possible outcome! *Marcus W., groomsman at Eric's and Tammy's wedding*

So glad all went well and chemo was uneventful! Yeah for doc's comments as well. Love and hugs for all. *Chick L., Village Life Group*

Olivia and I really enjoyed walking with Ellie to the bus stop today. She is a very sweet, smart and beautiful girl. She mentioned how excited she was to go to Hawaii. I hope you all have a wonderful and memorable time there! We are all sending good thoughts and prayers your way! Take care,   *Jennifer L. and family, neighbors*

Continuing to pray for you, Eric! I've been encouraged lately by Jer. 32:17, "Ah, Sovereign Lord, you have made the heavens and the earth by your great power and outstretched arm. Nothing is too hard for you!" Praying for your sweet kids and Tammy, too. Hang in there, and may our Living God bring you healing and strength! *Laurie G., Village*

Wednesday, Jan. 11, 2012, 10:54 a.m.

The chemo bus

First off, I just want to start by saying how thankful I am for God's provision in the midst of all this cancer stuff. So far with this chemo round, no ER and no hospitalization. The "bus" still hits hard, but as yet, it is all within the bounds of what I expect. The steroids, while helping block more severe symptoms, have their own set of side effects that I loathe. It seems like there are at least two blocks of time each day that I get hit hard and just have to sleep it off. Thankfully, the steroids end on Thursday night.

So many are praying for full healing for me this side of Heaven. Thank you for your prayers! In all this I know God will heal me. I just don't know how … taking me Home "early" or healing me physically here on earth. So … I prepare for both. It is a strange balancing act.

I'm still working on the details for Saturday's shoot for my special DVDs to Tammy, Ellie, and Timmy. We are so honored to have such a helpful team of friends. Ideally, I'll lock in on where we shoot the video today … got a few calls out.

As I get closer to the shoot day, I am realizing how hard it is going to be to say what I want to say. It is admittedly an odd exercise to think about "last words."

It feels like one of those corporate team-building exercises.

"What do you want written on your tombstone?"

"If you only had 30 minutes with your loved one before you died, what would you say?"

Yikes! Please pray that I would be able to share from my heart a message for each of my loved ones that can be a lifelong treasure to each.

Here's to taking things one day at a time. Blessings to all!

The videos are such a great idea, and I second the wish that you wind up watching them with your grandkids. If it were my dad speaking to me, I guess I'd want to hear how he loves me and wants me to be happy all my days. I'd probably want to hear him explain that, if leaving is in the cards, he didn't leave for lack of wanting to stay with me. I'd want to understand the lessons of life he learned, of dealing with ups and downs, of bouncing back and owning my own happiness. Pick your friends and mates wisely, as they can stoke the fires of your happiness, or drain the energy away. Education is the ticket to options and independence. Cock-eyed optimism is a far better outlook than the most informed cynicism. My two-cents. I know you'll do fine. It is a wonderful project and I hope you blog about what you decided to do. Good luck and miracles!

Mike F., Intel

Thursday, Jan. 12, 2012, 9:56 p.m.

Celebrating the small things

The good news ... no ER, no hospital, and I took my last dose of steroids for this chemo cycle. (Steroids on this chemo recipe have been the bane of my existence.) I'm on hold right now to schedule a pick up for the return of my oxygen supplies ... haven't needed extra oxygen since just after Christmas. And ... we are still a go for heading to Hawaii. We're all super excited.

On the not-so-good front ... I'm having a really tough time regulating my GERD (acid reflux). The meds that worked well are not allowed with the current drug cocktail I take, and the replacement med dosing for GERD is maxed out and not working well. The doc is flummoxed and has called on his pharmacist for advice. Hopefully, I get a call tomorrow that will give us better options. Today's diet has been rather bland ... bagels, crackers, water ... not a stellar menu. I tried a Jamba Juice... bad choice (though not as bad as the pizza yesterday ... ☺). God willing though, my stomach will repair well prior to Hawaii. I've got some good eats to have over there and I don't want GERD in the way.

As always ... thanks! Your support is overwhelming. We are surrounded by so much love and care. Thank you!!!

Friday, Jan. 13, 2012, 8:01p.m.

GERD is not my friend

Thanks for the notes and suggestions for GERD. This seems to be a very special flare up connected with the chemo and the change of GERD meds. The pharmacist/doctor let me go back to the old meds in conjunction with the new meds. I just have to be careful to keep the 8 p.m. to 12 a.m. window of time clear for a key daily chemo med. God willing, the combo will work well. I actually had dinner tonight ... Red Robin "to go" (tasted heavenly), Tums, and an appetizer of Omeprezole.

I am not paying too high a price yet, thankfully. Please pray that with each day further from the chemo, I get better and better with respect to the GERD and the other side effects ... including a fresh crop of acne all over my face just in time for tomorrow's videotaping ... sigh.

Today has admittedly been hard. Emotionally I am not nearly as stable as I would like. After reading Psalm 13 (thanks to my brother's encouragement) and really listening to the lyrics of a few songs on the local Christian radio station, I was reminded, multiple times, that ... this is all about God and not about me. King David, in Psalm 13, starts by asking why God has forsaken him, but at the end affirms his trust and love for God.

In Deuteronomy 31:6 we are reminded that God will never leave us or forsake us. So ... I cling to the truth of God's Word. He is good and big. He will take care of me through all the troubles ... including annoying GERD, chemo, and whatever else may yet come.

A little joke:
Q: "Why was the young girl afraid to fly on the plane?"
A: "She heard that Jesus said, 'Low, I am with you always.'"

Tomorrow I record my videos for Tammy, Ellie, and Timmy. I've written my outline and purposely not practiced much more than that. I feel so blessed to be able to record my thoughts while I still have good enough health. God willing, I'll watch these videos with the family in the years to come. We will keep asking for a miracle healing this side of eternity. Counting down to Hawaii! Blessings to all.

~ Responses from Family and Friends ~

Praising God with you for the small things and continuing to pray for a great Hawaii vacation and complete healing! I really enjoy your blogs and am walking with you and fighting for you in prayer the whole way! I'm running in a half-marathon this Sunday! You and others that are fighting cancer right now will be my motivation to finish strong! Have a great day!
Fred J., Intel

As always you give me cause for thought! My prayers are with you especially as you make the movies for Tammy, Ellie and Timmy. I pray that God gives you clarity of thought and speech and exactly the right words to say. How wonderful technology is when it comes to holding our precious memories. I pray you get good rest and gain strength for your 'funtastic' trip. Much love to you all.
Ruth J., Ellie's and Timmy's preschool teacher at Village

Eric, you continue to amaze me with your spirit and your soul. Prayers and positive thoughts continue to stream to you, Tammy and the family. May God continue to bless you with hope and healing,
Laura B., Intel

I'm so blessed to know you – you may never know just how much your postings mean to so many people. I believe God is using you in a very special way right now to further His Kingdom. You may never know just how much, but that's okay, because He does, and that's really all that matters. God bless you, and I will be thinking of you tomorrow as you make your very special videos. I continue to lift you up to the Father.
Terri B., Village

Glad you are celebrating the small things! So often we let the bad small things become magnified and annoy us, but don't go the other direction. Yea for Hawaii! We're praying for a wonderful vacation for all of you. Soak up some warmth for me...I'm freezing!
Dawn R., Tammy's sister

Here's to warm temps, gentle ocean breezes, lovely Hawaiian music, and a pleasant, relaxing vacation with your family! Aloha,
Marty L, Eric's aunt in Colorado

You are such an example of truth, faith and honest, heartfelt emotions. You bless us by your writings. Continuing to pray for tomorrow ... for strength and courage to say what you have planned. The warm ocean breezes are but a few days away. Love you guys!
Chick and Scott L., Village Life Group

Sunday, Jan. 15, 2012, 8:02 p.m.

Ready for a break

Quite the weekend ... Saturday morning went amazingly well. I had a whole film crew with me at Village to record messages to Tammy, Ellie, and Timmy. Huge thanks to Mike, Geoff, William,

 Andrew, Dennis, and the rest who helped.

The shoot was probably one of the hardest things I've done, but I believe God uniquely prepared me to do the videos. God willing, I can watch the DVDs for years to come ... with my family. If not, I know my family will have a really special remembrance of me.

The stress of the shoot did me in. The afternoon held a horrible nap time with nasty dreams. By the time the kids were down for the night, so was I. After a few hours of debating whether to go to the ER or not, I did go. Thankfully, the ER didn't find anything huge and was able to get my symptoms under control. By 3 a.m., I was back home. Oh joy!

The doctor on call for my cancer clinic believes I am overloaded on the daily oral chemo med, Tarceva. He instructed me to discontinue use for now. I didn't argue. Side effects include GI tract distress and major acne – of course, it all shows up when I'm shooting for the DVDs.

Today was decent ... I made it to church and even was able to visit Tammy's side of the family. I'm up now from a major nap ... my stomach is on edge and my head hurts. We've got two days for my body to recover more from the chemo. I'm asking God to do amazing work in righting the nasty chemo effects before we fly out.

Aloha-time starts on Wednesday. We so need it. Please pray

that I'd feel tons better and that our family would make wonderful memories on the Big Island. Pray also that I would exercise wisdom in choosing how active to be or not to be. I don't want to overdo it.

p.s. It snowed here today ...☺. It breaks my heart to have to fly off to 80-degree weather and hang out on a beach ☺. ... The things we suffer.

p.s.s. Please keep the kids in your prayers ... especially Ellie. She needs to keep processing what is going on and I know she would much rather just "stuff it." Timmy is mostly clueless ... but that is age 4 ... ☺.

~ *Responses from Family and Friends* ~

Oh, sure, rub it in. Leave us freezing in the not-enough-to-be-fun-but-just-enough-to-be-annoying snow and jet off to the islands. Harrumph! Glad the video shoot went well, Eric. Hope you get some good rest the next day or so. Enjoy some serious R&R starting Thursday A.M. when you awake with the ocean breeze in the palms. Sweet! Take care!
Mike F., Intel

Praying for you guys! Two days to heal enough to get on that airplane ... ! God can do it. You're all doing an amazing job. Big hugs and lots of prayers for all of you.   *Leah K., missionary friend in India*

Praying for chemo recovery in time for your trip ... for organization/ relaxation for Tammy ... understanding/openness/communication for Ellie ... a fun family time in Hawaii.   *Colleen H., Tammy's friend*

Eric, Tammy, Ellie, and Timmy, Wayne and I will be praying that you have a wonderful time in Hawaii. Ellie, I look forward to you telling me all about your time on the Big Island. A big hug for each one of you.
Donna T., Village

I am not sure if you remember me or not. I work in consumer campaigns with Alex, Elizabeth and Tim. Alex told me of your struggles, so I wanted to let you know I believe strongly in prayer and will be praying for a full and complete healing, and for your dear sweet family for strength and encouragement through this difficult time. Blessings to you and your family!   *Renee W., Intel*

Tuesday, Jan. 17, 2012, 12:52 p.m.

Less than a day

The countdown is on! I am feeling better today and actually had energy to do some packing.

The acne/rash side effect of a now-discontinued med is itching to beat the band, but other than that ... I'm doing pretty well. At least I have a gel to help with the rash ... it should clear up sooner than later – please.

Tammy is at work, and the kids are out of the house, too. While I sit here and type, a very nice woman is cleaning our house for us. … another wonderful provision from friends. My parents are running a few last minute errands for us. Our bags are essentially packed and we have boarding passes at the ready. In less than 24 hours we will be in the air on our way to Hawaii!

We're watching the weather closely – may need snowshoes to get to the airport ☺. The kids are loving the snow though, and I don't believe a little snow will keep us from our vacation. We so very much need this break, and we are so thankful that we can take it.

Family on the Big Island – Dad's cousin Dave and his wife Ginny – is showing such great hospitality already. Thanks to their local persistence we now have guaranteed adjacent [with Eric's brother Brian] rooms for our stay at the Hilton. The hotel doctor is on standby … already spun up on my health challenges. Dave and Ginny will meet us at the airport. From the airport, we'll follow them to our hotel where we'll find a stash of favorite snacks at the ready for the kids [provided by Dave and Ginny from a list they requested Eric and Tammy to make]. Now that is Island hospitality!

This cancer truly stinks and we are so ready for God to miraculously heal, but we know His timing and His plan is perfect.

"This is the day the Lord has made. We will rejoice and be glad in it." In fact, we are so richly blessed by all the generous gifts we are receiving. Thanks be to God from whom all good things come.

Until the next entry ... Aloha! Likely the next journal entry will be from Hawaii ☺.

126

Thursday, Jan. 19, 2012, 1:11 a.m.

Made it!

Wow ... a very long trip, but we made it safe and sound (minus my iPhone ... it met its untimely demise in the Hertz rental lot). We're all tired, but after sleep tonight, we should be good to go for some hardcore rest and relaxation tomorrow.

I do have a head wound – one of the sites from a halo screw, used during the gamma-knife procedure – that doesn't seem to be sealing up well. Also might have something to do with my youngest hitting me right on the bandage this morning ... maybe? I'm walking around with red gauze on my forehead. The Hertz Rental rep asked what I'd done. I paused for effect and said, "Well to be completely serious ... brain surgery." Stopped him in his tracks. ☺

A huge thanks again to cousins Dave and Ginny ... such hospitality. Our rooms are very nice and we even have a pass-through door between them. Thanks, Uncle Brian, for being here with us ... such a HUGE help.

Tomorrow I'll figure out the borrowed Flip HD camera and start recording more memories. Today was already memorable and I'm sure this trip will fill itself with special memories for our whole family. Thanks for continued prayers and encouragements.

Signed,
Nearly Comatose in Hawaii

~ *Responses from Family and Friends* ~

Awesome extended family photo!! Thanks for taking it, Brian. What great joy and peace to have loving family preparing the way and greeting our dear ones there in sunny Hawaii. Way to go, Dave and Ginny. Love to all,   *Sally H., Eric's mom*

Your smiles are contagious!!! Praying for you and love you all so much! "Yur Sis,"   *Cyndi F., Eric's sister*

Sorry to hear about the iPhone and the ouchie on your head, but I'll bet a Hawaiian sunrise and some time at the pool or on the beach and you'll forget about the phone and the ouchie will heal up very nicely! Have fun. The Flip is about as easy as they get to use. Just turn it on and press the record button. And editing is super easy, and super fun, too.
Valerie H., Eric's high school friend

Hi, Eric. My husband and I came over [to your home] in November to take your family pictures. I just got caught up on how you are doing. My prayers are with you, Tammy, Ellie and Timmy. I am glad you made it to Hawaii. I hope you are all having a wonderful time. I pray for your healing. I pray for strength so you can enjoy every moment. Most of all I pray for God's special hand on Ellie. I have daughters her same age. I know that this cannot be easy for her, but I also know that God loves her and will use these challenges to draw her near. Blessings to you.
Amy S., friend of a friend

Saturday, Jan. 21, 2012, 1:17 a.m.

"A-LO-HA!"

Dolphins … check.

Luau … check.

Creating lifetime memories … check.

Overall, we are having a great time in Hawaii. A number of times I have found myself asking God to fill me up with all the prayers that I know are being offered up on our behalf. Thank you so much for praying us through this trip. With strategically placed naps, my energy has held out well. About the only things I've missed is pool time [More sunshine than is healthy].

128

Thankfully, Uncle Brian has been a HUGE help. Tomorrow is a fairly unscheduled day ... lunch with Dave and Ginny, and then maybe even some date time for Tammy and me during the kids' naps. On Sunday we do the helicopter ride to see the volcanos/lava. On Monday we leave.

Each day is a gift from God. Here in Hawaii, it is all the more apparent how amazing the creation around us is, and how amazing our Creator is. The God who hung the stars in the sky and calls each one by name, the same God who knit each one of us in the wombs of our mothers, is the same God who will heal me of my cancer. Of that I am sure.

We continue to pray for healing in the here and now and not just for eternity. That said, regardless of outcome, we know God is big and good, and we do our best to embrace each day for the gift it is. Blessings to all, and a very warm "ALOHA!"

~ Responses from Family and Friends ~

We are loving the adventures of your family. He delights in YOU, your family, and in all that is His. Enjoy it all to the fullest. We lift you up daily asking for God's hand to give you His best and more ... may that include healing on this side of eternity – only God knows our days. We rest in that truth. He is our mighty Warrior King. Much love,

Dan and Kathy C., Village

Hey there family, Everyone OK after the 5.0 [earthquake] on the big island? Saw the news a bit late (since we're on Europe time – GMT +1), but thought we'd better check in. Praying for each of you.

Krista and Jim S. and kids, missionary friends in Belgium

Praising God for the blessed time you are already having in Hawaii! Praying for more! Enjoy it brother! *Fred J., Intel*

Glad vacation is going great. Enjoy the helicopter ride Sunday. Take care man. *Hector L., Intel*

Hi Eric, I heard about your situation and wanted to lend my support. Please enjoy your trip and continue to focus on your health. You are a strong person with a powerful mind. You will be in our family and my personal prayers. Please try to derive strength from all the support and never doubt your ability to overcome this. Best wishes for a speedy recovery! *Phil K., Intel*

Tuesday, Jan. 24, 2012, 3:54 p.m.

Back to reality

Last night, we made it safely back to rainy, cold Oregon. The vacation was GREAT!

On Sunday, we got a two-hour helicopter tour of the Big Island. Wow! All four of us really enjoyed it. (I'd love to have heard what Ellie told her friends at school today.) We even flew close enough to an active volcanic caldera to see the glow of the lava tube as it pumped out a huge plume of smoke. A trip to Hawaii, like we did, is a once-in-a-lifetime undertaking … Thanks be to God that my strength held out for the whole trip; we were able to do everything we planned, and I walked way more than I would have thought possible.

Now that we are back home, my medical schedule resumes. Tomorrow is the PET scan ... based on how I feel, it should show good progress in the battle against this insidious cancer. Then, on Monday, I get my next hit of chemo meds. Hopefully somewhere between now and Monday, I will get some advice from the neuro-surgeon as to how to stop the bleed on my forehead. I've got my own little "volcano" on my forehead – residual damage from the gamma knife procedure. Once I make it through the next chemo round, I've decided to reward myself with a fancy steak dinner. … figured goals and rewards are a good thing.

Looking ahead to the next week, here's what is on my mind: How do I process all that is going to happen? Even if the PET scan shows good progress ... how long can the meds fight off the fast-growing cancer? If God doesn't choose to miraculously heal me here and now ... how do I endure the repeated chemo doses and the ongoing stress of being so atypical (up to a dozen ER trips so far)?

I know I shouldn't borrow trouble from tomorrow and yet, at the same time, I want to mentally prepare myself for whatever might come. I'd welcome your prayers in this particular area ... though I'm not even sure exactly what to ask of God. Thank you for staying with us. I feel a nap calling my name, so I don't think I'll get to posting more this afternoon before the kids get home. ☺.

~ *Responses from Family and Friends* ~

We are so glad your trip was everything you hoped and that your stamina and energy were good throughout. We continue to pray for God's healing, and will pray for your spiritual, physical and mental perseverance.   *Jim and Jessie N., Village*

Like everyone else, we are so happy to hear about the great memories your trip provided. I personally was very happy to see you did NOT have daily posts and by that I knew you were having a good relaxing time not focused on cancer. We pray for you to have strength as you take the next steps and get results. Whatever plan God does have for your future, take every day on its own, loving those that are close and continue making the memories. You're an amazing man, husband to my sister, and brother-in-law to me! We all love you.   *Cary M., Tammy's brother*

Welcome Home! We echo everyone else here in saying how glad we are that your trip was filled with so many wonderful times. Like Cary said, we knew that the lack of posts meant you were fully enjoying every minute and that made us happy! We will be praying for all you have written about. I know that all the questions weigh heavily, but I also know that God has the answer to each one.

Dawn R., Tammy's sister

Thursday, Jan. 26, 2012, 7:39 p.m.

"Ewwww!"

It can't be good when the doctor's assistant pulls the bandage off and says, "Ewwww," with a disgusted look on her face. As she left, she handed me a gauze pad to catch any drips before the doctor came.

This morning I went in to the neurosurgeon about my weeping forehead wound from the three-weeks-ago gamma-knife procedure. When the doc saw the wound, he informed me I needed a stitch. Out came the suture and – without any numbing agent – I got a stitch and a bandage. On the way out the door, the doctor commented, "Aren't there hospitals in Hawaii?" I guess we should have dealt with the wound sooner. Hopefully by tomorrow, the pain will subside. Today seems like yet another example of my being "atypical." Who else gets a "volcano" wound coming out of the gamma-knife procedure?

With all the unpredictability of this sickness, I find it hard to commit to anything that requires a regular schedule ... like working again. On the work topic, I've decided not to commit to any formal hours. After next week's chemo, I will attempt to own parts of projects and work an irregular schedule, putting in time as I can. As long as I get the work done in a timely way, I should be good to go. Helping Intel without the stress of a formal commit feels like a good compromise. I'll give it a try for a few weeks and see how it works.

On a different topic, the PET scan yesterday was uneventful. I actually got a few good naps during the procedure ... ☺. I don't have the results back yet, but might hear something tomorrow. Worst case, we get results on Monday right before the chemo starts. Both Tammy and I expect to hear good news and for the chemo to continue with the current "recipe." (The swollen lymph nodes on my neck appear to have reduced a bunch.) If our expectations are met, we should have another 12 weeks (4 Rounds) of this chemo recipe to knock down the cancer.

As I'm often reminded, nobody has a guarantee of tomorrow. So, I'll try to not worry about tomorrow or the next rounds of chemo even. My God is in control and He is good. He continues to bless us in amazing ways – so many people praying, giving, caring ... not to mention our wonderful trip to Hawaii. Thanks be to God, and thanks to all of you as well. Your readership [on CaringBridge] – nearly 21,000 visits at last count – and comments are a huge encouragement.

~ *Responses from Family and Friends* ~

"Ewwww" is never a good sign. Hopefully now that it's clean and stitched, it will heal quickly. These verses were the focus of my devotions today and as soon as I read them, your name came to mind. So clearly God wanted me to share them with you. We serve such a faithful God! Psalm 73:23-26, "Yet I am always with you; you hold me by my right hand. You guide me with your counsel, and afterward you will take me into glory. Whom have I in heaven but you? And earth has nothing I desire besides you. My flesh and my heart may fail, but God is the strength of my heart and my portion forever."   *Lori H., Village*

Friday, Jan. 27, 2012, 9:12 p.m.

Catching a break

Some days are harder than others. Timmy is challenging ... to say the least. My forehead still hurts, a lot. And during dinner, while chewing bread, a molar broke. I see an emergency dentist at noon tomorrow. Oh ... and we have chemo on Monday. Still no word on the PET scan results. If screaming were helpful, I think I might. Both Tammy and I are "done." Fortunately the truth of God's goodness and sovereignty doesn't change based on my daily situation. I know even with trying kids, a broken molar, and more tribulations ahead with cancer, God remains good and in control. Hard to see tonight, but I choose to believe. Thanks as always.

Saturday, Jan. 28, 2012, 8:49 p.m.

Some answers

It's 24 hours later – two cavities filled and the riddle of the forehead pain is at least understood ... not solved.

First thing this morning, I headed to Immediate Care. Amazing how prompt the service is for a Stage IV cancer patient. The doctor who saw me said the forehead wound is healing well. Likely the persistent pain is because the stitch went through a nerve. I'll ask my cancer doc to pull the stitch on Monday and switch to a butterfly bandage. In the meantime, I just need to tolerate the pain.

After the Immediate Care trip, I went to see the emergency dentist ... 90 minutes later, I had a numb mouth and two new fillings. Fortunately the broken tooth wasn't crown-worthy and could easily be fixed with a filling.

Yesterday was a bummer day, but in hindsight, I am thankful we weren't in Hawaii when all this happened. I can't imagine the complexities of a painful forehead and broken tooth in Hawaii. It would have surely put a damper on our fun. I thank God for His good timing. So ... one day at a time.

We'll do our best to ... trust God with all our heart and lean not on our own understanding, but in all our ways we will acknowledge Him and He will make our path straight (Proverbs 3:5, 6). Thanks for the notes ... and screams ... ☺.

~ *Responses from Family and Friends* ~

So sorry you have another bump in the road. With so much going on, anything is just one more thing on the pile isn't it? Thankful that you were spared some of these bumps during your trip. Praying as always for quick and miraculous healing.   *Kris K., friend*

It's so hard when trials keep coming at you, one after the other. It's like you don't have time to catch your breath sometimes. Praying for God's strength to uphold you and His peace to give you comfort and rest tonight ... and for healing in every way needed!   *Teckla A., Village*

In all situations, I have resolved that God is good. Praying for you today and always,   *Jim and Jessie N., Village*

Thanks for the update, and we join you in praising God for His excellent timing!! So thankful for doctors, hospitals, medicine and loving nurses. Please know that we continue to pray for all of your family. May His love continue to strengthen you on this road you are on now. As always,   *Wanda K., former co-worker of Eric's brother*

Eric and Tammy, We are praying continually. We will be praying you get some relief from the pain on your forehead and molar very soon. Hang in there.   *Melissa and Brian L., close friends*

Hello Eric, I am keeping up with your postings. It's Renee, I work with Alex C. Love your great, positive attitude and your awareness of being prepared for whatever will be. Know that you and your family are in my prayers ... and I pray for a full and complete recovery.CANCER GONE! Can't wait to see the Hawaii pictures. It's my favorite place to vacation and I am taking my daughter back in May! Blessings,

Renee W., Intel

Sunday, Jan. 29, 2012, 8:57 p.m.

Chemo ... again

Today is "chemo eve." Tomorrow, we find out PET scan results and, we assume, I get Round 5 of chemo drugs. It is hard not to dread the week ahead. As I've been reminded though, we're taking things one day at a time. I'll plan to post from the chemo room tomorrow. We should have about five hours to "hang out."

134

Monday, Jan. 30, 2012, 1:10 p.m.

Results are in ... and encouraging

Thanks for all your prayers. After two rounds of this chemo cocktail, the PET scan results are extremely positive. If you remember, there are two measures in the PET scan ... activity/heat, and size of cancer. For activity, the magic number is less than 2. A number of sites moved from the 5-9 range down to 2 and under. For size, my composite measure shows a 25-percent reduction in size. Dr. Andersen said the results, "made his Friday."

So ... therapy continues with the current recipe of drugs. Thankfully we can drop the Tarceva, the daily oral med that caused such a strong reaction ... massive GERD and a huge acne outbreak. I will need a white blood cell booster shot tomorrow, but all is effectively good to go. (Shot tomorrow is likely to cause bone pain ... oh joy.)

Longer term, we will max out the number of useful cycles on this chemo mix (think logarithmic curve). The maximum expected is six rounds, although it could be as short as four rounds total, before the effectiveness of the drug wanes and/or my body's ability to handle the toxicity drops. Hopefully, the cancer will continue to shrink and decrease in activity while on this cocktail. If we decrease the cancer enough, then we can go on maintenance meds for an indeterminate time.

Obviously, the best outcome goes beyond simply lowering the amount of cancer or even a NED (no evidence of disease) finding. We are looking for a full-on miracle – no cancer at all. While the doctor is encouraged, he is still in "treatment" mode. So we look to our All-Powerful Doctor for a cure.

In the days ahead, please keep praying for full healing. Also, please pray for endurance for our whole family. These last four months have taken their toll on me, Tammy, and the kids. And we still don't know which way the ball will bounce. So ... one day at a time.

And one other prayer request ... the neurosurgeon who stitched through a nerve in my forehead is out this week and, according to his nurse, doesn't have coverage. My oncologist is hesitant to remove the stitch ... specialists don't like to mess with each other's work.

He is trying to find out who actually is covering for the neurosurgeon so I can get this stitch out and reduce the head pain.

Each cycle gets harder from a mental perspective. The more it seems that full healing is not happening, the more the treatments feel like rearranging deck chairs on the Titanic. I know I need to fight, and yet, if given the option of Heaven or more chemo ...

Blessings to all.

~ *Responses from Family and Friends* ~

I am glad to hear that the trials of the last few months are showing some positive results. I know it is difficult to face the effects of the treatment when no cure is guaranteed but surely it is a tiny bit easier to "suck it up" and go through the chemo knowing that the cancer is getting beaten back. May each day bring you a glimmer of the investment you still have to make in this world, as we pray for complete healing. All the best.   *Kris K., friend*

So grateful for a move in the right direction. I will continue to pray for a full-out mind-blowing miracle! Will continue praying for God's very best for you and for joy and strength as you walk this road. Thank you for being honest with us, we wouldn't want it any other way. Blessings, friend,   *Kathy B., Village*

Praise God for this answer to prayer!! It may not be the finish line but in this marathon journey, every step gets you closer. You made my Monday. =D And I'm praying that you have an atypical response to the neupogen and avoid the joint pain. "Atypical" has to work for good too, right? Keep the good news rolling!! Sending your family prayers, love and support.   *Lori H., Village*

[There were 215 responses in the guestbook
from January 1-31, 2012.]

February 2012

~ *The Fifth Month* ~

Wednesday, Feb. 1, 2012 – 10:22 a.m.

"Animal Strike at the Zoo"

Wednesday is here and the sun is shining. Tuesday is a bit of a blur – I slept most of it away. Fortunately, sleepiness has been the only major side effect of this round of chemo, and my stitch pain is not beyond my tolerance. (The doctor wants the offending suture in for three weeks … ugh.) To his credit he did get back to me even while on his vacation. If the pain gets to be intolerable, I can go to the ER and have them fix the stitch. Though right now with chemo week, the stitch pain isn't even on the radar … either better, or just the lesser of two evils.

One of Timmy's favorite books right now is "Animal Strike at the Zoo." The zoo animals get greedy and demand all sorts of perks – peanuts are no longer enough, the living quarters nowhere near as posh, etc. So, the animals refuse to do animal things in front of the visitors. It takes the tears of a little girl to break the strike. The animals realized doing what they are made to do is way better and more fulfilling than the strike.

A few days ago, I had a parallel thought ... If my being so ill and writing about it on CaringBridge is "blessing" so many (your words, not mine), then why don't I "go on strike" and force God's hand to heal – I've never claimed to be 100 percent rational all the time ... ☺. As I pondered how to "manipulate" God, I was reminded of Timmy's book. I honestly believe it was a prompt from God's Spirit.

When I, the created (just like the animals in Timmy's book) do well the things that I do today – for the glory of God – that is when I am most fulfilled. There is no guarantee of tomorrow, for any of us, so let's do today what we do well for the glory of God. And as God's Word is oft to remind, don't worry about tomorrow. Easier said than done some days … especially when I feel horrible on chemo week, or when I realize that apart from a miracle my lifespan is much shorter than I'd ever have planned. That said, I purpose to keep my focus on God, trust Him for each day, and attempt to follow His leading. Right about now, I feel a nap coming on ... ☺.

♦ WAYS TO PRAY:

Full healing ... either here or in eternity;

Better chemo week;

Restful sleep without horrible dreams (two nights ago I had what is best described as a demonic dream ... last night's sleep was way better);

Wisdom parenting the kids through this huge life stress;

Endurance, especially for Tammy;

Making the most out of each day ... especially as I look to add Intel work in for chunks of time next week.

~ Responses from Family and Friends ~

Yes, we will continue to pray, and will pray as you indicate. I think I need to read Timmy's book! Hugs,   *Jerrilyn K., friend*

You are such an encouragement! I look forward to reading your posts. Your life (though I don't even know you, just your sweet wife) has challenged me to be more for the Lord. To lay aside fear and even laziness and do what the Lord wants me to do ...win the lost to Christ! It's easy to take my time here on earth for granted thinking I will always have tomorrow. I admire your strength to keep writing through it all. My family continues to pray for you daily ... even several times a day at times. We pray for miracles to come your way along with your other requests. God always wins. Whatever that looks like, He is greater and we trust that! May you be strengthened with the joy of the Lord!

Anne B., Tammy's friend

Eric, you will never, ever know how I needed your blog this morning. You are exactly where God wants you right now, for so many reasons. I count it a blessing to know you, and through you get some needed encouragement. Wherever God leads you (and me) is the right course – all for HIS Glory. Again, thank you for the reminder, Eric. As always, praying for a miracle of healing for you NOW, and knowing that He is able, in His timing. God bless you, friend.   *Terri B., Village*

Friday, Feb. 3, 2012, 12:36 p.m.

The truth is hard to live

This cancer is by far the hardest thing I've dealt with in my life. I don't have a clue as to how/when this cancer battle will end. My "Type-A" personality wants to plan ahead, exert control.

♦ A HUGE PART OF ME WANTS TO KNOW
WITH CERTAINTY:

How much longer? … Days, months, years?

How many more chemo cycles will I have to endure? … I think I hit the low point for this chemo round last night.

When will the good days be outnumbered by the bad days?

Will God heal me physically now or simply take me Home?

How much more suffering?

♦ IN ALL THE QUESTIONS,
I'M REMINDED OF WHAT IS CERTAIN:

This cancer is more than I can handle alone ... Thankfully I have a huge support network, you, family, church, friends; and most importantly … my God is sufficient for what comes each day. So while I am beyond done with suffering, I trust in God's daily provision … or at least I try ... easier said than practiced.

I don't know what is coming beyond today … and fearing tomorrow only robs me of enjoying today. God knows tomorrow and will work it all out for good because He loves me deeply.

I am so limited in my knowledge and power ... It is ridiculous for me to think I can "help" or do a better job than God can at working all this. He will reveal what I need each day. I am not God … thankfully.

I'd much rather not deal with the daily suffering ... I'd love to find an easy out, but I know the easy way is often fraught with ugly consequences. I need only look to Adam and Eve – their easy way out brought separation, shame, blame, toil, pain, deceit, and death. Jesus, on the other hand, embraced the suffering of the cross and the weight of the sins of the world, and through Him came reunion, restoration, forgiveness, eternity, truth, and life.

Thanks to all for your continued love and prayers. Here's to embracing today and leaving tomorrow in God's hands. Nothing of what is happening to me and my family is catching Him by surprise.

~ *Responses from Family and Friends* ~

Eric – my friend, my desire is to share with you a secret formula, "The best and easiest way to live with and battle cancer." We all know that is not possible. You have done such a tremendous job of fighting the good fight. You have kept your head up and persevered in the face of daily challenges and unknowns. I am humbled by your will, drive, and relationship with Christ. We will continue to hold you up in prayer.
Mike T., Intel

We continue to pray here and I have shared your story so that others are praying across the country. I have been so thankful for your outlook and your focus on God. This post is amazingly written. I shared it with my closest girlfriends (five pastors' wives scattered around the U.S.) whom I communicate with every day on email. They have been praying and they too feel blessed and inspired by these words. May God grant you strength and peace. *Kristina W., Eric's college friend*

We love you, Tammy, and the children so much. You are being lifted up continuously by our family and in our small group bible study. We agree in prayer for your complete healing. May each test show more and more evidence of this healing! May He wrap His arms around all of you in loving strength and support. Love,
Bonnie and George J., Tammy's aunt and uncle in Arizona

My heart just aches for the pain you and your family are enduring. I share your confidence that God knows and will sustain you through this. I'm praying that you find rest in the midst of these trials.
Lori H., Village

Eric, no words for what you are suffering. What we do is sit beside you in our own cyber way, mourn with you, rejoice with you and pray over you. Praying God's presence will surround you and His mighty arms uphold you always. Much Love, *Kathy B., Village*

Saturday, Feb. 4, 2012, 10:35 p.m.

Resolved

Nearly through another day. I'm feeling weary in both body and mind.

This morning my parents came by and I had a nice slow walk with my Dad through our neighborhood. I can recover from the chemo effects faster if I get up and move around each day, or so they say.

Despite the sunny weather, I had quite a cloudy disposition today. Not feeling great and being cooped up was a bad recipe. Thankfully those around me encouraged me to buck up. Our neighbors came by and spruced up our yard – huge thanks! Ellie's friend came by and the kids went out to play. And then we all loaded up in the van and headed to Washington Square for dinner. I ended up using the walker through the mall ... it helped enough. I think everyone had a fun time and the evening passed by a little more quickly. We even had my niece as the "sandwich artist" at the Subway where she works... hadn't planned on seeing her tonight.

So, my big challenge ... take one day at a time. I'm not doing so well today, but with God's help I'll have lots more days ahead to practice.

Monday, Feb. 6, 2012, 1:31 p.m.

Battle on

Where did the weekend go? I guess most of yesterday was Super Bowl. Was I the only one underwhelmed by the commercials this year? (I did like the Doritos ones, and Honda's Ferris Bueller commercial was pretty good.)

On the health front ... I'm one week past chemo. This morning I am still tired and had to layer in more anti-nausea meds before heading to a regularly scheduled doctor appointment (naturopath), but on the whole, things are improving. Hopefully, now I can have two good weeks before the next chemo hit. Ideally, I'll get the forehead stitch out this week, too ...one week earlier than planned. I'd love to lose the pain.

The most challenging element to overcome these days is

my mind. Seizing-the-day ... one-day-at-a-time ... seems to be a nearly impossible daily mission. As I look to the Bible for guidance. I am told to stand firm and remember that my fight is not against just what I see, but against a broken world system ... and against the Enemy of our souls.

Ephesians, chapter 6, uses battle language when talking about taking on our daily challenges. We are to put on our battle armor each day ... belt of truth, helmet of salvation, breastplate of righteousness, feet ready to share God's good news, shield of faith, and the sword of God's Word.

So ... time to get dressed for the day and hold on to the whole truth. I'm in a battle I plan to win, even if I lose against cancer.

One final thought ... here's a shout out to all my Intel friends at ISMC this week.

I miss the chance to see you face to face.

~ Responses from Family and Friends ~

Greetings from ISMC. Carpe Diem is the conference theme. It means Seize the Day. Interesting that you used that phrase in your recent post.   *Hector L., Intel*

Eric, we miss you here at ISMC, too. Congrats on your Marketing award for Score with Core, well deserved!   *Tim W., Intel*

As I read today's post, I can really hear you rallying for the fight. I'm glad to see you throw off some of the gloom that weighs so heavily on your shoulders. I know some days are better than others, and it's good that today was a "better" and not an "other." You have an army of friends in your corner who celebrate every victory you achieve, big or small. (And if it makes you feel any better, I didn't get a ticket to ISMC either. I'm sulking about it)   *Mike F., Intel*

Ahh Eric, true fighting words. Battle on my friend, we battle with you, beside you. Keeping you in my prayers and always your family.
                                                        Debbie M., Intel

One of my favorite Petra songs was "Get on your knees and fight like a man!" Keep up the good fight Eric. Your faithful witness to God's presence in the midst of horrible circumstances will be rewarded.   *Becky J., formerly at Village*

Tuesday, Feb. 7, 2012, 11:00 p.m.

Fuzzy wuzzy

I'm making progress ... clawing my way out of the chemo hole day by day. This week, in particular, has been hard because of persistent depression/anxiety that has been hard to shake off. I am dealing with more than just simple worry. It seems like with all the meds, the chemo, and the cancer, my brain is unable to handle the pressure.

After my usual afternoon nap, I awoke feeling extra anxious. My heart rate was up and my mind was unfocused. I tried napping more, but that didn't bring relief. Fortunately, I have a "take as needed" medicine specifically to help with anxiety. After taking that earlier this evening, I'm feeling much better.

Having never really dealt with what I believe to be truly mental illness/disability, this is a learning experience for me. Through this, I think I will develop more empathy for those who struggle daily with chronic mental illness/disability. It is a strange feeling to be anxious and down without really having any control over the feelings whatsoever. (Longer term, I'm able to double up my anti-depression meds ... that should help me have a more stable base, ongoing.)

On a separate note, tomorrow I get the stitch out of my forehead. I'm jazzed to have that pain stop. Hopefully, the surgeon won't argue with taking out the stitch. Thanks as always for sticking with us on this journey. We so value your prayers and notes.

Shout out to my Intel ASMO buds at our sales conference. Hope you guys are having tons of fun at Disney! I miss you.

~ Responses from Family and Friends ~

Checking in from [Intel] ISMC ... funny how the conference theme of Carpe Diem is what you have been living and role modeling for all of us. I'm sure you've heard that your team was recognized at the ASMO Geography update as the "Marketing Excellence" winner. We were able to see your photo – the cheers of congratulations were loud and "big" ... just like our cheers of encouragement to you!!! Prayers for "calming" and rest so you can build strength!
Laura B., Intel

Friday, Feb. 10, 2012, 7:08 p.m.

A little help

After months of avoiding my primary care physician (PCP), I went back to see him today. Yesterday I tried to change to a new PCP, but everyone I called was booked months out.

[Ed. note: In September of 2011 Eric found himself suffering from an excruciatingly painful lower left leg. It had been diagnosed and was being treated as Achilles tendinitis ... it turned out to be something much more insidious.]

After a good visit with my old PCP, I have a prescription for some meds to help me through the anxiety. Yay!

In general, my emotions – and my family's emotions – have worn thin over the months of this cancer fight. If curling up in a ball and pulling the covers over my head would help for any extended period of time, I'd be in that position a lot.

One night this last week while I was having an especially hard time of it, the following question came to mind, "Do I trust God?" The answer might surprise some, as in that moment, I said to myself and to God, "No."

Now don't get me wrong ... big picture, I trust God. I wholeheartedly believe He is good and in control. I have only to spend any time looking at His creation or reading the Bible to see His overarching goodness. That night, as with other moments, my lack of trust was much more personal. This cancer sucks. Chemo is harsh. And, with each new problem, I grow more weary. Even the successes ... 25 percent reduction in tumors and great PET scan numbers ... lack impact under the combined weight of the "suckiness" called cancer.

In those moments, I question God's personal goodness to me. At times, God seems almost capricious, mean-spirited. I don't trust Him to be personally good to me – when measured by how good I feel. My lack of trust reveals just how deeply ingrained the gospel of convenience and the culture of personal peace and affluence are in my life.

The Bible is full of "suckiness" (a theological term –☺) – that the saints suffer in this world. In fact, I know I am guaranteed suffering this side of eternity. In my weakness, or maybe humanity, I want to have everything go my way – I want the promises of Heaven now.

When things don't go my way, I feel like God has betrayed me, left me high and dry.

The truth is so far from betrayal.

♦ HERE'S WHAT I TELL MYSELF NOW,
and when I feel like God is against me:

Suffering is guaranteed. God suffers with me as I go through hard times. He is not the author of evil things, but rather the source of all good things.

The Enemy wants me to doubt God's goodness ... Since Adam and Eve, Satan has been working hard to wound God's creation. I must be careful to not attribute the work of Satan to God.

Jesus loved me enough to willingly suffer beating, scourging, crucifixion, and even separation from the presence of God as He took the penalty for the sins of the world.

God is personally good to me ... even if I don't feel it. Each day, He offers me His very presence. I just hope I understand more of what all that means in the days ahead.

May we all personally experience more of God's presence and goodness in the days to come. Thanks! Here's to choosing to trust God on all levels.

~ Responses from Family and Friends ~

After reading today's journal entry, I just had to say, "Wow!" You hit the nail on the head: We must cling to what we know to be true, and not let what we feel sway our beliefs. While we can't deny the reality of experiencing our feelings, they are not the ultimate truth we trust. Thanks again, brother, for such encouraging words. Praying for peace and assurance to be very tangible to you, Tammy, Ellie, and Timmy.
Celeste H., Village

Eric, Your honesty in sharing the "suckiness" of cancer is amazing to me; and the truth you speak, in spite of everything, is beyond amazing! God is using you to encourage me every time I read one of you journal entries. Thank you!!! I continue to pray for you, Tammy, and the kids, that God wraps you in His peace, love and perseverance through all!
Nancy O., Village

Saturday, Feb. 11, 2012, 12:09 p.m.

Pondering eternity

I want Heaven! If cancer is going to claim my life, and if the process is going to be heinous, why not hope for a fast end to all of this? Why am still I here on Earth?

♦ HERE ARE SOME ANSWERS I'VE HEARD OTHERS GIVE:

> We are here by chance ... evolved from amoebas. There is nothing beyond this life, so live to the fullest ... Create fame and pleasure for yourself. If it feels good, do it.

> We are all interconnected to "Mother Earth." Tread softly and do our best to preserve this world. When we pass, our energy joins the greater pool of energy that exists.

> This incarnation is our chance to do better and do penance for our past-life mistakes. If we are really devout, we will ascend and our energy will join the great nothing. If we need more practice we come back as something more lowly ... a bug, or something more holy ... a cow.

> If we believe and do the right things in this life ... we will be creator gods ourselves and have our own worlds to manage someday.

> Our eternal reward or punishment is conditioned on the works we do here and now, so we strive to have the good we do outweigh the bad.

> This world is not real at all ... in fact it is just Adam's dream, so live in light of that reality, sickness can be willed away, no need for doctors.

> Even for those of us who call ourselves followers of Christ, why not just do a big "Jim Jones" and get a head start on eternity?

♦ IN PONDERING THAT, I CAME UP WITH TWO ANSWERS

FIRST: As Christ's ambassador to a lost and dying world ... I have work yet to be done. Work prepared in advance for me to do.

> "For we are God's handiwork, created in Christ Jesus to do good works, which God prepared in advance for us to do" *(Ephesians 2:10).*

The main work for us is to testify to the truth of God's Word ... I believe God desires that none should perish but that all might be saved; and how are people to be saved if not by hearing from those of us who know ... testifying to what we know.

SECOND: Each day this side of Eternity is an opportunity for me to send treasure ahead. As it says in 1 Corinthians 3, we build upon the initial reward of our unconditional salvation, and we speak out about the goodness of God ... even in our weakness. What we build will be tested and those things which survive the testing ... gold, silver, and costly stones ... vs. wood, hay, and straw ... will be cause for eternal reward.

> "Therefore we do not lose heart. Though outwardly we are wasting away, yet inwardly we are being re-newed day by day. For our light and momentary troubles are achieving for us an eternal glory that far outweighs them all. So we fix our eyes not on what is seen, but on what is unseen, since what is seen is temporary, but what is unseen is eternal."

So, 2 Corinthians 4:16-18 makes more sense to me today than ever before.

Each day I have is less about me, and more about God receiving glory through more lives being drawn to Him ... those who believe being transformed to be more Christ-like; and those who have yet to enter into God's forever family, hearing the truth and responding to the Spirit's prompting to believe and be saved.

So today, by faith, I look for those opportunities to store up treasure in heaven. I join you and many others asking for my healing on this side of eternity. There's a lot more work to be done, and I'm greedy ... I want a huge stockpile in Heaven. ☺

Have you put your faith in Jesus for your salvation and transformation? If not, let me encourage you to consider it today.

Thanks as always for the notes, prayers, etc. We are blessed by you.

~ *Responses from Family and Friends* ~

I was reading earlier today that "suffering is the school of faith." Clearly, it is a sucky school, but school none the less. Thank you for sharing your hard won faith lessons with us ... in the midst of suckiness, much ministry is being done. Your earthly vessel of a body is being ravaged, and yet you find the courage and strength to share with your community the hard won lessons of this grinding trial. There are a multitude of eternal rewards awaiting you for your transparency and your witness in this trial. Your ability – DECISION – to keep the truth before you, and before all of us, is honoring to God, and humbling to me. I will continue to pray for your healing, and your peace and trust in the Creator, praying that those truths of His love and goodness for you personally seeps deep into your bones, even to the depths of your soul. You know He loves you. My prayer is that you and Tammy would feel His love during the lowest points in all of this.   *Tracy L., Village*

I just took a few hours and read your [whole] journal and got "caught up" with the past 4-1/2 months. Wow. You have really been through it. "Hard pressed on every side" is what immediately pops into mind. Praying for a miracle of healing, first of all! And until then, praying that you will continue to know God's presence with you on this journey you are on. "May the God of hope fill you with all joy and peace as you trust in him, so that you may overflow with hope by the power of the Holy Spirit" (Romans 15:13). Thanks for the words that you've shared with us – you have deepened my perspective on life and reminded me again of what is most important. Blessings on your entire family! With love,
        Bonnie and Kevin O., missionary friends in Burkina Faso

Monday, Feb. 13, 2012, 10:31 p.m.

A lighter fare ...

No bad news today. Whoo hoo!

After a more strenuous day yesterday (hosting a birthday party for my side of the family), I slept a good deal of today – planned and unplanned naps ... ☺. Beside the naps, I also did a number of things that show great progress. For example, my dad and I made two laps around our neighborhood. In previous days I was pushing to do just one slow lap. Tonight I also spent a long time standing ... making a Valentine card.

God willing, I'm in for a good week. The only procedure scheduled is my brain MRI on Wednesday to make sure the cancer in the brain is gone. Our assumption going in is that the cancer is gone from my brain. We're not seeing any symptoms of lesion growth at all.

So, for those not on Facebook with Tammy, I'll close with a funny. Saturday, after getting my anti-anxiety meds, I was feeling the onset of anxiety. As I reached for the pill bottle, I was reminded of the doctor's cautioning about negative side effects ... addiction, amnesia ... I hesitated to take the pill; then I started to laugh.

Q. "Why didn't you take the anti-anxiety pill, Eric?"
A. "I was anxious about the side effects." ☺

The irony was not lost on me. I took the pill. Thankfully the anxiety has lessened overall too. Hope everyone has a wonderful day tomorrow celebrating Valentine's Day.

Wednesday, Feb. 15, 2012, 5:59 p.m.

Steak!

Dipping my toe back in the Intel waters. We'll see what I can do. I've been pretty much offline since October, with only a few hours last year as the exception. Hopefully, I can successfully take on a few key projects and really help my teammates out [working from home]. There's a ton to be done in 2012 and we've got some exciting projects. I was really pleased to hear that the strategic choices my team made before I left on medical leave are panning out well. What a huge encouragement to know we set a great foundation. Now to keep building.

As a celebration of making it through this last chemo cycle, Tammy and I are heading out tonight ... sans kids ... to have a nice sit-down dinner. It isn't quite Hawaii, but I will thoroughly enjoy a steak dinner with my bride.

The rest of the week should be somewhat quiet, especially with today's brain MRI done ... results by Friday, or for sure Monday. Hopefully, I can keep a good attitude and look at each day as the gift that it is. I'll leave the Monday chemo for Monday. I don't want to borrow trouble.

Friday, Feb. 17, 2012, 8:31 p.m.

Seize the day

Another day passes. The highlights of today are the visitors we had ... my brother, a coworker, and a friend from church with dinner in hand. My naps were good, too. On the not-so-hot side, the nausea and fatigue were back stronger than I would have expected for week three. There was a remote chance that we'd have heard the brain MRI results before the weekend, but we haven't heard anything. We'll assume no news is good news. The doctor will share results first thing on Monday morning ... before we start chemo.

On the mental/emotional space, I'm doing okay, but not great. Adjusting to "chronic sick" is hard. I remember my pre-cancer abilities, and even though I am doing better than in October, it is all too easy to measure against the 100-percent-healthy-Eric baseline.

Another struggle is living "carpe diem" vs. borrowing trouble from tomorrow. Knowing Monday's chemo is coming can be very discouraging. It is hard to stay positive in the face of another week of feeling horrible. At least in a few weeks we'll have another PET scan and know how well chemo is working.

◆ WE HAVE SO MANY AROUND US
who continue to encourage us:

I got an amazing card from my coworkers, they all had signed it at the recent sales and marketing conference.

Meals continue to stream in.

The guys helping with my "family" video project have the edits all done; just need to "sweeten" it with other pictures, etc. (For that to work though, I've got to have enough mental/emotional reserves to spend the time needed to round up the photos.)

Family continues to help in so many ways, especially with watching the kids.

Tammy and I had a wonderful meal out a Stanford's earlier this week. I had filet mignon … mmmmm. Next chemo cycle, I'll look forward to a yummy Indian cuisine meal.

We love all the notes ... If I wake in the middle of the night I'll check CaringBridge for new notes or read old ones. The encouragement goes a long way.

So many are praying us through this ... I imagine a giant bowl in Heaven that collects all the prayers of the saints for me and my family. As we have need for God's special help, I imagine the bowl pouring out blessing on us … and the list goes on.

Thanks! Have a great weekend!

~ *Responses from Family and Friends* ~

I simply love the image God has given you (I have to give Him the credit) about the prayers being collected in a big heavenly bowl and poured out as needed. Simply beautiful.   *Libby S., Village*

I know the temptation to compare what used to be to what is. Compare to October and smile at the progress. (I know what you're thinking: "That's easy for you to say." But, perspective is everything. We are thankful that this week has held some happy times and we pray that this weekend will hold even more.   *Dawn R. and family, Tammy's sister*

Sunday, Feb. 19, 2012, 9:14 p.m.

Seventh time is the charm

Thankfully the weekend flew by. Yesterday [Saturday], I drove myself to and from Costco. While in Costco, I forwent the electric cart and instead pushed a normal cart through the aisles. My legs still hurt from yesterday, but my health is so far ahead of where it was just a few weeks ago. I am claiming improvement.

Between church and time with my dad at a movie, "Mission Impossible" ... two-plus hours of non-stop adrenaline, today flew by, too. As I type, the kids are upstairs in bed and we only have a few more hours to pass before bedtime. On the whole, I appreciate all the "distractions" from what comes tomorrow.

Early tomorrow, Tammy and I head out to meet with Dr. Patton (*radiation expert*) at the Rose Quarter clinic. There we'll find out the results of last week's brain MRI. Hopefully the brain MRI shows no sign of cancer. Once we are done with Dr. Patton, I head ... no pun intended ... to the oncology clinic and undergo chemo – assuming my blood tests out okay.

♦ TOMORROW WILL BE ROUND 7
  in the chemo room [Reflecting back.]

Round 1 – on the first recipe;

Round 2 – the failed attempt that left me in full-on anaphylactic shock (I have now added one more med to my allergy list). Taxol is evil ... we even just saw a murder mystery on TV where the murderer used Taxol to kill his victims (Hello?!?)

Round 3 – with a modified first recipe ... avoiding the near-death side effects of Taxol;

Rounds 4, 5 and 6 – with the current recipe ... part of that time with nasty side effects from a daily oral med that was to improve the chemo impact ... ha ha.

Also included ... was one round of post-PET-scan results showing less overall cancer activity and [some] cancer shrinkage.

Even with a positive PET scan under the belt, each round of chemo seems to get harder and harder. To say, "It is a challenge to willingly have poison pumped into your body," would be a major understatement. Tonight though, I do my best to keep tomorrow in its box. I choose to enjoy tonight ... as much as that is possible.

As for tomorrow, I know who holds tomorrow. Like Psalm 17:15 says, "...when I awake, I will be satisfied with God's presence." That is my goal. I want to fix my eyes on Jesus, all the more with my health as it is. God is with me through this, and He will get me through this – one way or the other. We all continue to pray for full healing and hope God chooses to heal me this side of Heaven. In the meantime, I take it one day at a time – seeking what God has for me each day He gives me.

I plan to write more tomorrow from the chemo room. Stay tuned. Here's to a week that exceeds expectations ... for me, and for you.

p.s. As always, thank you!

Monday, Feb. 20, 2012, 12:14 p.m.

Good news – brain lesion shrinking

Here's the latest from my chemo chair ... The brain MRI showed a great response to treatment. The lesion size has decreased significantly and I won't need another brain scan for two months. So, my brain is "normal," – if you listen carefully, you can hear Tammy snickering in the background ☺.

The pre-treatment meeting with Dr. Andersen, or in this case his Physician Assistant Kim, went well, too. My white blood count is still lower than they would like, so tomorrow I come back and get a booster shot. Hopefully the side effects they say can happen, won't happen. Last cycle, the extreme bone pain from the booster shot didn't happen, thankfully.

Thanks again for all the prayers and support. FYI, the next major milestone will be the PET scan March 7. Now to chill in my recliner and let the meds flow. Might even get in a nap or two ... ☺.

Wednesday, Feb. 22, 2012, 10:02 a.m.

Fatigued

So, Wednesday after chemo Monday – on the whole, things are going reasonably for a chemo week. Splitting the steroids and eating food with each dose appears to be helping. I'm still sleeping a ton, but there are worse things. I am nowhere near having to go to the ER/hospital with this chemo round. Two more days with steroids. Friday should be much better ... I hope.

I know my head/emotions are more "messed up" with chemo week. I may write more on that at some point later, but I should probably let the bias of the chemo meds abate some. In short, the more this goes on, the more just being done with the whole thing appeals, and having a long future post-cancer seems scary.

Thank you for all the support. We are having so many yummy meals. Last night we even got a bonus breakfast delivered ... oven-baked French toast for this morning ... mmmmm.

Please feel free to send notes on the guestbook or email. I'd love to hear from you. Don't worry too much about what to say or not say. Having been on the other side of CaringBridge, I realize it is hard to come up with notes that are "meaningful" and not "trite." That said, I'm just good with hearing from you. It doesn't have to be deep at all ☺. Oh ... and feel free to send notes to Tammy too; she's got a huge load to carry in this as well. Blessings to all.

~ *Responses from Family and Friends* ~

I'm so glad to hear that chemo week is going better than "usual!" I just wanted to let you know that I am thinking of you and your family often. It's nice to see Tammy and Ellie at the bus stop every day. Today, Ellie and Kaitlyn [Jennifer's daughter] were walking around together kind of forming a train. It was cute and they were having fun! Thanks for the reminder that we don't have to write deep meaningful stuff every time we sign your guest book ... it's just what I needed! *Jennifer L., neighbor*

154

Thursday, Feb. 23, 2012, 10:04 a.m.

Oops – OD'd, but OK

Today is off to a "fun" start. In the grogginess of taking my morning meds out of my pill box (*7"x4" lidded slots*), I ended up taking a double dose of my morning meds. Oops.

Somehow I opened the Thursday- and Friday-morning bays. It did strike me that I had quite the handful of pills, but I didn't catch what happened until the pills – all the pills – were well down my gullet.

We called Dr. Andersen, who I'm sure is no stranger to such calls. He wasn't concerned. He said I may be extra tired, but no need to rush to the hospital and have my stomach pumped. Brain fade ... Case in point – I just had Tammy search upstairs for my cell phone, only to find after calling it that it was in my pocket all along. Duh!

On a somewhat more serious note, I was just thinking about the verse that says, "God loves a cheerful giver." So, in addition to "one day at a time," I am also called to be cheerful in serving God each day. He has a plan and a reason ... my days are numbered, and only He knows when my days will end. So each day I have left should be one where I am thankful ... even in the midst of hideous cancer and vile meds.

Moreover, 10-plus years ago I made a vow to Tammy and to God that I would love Tammy ... in sickness and in health. (I always thought it would be Tammy getting sick and me being healthy.) While Heaven is a great opportunity and the desire of all our hearts, I need not rush off this mortal coil. Each day God gives me here is a day to joyfully serve Him AND my family. Way easier said than done, but that is going through my extra-drugged-up brain this morning. As always, thanks for reading, supporting, loving, etc.

~ *Responses from Family and Friends* ~

For many years I have thought about the part of the marriage vow that says "in sickness and in health," specifically how you refer to the obligation it places on the person who is sick. Within the battle you are waging, and even during your hardest times, I have observed how you love Tammy. Thank you for that.   *Chip M., Tammy's dad*

155

Friday, Feb. 24, 2012, 4:34 p.m.

Best chemo week

Huzzah! Steroids ended for this chemo cycle yesterday; and today I am doing pretty well. It's all relative, but compared to previous chemo cycles, this has been the most benign – no ER or hospitalization. My brother and I even ran two small errands this morning ... had to have a one-hour nap in between, but ...

It is encouraging to have an easier chemo cycle. Perhaps it means the PET scan will bring with it more good news. On an even more festive note, "Happy Birthday" to my lovely wife. Both sets of parents are coming tonight; we'll do dinner, dessert, and presents. Well ... time for a nap ...again. One day at a time.

Saturday, Feb. 25, 2012, 2:48 p.m.

Grumpy

To say I woke up on the wrong side of bed this morning would be a gross understatement. I'm sure the emotion has a lot to do with chemo drugs pulsing through the system. Fortunately for Tammy and the kids, they were able to be out of the house ... away from me. My poor parents, on the other hand, had to deal with grumpy me.

♦ WHY AM I GRUMPY? Here are a few thoughts:

I am tired, hungry, and on drugs ... ☺. I just ate lunch and that has taken some of the edge off.

Cancer sucks! Even with cycle-on-cycle improvement I am pounded down on all fronts and there is no obvious "break" or "off ramp."

The progress made in my health seems almost like a tease ... assuming God doesn't fully heal. I lose perspective all too quickly when I look beyond today and count the "bad" days that are "sure" to be ahead. I count the suffering and discount the blessings, finding myself afraid to survive. Just imagine, how would you choose ... Heaven vs. a future of arthritis, dealing with rebellious teenagers, the onset of dementia, etc. ...

Like many who choose to check out from responsibility … quitting a job for the wrong reasons, filing for divorce as the easy way out, etc …. I, too, am sorely tempted to punch out, at least on some level. There has to be some respite, some release from the commitments I have here and now. And yet, my marriage vows stand, in sickness and in health; my commitment to deeply love and cherish my children remains.

So … I have a bad disposition this week (and especially today) because of meds. And I know the Enemy of my soul would love nothing more than to piggyback on that and encourage me to wallow further in my grumpiness.

Rather than wallow, I must choose thankfulness. God is good and in control. He has numbered my days already … and that number is His to know, and not for me to know. As such, I try to live one day at a time. Hopefully with a few more days away from chemo meds, it will be easier to "carpe diem." Thanks for your prayers. This is a battle. I know how the war is won … the Bible is clear on that … but I need God's help in the daily skirmishes. It is hard to keep up the good fight.

~ Responses from Family and Friends ~

I can only imagine your frustration. Being a bit grumpy is more than understandable. Your passion to fight through this has been inspiring to watch. An hour at a time is sometimes the only way to get through it. Hang in … we are proud of you, and your Intel family is right behind you. Continued healing prayer coming your way.   *CJ B., Intel*

Thank you for sharing your journey with us Eric! It helps me know how to pray. It also helps put this life into perspective so many times. You are running a great race and you are running it well. I don't always know what to say but you are both in my heart and prayers. We pray for you daily and are blessed by you and the lessons we learn from your journey. We love you guys,   *Lori O, Village*

Eric, you are an inspiration to me and many others. Thank you for being real and transparent through this journey. I am praying for healing, peace, comfort and joy for you. In Christ,   *Amy B., Village*

Monday, Feb. 27, 2012, 4:47 p.m.

Sleepy in Portland

As far as side effects go, sleepiness is pretty tame. Happily, that is the major side effect of this chemo cycle. Today after a brief meeting with the naturopath, I came home and fell asleep in my chair … not planned, but the sleep was good. Later, I'll try to do a leisurely loop through the neighborhood with my dad. We'll see how much walking takes out of me.

My most recent discovery is that the "grumpy" and "anxious" feelings all seem to be basically from the same root, and they are not just a product of letting my mind wander the wrong direction, rather they seem to be very chemical in nature.

Without creating addiction (hopefully), I am learning to take the anti-anxiety medicine sooner than later. The one little green/blue pill seems to cut through the bad feelings … if only for a few hours. The naturopath affirmed that the meds were a big contributor to how I am feeling ... good to have confirmation that I am not a complete loon.

This week I will try working a bit for Intel … something I approach with very mixed feelings. Hopefully though, thinking about something other than cancer will be good, and I definitely welcome the chance to engage with my teammates again. Everyone at Intel has been so very encouraging.

So for those praying ... please pray that my emotions will even out this week, and that my family would have the endurance needed. Poor Tammy gets saddled with so much of the burden.

In all this, of course, I trust God who remains good and able. None of this catches Him by surprise. As much as I like to think it is "all about me," I know it has always been about so much more. Here's to seeing how God's plan unfolds each day ahead. May He find me faithful today and in the days ahead … however many more He chooses to give me.

Tuesday, Feb. 28, 2012, 8:06 p.m.

Sleepy, continued ...

I slept away most of today, and yet I yawn as I write this. Hopefully, all my sleep means there's good cancer fighting going on … that's what my optimist wife says ☺.

My mood remains a struggle. Part of the challenge, I believe, is that I am physically feeling better (vs. other chemo cycles), but my overall health won't allow me to do much. Compared to my pre-cancer days, I am hardly doing anything. Pre-cancer, if I were prone to feeling blue, I'd pick up a project and pour myself into it. Both the action and the accomplishment of the project would help me feel better. Unfortunately, I don't have a good distraction to help me.

I am reminded of Brother Lawrence, who wrote about "Practicing the Presence of God." He turned everything into a dialogue with God, a chance to enjoy God's company – even when he was scrubbing floors or peeling potatoes. Perhaps in the days ahead I can learn all the more to experience God in even the small things of each day.

Thanks for your continued prayers. Beyond all the normal requests, I'd appreciate specific prayer for my mood. It feels like the grumpiness/anxiety/bad mood is much more present the last few weeks than in other chemo cycles, and it seems to be more chemical than a simple act of will. Thanks!

~ *Responses from Family and Friends* ~

Thank you for your sleepy post ... I think your Brother Lawrence track could really gain some traction ... sleepy lessons in "sucky school." One thing I know... God is using all of this ... especially the sucky parts. I will pray that this discouraging mood lifts so you can feel all the love and support coming your way. In the meantime, I pray you would experience His presence IN the midst of the blues. Once again, thank you for your willingness to share your burden so we might know how to lift you and your family up in prayer. So good to hear that your physical self is feeling better. In Him,   *Tracy L., Village*

I am so blessed by your desire to TRUST even when ... I love sharing quotes from you with others who are struggling after I have digested them myself. Thank you for being so honest about how hard it is.
                    Karen R., friend of a friend

Wednesday, Feb. 29, 2012, 10:18 p.m.

An easy day

Nothing major to report for today; and that is great news. The bad mood stayed away for the most part. Tonight, while the kids and Tammy were at AWANA, a friend and I had a movie night here at the house, "Real Steel." It was a fun way to pass a few hours. ... I am so glad it wasn't more HGTV or Food Network. ☺

On the work front, I am navigating tricky waters to be able to officially work part of the week. The disability administrator wants me to commit to specific work hours each week, whereas I'd be much more comfortable committing to projects and flexible work hours. We'll see what can be worked out in the end. I'm so thankful that figuring out how to work a few hours is the sum of our issues ... Intel has been very generous.

Each day is a challenge. I am amazed at how quickly my energy reserves deplete. Even with physical improvement, I really have no guess as to how the PET scan will turn out next Wednesday morning.

I wish I knew how this all turns out, but I'm only given one day at a time in this life. Tomorrow isn't even a guarantee. So I look to tomorrow with curiosity. I wonder what God has in store. Hopefully with whatever comes, I will be found faithful.

[There were 200 responses in the guestbook
from February 1-29, 2012.]

March 2012

~ *The Sixth Month* ~

Thursday, March 1, 2012 – 6:55 p.m.

Bienvenidos ... Benvenuto ... Welcome

I'm famous now ... well, sort of. ☺ My brother, Brian, just published his "quarterly" family newsletter – "Grand Central" and invited all of his readers to join in our CaringBridge readership. If you are in the sizable group of "Grand Central" regulars, welcome. Feel free to browse our story.

There have been lots of twists and turns since Oct. 1, 2011. You'll find my story to be full of the "atypical" – almost a dozen ER trips, multiple hospital stays, anaphylactic shock, a broken tooth; Hulk-like radiation treatments taking me from wheelchair, to walker, to no-help-needed; a glorious trip to Hawaii, good and bad chemo results, difficult conversations with our kids, brain surgery, depression, anxiety, and lots more.

Some months ago, I wrote about "why I blog" – and it's not just because it is cheaper than counseling ☺.

Beyond a way to help me process, this is a great way to keep a large group of people in the loop so prayers can be focused for the needs at hand. Along the way, a number of people have mentioned that they personally have been touched by something I've written. I am glad that God chooses to use the things He is teaching me to touch others. Although, if God were to give someone else a turn for a while, I wouldn't object. We'd take healing any time ... ☺.

So, to both those who have been with us since day one, and to those who are just joining ... welcome and buckle up. Here's to taking this one day at a time, not knowing the outcome, and in all this, trusting God is good and big enough to heal should He choose.

In closing, please lift up Tammy's health. She's got a cold that we'd love to see go away quickly and not be shared with the rest of the family (especially me). Thanks!

Just checking in to say hello and to let you know that you continue to be in my thoughts and prayers. In case you haven't looked lately – your number of visitors to your guestbook is now 26,699!!! You've got a huge following across the globe, and we are all with you on your journey!! *Laura B., Intel*

Always thinking of you. I've shared some things you've written with a close friend of mine who is going through what you are. Your words are very inspirational and she is overwhelmed with your insights. She has found great comfort in what you write ... you understand where no one else really can. Stay strong and know that so many, some of whom don't even know you, are gaining strength from you. Always, praying for you and your family. *Sue B., friend*

Friday, March 2, 2012 – 5:01 p.m.

To boldly go

Hard to believe I've been sick for five months already. The good news is that my health seems to be improving. Far better than what my primary doctor thought – six months of life tops. The flip side of the good news is a challenge. How do I spend my time?

It's not like I have tons of energy and tons of brain power, but I have comparatively more than I did a few months back. Two weeks ago, I actually walked through Costco. That's impressive. Today I even walked 2.5 laps through our neighborhood. Last night I watched a "Miss Marple" murder mystery ... two hours, and I actually followed the story line. Things are improving.

In the past few weeks, I've felt as though God has been encouraging me to take things "one day at a time," for tomorrow has enough worries of its own. While that is still true, I start to wonder about "longer-term" commitments. What could I do to add more purpose/impact to the days ahead?

I'm still working with Intel to figure out how to come back to work. Last dialogue with the Intel nurse suggested that a 20-hour work week is a good minimum guide for when folks are ready to return to work. I'm good for maybe a 4-hour work week ... Hmmm.

While many are encouraging me to go back to work, a piece of me really would be okay putting off my return to work. Not sure which voices to listen to.

Beyond Intel, are there investments of my passions and talents that would be scaled right for what I can give now? Should I take up knitting, Bridge, fantasy sports? ☺ What activities could add more purpose to the days ahead and at the same time keep my wife from losing all patience with me? All day with me and the kids can be tiring to say the least.

There are lots of variables in all of this, and I know I won't ever get a crisp road map to follow. I'd love some additional clarity though. I want to know I am using the time well. Please join me in praying for God's wisdom and clear guidance in the days ahead.

Please also keep Tammy in your prayers. The cold has grabbed hold strongly. Overall she is just worn down. I'd love for her to find renewal.

As always, thanks for your support through this. The notes, meals, prayers ... all mean so much to us. We are blessed to not be going through this alone. I shudder to think what some patients must go through without strong support. Thank you!!!

~ *Responses from Family and Friends* ~

Eric, Your post actually made me laugh today! Take things day by day ... you are doing awesome! Maybe you can give Tammy "chore coupons" for things like folding the clothes? or organizing one drawer/kids play-toy bins? or a hand to be held:) it's the small things that mean so much ... esp. if she's feeling sick. Prayers continue to flow ... you will get your mojo back :)   *Laura B., Intel*

Praying for you all, and especially Tammy. Glad to hear you are feeling better. God has a purpose for each day that He keeps us here on earth. Praying for clarity on His purpose for you.   *Mythraie G., Village*

Hi, Eric, You are humbling me with your concerns about feeling grumpy! You wouldn't believe the ridiculous things I have the audacity to complain about. You are amazing no matter what mood you are in, and we are a better world every day you are in it! :) Love and hugs,
                    Carissa H., Intel

Sunday, March 4, 2012 – 8:23 p.m.

Wednesday is coming

Another day of napping nearly done. The good news is that this week I didn't nap through the sermon (apologies to Pastor John for the times I did). The anxiety/grumpiness about which I've written recently is only there off and on; I only had to take one "blue" pill today.

If it weren't for the general tiredness, I'd be even more optimistic for the PET scan results. Everyone who sees me notices distinct improvement week on week ... including some hair growth. God willing, we'll have PET scan results in hand by Friday and then back to chemo on Monday. I've got a full week ahead of not feeling horrible, and that's great news. Perhaps on Wednesday night Tammy and I can do dinner out, just the two of us, at a local favorite East Indian restaurant. We'll celebrate another chemo done and one more PET scan under our belts.

As I've considered how to better use the talents and gifts I have each day, I've had several suggest I write a book about my experience facing down Stage IV lung cancer. I could title it something like, "Cancer Sucks, God Doesn't," or, "Carpe Diem or Crappy Diem?" ☺ I'm not sure writing a book is my passion, but I am talking with God about what I should do.

I'll stay watchful for open doors. Work and play that tap into my passions/talents will be therapeutic, and I believe God has more for me to do than sit in my Lazy-Boy recliner.

NOTE: The control freak in me wants a road map and answers right now. I even worry about finding the right thing(s) to do. I admit that is totally the wrong demand, and I am actively working to just settle down in God's presence and allow Him in His timing to show me what He has for me to do. He has been more than faithful so far. How silly of me to think He'd stop leading me now.

Here's to a great week ahead. We'll keep asking for the specific miracle of full healing, and daily watch for the miracles all around us – the sun that rises, each breath we breathe, the verse we read that speaks right to our hearts, the atheist who puts their faith in God, the innocence of a child, each answered prayer, unmerited forgiveness.

Thanks and blessings!

I appreciated your encouragement a few days ago: "Don't worry too much about what to say or not say," so I'll just say the usual – we keep praying for you for full healing and for you and your family for endurance.

Annabelle and John P., Village

Amen! You already have the bare bones of a wonderful book Eric. Fill it in, add more anecdotes and there you'll have it – a fantastic testament to one man's faithfulness to the Lord during a horrible trial that would make mere mortals tremble in utmost fear. Thank you again for your honesty and openness in sharing your experience. You have truly encouraged and blessed my walk. Still a fan of Jesus through you.

Ella B., Village

[Ed. note: With Eric's permission, his writings became the basis for this book, "There was a Man."]

Monday, March 5, 2012, 9:05 p.m.

Downhill day

As I write, the pain in my leg is pretty bad, my head aches, and my overall body is just feeling "ick" … may possibly have something to do with me missing my 7 a.m. meds. Sigh.

Tammy is soldiering on through a huge headache and massive tiredness. I'm glad the "perfect storm" doesn't hit often, and I was glad to have my parents come over for a bit. That allowed Tammy to get an hour nap, and they took care of bringing dinner. Hopefully, tomorrow will be a better day. In less than an hour the kids will be down for the night and we grownups can crash.

Earlier today I slept a ton, but was able to … by myself … get Ellie from school for a doctor's appointment, then back to school. That was a pretty huge accomplishment. Ellie is just fine, and we now know how to help her intermittent stomachaches. In my more lucid moments, I am trying to think through the PET scan results due Monday worst case, or Friday best case.

Tammy has asked me, "What would the best result be? What would make you happy?" I'm not sure how to answer.

I know that all in all I am tired of this whole process and I just want to be "done" – whatever that looks like. God, however, in His wisdom and timing hasn't called me Home yet, and He hasn't cured me yet. So – we keep praying, seeking, and trusting.

Thanks for your prayers. I am often reminded that while our problems seem huge, each family has their own set of challenges – both small and large. I appreciate everyone who has taken a break from their challenges and stepped into our world to help in so many ways. May God bless each of you richly.

~ *Responses from Family and Friends* ~

Our prayers are with both of you, that you will make it through these difficult days! Hang in there – and thanks for the frequent updates to let us know best how to pray for you! As we say out here in French when someone's going through a tough time – *Du Courage!* (If my memory serves me right, Tammy took French in high school ... :O) Blessings on your family!
Bonnie and Kevin O., missionary friends in Burkina Faso

Eric and Tammy, know that Brian and I are praying for you as God brings you to our minds many times throughout the day. Thank you for keeping us updated so regularly. Praying that today is a better day and that you both are feeling well for your Wednesday night outing. We look forward to getting to see you guys soon! *Melissa L., close friend*

Wednesday, March 7, 2012 – 1:23 p.m.

Keep your distance ... radioactive for the day

PET scan is done. Now we wait – something I don't do the best. I honestly have no clue as to what the scan results will be. Based on how I feel, a NED (no evidence of disease) finding is unlikely, but not impossible with God. I think we're hoping for continued progress and a green light for chemo on Monday.

Regarding my health, the last two evenings around 4 p.m., everything seemed to go bad. Two days ago I attributed it to missing meds in the morning, but yesterday, I had nothing to blame. I'm asking God to give me better health tonight so I can go out on a date with Tammy. We're planning to go to a local East Indian restaurant. I can almost taste the chicken tikka masala already.

166

On the work front – at this time it feels as though doors have been closed for returning to work, even for only a few hours each week. Assuming my health improves, I can head back to work as early as I'm able to work half time. Having that decision made relieves me. Now, if I do have a few spare moments of lucid thought and physical energy, I'll find other areas in which to invest. As I've said in other posts, I'm trusting God to show me other open doors.

As I write, lunchtime is upon me and the sun is shining. So ... it's time to eat, enjoy the sun, and then catch a nap. And as always, thanks for loving on us!

Thursday, March 8, 2012 – 9:55 a.m.

Date night

Thanks for praying for us to be able to get out and enjoy a date night last night. We had a great time and thoroughly enjoyed our East Indian meal. For the third week after chemo, the outing took more out of me than I would have expected, but thankfully it all worked out well.

I'm still waiting for the PET scan results. What will the results be? I wonder, and at times worry ... though I know the worry does me no good. There's an outside chance we'll hear results before the weekend. Monday is chemo and we'd for sure get results in our pre-chemo consult with Dr. Andersen.

"Wait, wait, wait." Or maybe I should say ... "Wait, wait, weight," ... nervous dessert consumption has definitely increased. ☺

~ *Responses from Family and Friends* ~

Hey, don't worry about the desserts!! Sweeter the better is my motto! Prayers for a great day and a great PET scan result!   *Laura B., Intel*

Thank you Lord for Eric being able to again enjoy a variety of foods, and for special time with Tammy!   *Chip M., Tammy's dad*

Let him eat dessert! So glad you had a great date night. Prayers, love and big hugs coming your way.   *Chick L., Village Life Group*

Saturday, March 10, 2012 – 2:45pm

Feeling better than expected

I did more yesterday than I've done in quite some time. In the morning my brother and I worked on a project that has been waiting to be done since before the cancer diagnosis. I had all the supplies, but was missing the gumption and a few tools to build a spice cabinet for Tammy.

As of lunchtime yesterday, all the cuts were done and the cabinet was assembled. When I have "spare" energy, I'll work next on the sanding and painting so, when my brother comes next time, we can pop the unit into the wall. Very fun.

In addition to the spice cabinet project, Tammy and I spent some really fun time with a couple from church talking and playing "Phase 10," well past 10 p.m. It felt like old times before we had kids and would play games with friends until late on Friday nights. It is pretty amazing that Friday went as well as it did, since Thursday afternoon I was fully prepared to head to the ER for shortness of breath and some other neurological symptoms – frequent twitches randomly happening all over my body.

Thanks to those who saw my Thursday Facebook post and joined with us in prayer. I truly believe God answered with taking away the shortness of breath by Thursday bedtime.

As of today, no PET scan results. Monday morning will be when we get them (what we expected, though we had hoped for earlier news), and likely we'll have another round of chemo starting.

SIDE NOTE: I am still thinking about how to use the limited "up time" I have. Mostly though, I am just going one day at a time and trying not to worry about planning too much. Opportunities will come.

Thanks as always. Just yesterday alone we had one family come and mow our lawn, and another came with a yummy soup for dinner. It is still humbling to receive so much love and help.

It's as though there is a "genie" – someone who comes to the family whose life is on autopilot – where everything is going "okay," (except for the daily challenges of just living).

168

♦ THIS "GENIE" OFFERS GREAT THINGS:

Paid time off from work for at least six months, so finances will not be a worry for you at all. In fact, you'll even get awards while you are away [See Responses Feb . 7, 2012].

All your chores will be done by others ... trash, mowing, cleaning ... people will bring you delicious meals for months on end.

Time with the ones you love will be abundant.

You'll have a dream vacation to Hawaii for nearly a week.

Your relationships with extended family and friends will deepen ... as a result of the time spent together, you'll know people in ways you never knew before.

You'll have people from all around the world listening to what you have to say; they will pray frequently for you, send you encouraging notes and tell their friends about you.

You'll gain new insights into the Scriptures and the person of God – concepts that once were abstract will be understood firsthand.

That new understanding will in turn help you minister to those around you. You'll have many chances to share the good news of Jesus with hundreds – even those at your workplace.

Beyond the earthly riches, you'll have treasures storing up for you in eternity.

Of course the only catch with all these blessings is ... they come through suffering – Stage IV lung cancer.

I don't fully understand how God is working in all of this, but I do see His blessings. My wish is that I wouldn't have to suffer to get the blessings ... but, I know that many of the blessings above would never come without the suffering. (That said, I'm ready for someone else to take a turn "being blessed" so much. ☺)

[Ed. note: In the midst of pain, heavy medication, the unknown, and weariness, Eric's frequent entries on CaringBridge continue to be extremely well written, theologically sound, humorous at times, amazingly to the point, and used to bless and build up others along the way – genuinely a gift from God.]

Monday, March 12, 2012 – 11:27 a.m.

"I am thrilled!"

"The PET scan results are very good – I am thrilled," Dr. Andersen said.

While the report doesn't show NED or a full-on cure, it does show the cancer dropping down in size and activity levels such that we have the option to enter a maintenance phase.

If you can imagine a bathtub-shaped curve, we started with tons of very active cancer … left side of the curve, high. With this recipe of chemo, we've driven the cancer down substantially. At some point, we enter maintenance – bottom of the tub. I'll still have meds and scans, but no chemo hits. Then, from a purely medical perspective, the maintenance will stop working at some point and the cancer will ramp up again – right side of the tub.

Tammy and I opted for another chemo round today. The idea being to push the cancer size and activity even lower than it is now. Hopefully, with a "bathtub bottom" closer to 0, we will see maintenance work better and longer. No guarantees, but we felt like we needed to go hard after the cancer, even if it means another few weeks (or cycles) of hideous chemo.

Regarding the fatigue and mental state I'm in, Dr. Andersen said it is likely the cumulative result of all the chemo/etc., and less about my cancer. I can push for more activity "to tolerance."

Thank God for continued healing and the hope of more days ahead, especially healthier days. It looks like we have a longer road ahead as full healing hasn't occurred as yet. That said, God is faithful and good – regardless how this cancer battle turns out. Thanks for praying and caring. Now for a nap. ☺

~ Responses from Family and Friends ~

That is awesome news! Now, of course, you will have to figure out what normal looks like while at the bottom of the bathtub. Praying that is an extra-long bathtub. All the best.   *Kris K., friend*

Praising God with you for this amazing news! Praying for another round of chemo that is smooth for you and hideous on any remaining cancer! Keep fighting Bro!   *Fred J., Intel*

Wednesday, March 14, 2012 – 12:21 p.m.

Paradigm shifting

It is Wednesday morning after Monday chemo. Given past cycles, I'd fully expect to be feeling physically worse than I am. Thanks be to God, though, that "the chemo bus" hasn't found me yet. I'm tired and not the sharpest knife in the drawer, but I am so much better than in other times.

Between the better-than-expected chemo and the PET scan results, we have lots for which to be thankful. You'd expect me to be over-the-moon joyful. Oddly enough though, I am feeling more pensive than joyful.

It is strange, but I believe much of my mental energy from October on has been slanted toward preparing for death and looking forward to eternity.

Now, I've known God can heal here and now; and, along with so many others – easily over 350 readers [who check in to read over and over] on CaringBridge, alone – we've been asking God for complete healing. Everything seems to be heading in that direction. So, why the thoughtfulness now that I am so close to maintenance mode?

Here's the thing … maintenance mode is just that … the cancer is less active and the tumors are much smaller, but the cancer is still there.

Hopefully with this chemo cycle and the 6th and last chemo cycle on this recipe (*Cisplantin Alimta*) coming up after Easter, we can drive the cancer down as close as possible to "no evidence of disease" (NED). Even with all that – apart from complete healing from God – the maintenance mode will come to an end. Dormant cells will exert themselves at some point … and we will be back to actively fighting lung cancer. Unless there are more medical breakthroughs, there will remain a finite number of chemo recipes that will combat the cancer.

Put another way, I'm still not in the space of buffing up retirement plans. It's likely not the same very short prognosis as back in October – Yay! But … it is still relatively short.

That leads me to the crux of it – I'm a control freak, and God has thrust me back into a great big space of unknown, uncontrollable variables. My God cannot be put in a box, easily defined, understood, and predicted. "For My thoughts are not your thoughts, neither are your ways My ways," declares the Lord. "As the heavens are higher than the earth, so are My ways higher than your ways and My thoughts than your thoughts" (Isaiah 55: 8-9).

The Enemy of my soul would much prefer that I worry and try to control everything rather than rest in God's daily guidance and provision. As I think of the themes in what I've previously written, here's what springs to mind.

♦ TRUTHS TO COMBAT THE LIES:

God is so loving, He won't waste one minute of my suffering.

God is good and big; His character will never change.

God is with me, "the Lord is near" and brings peace beyond understanding (Philippians 4:5-7), I need only fear Him.

Each day here on this side of eternity is an opportunity to be an ambassador for Jesus – sharing the good news of salvation through belief in Christ alone.

Each day is a chance to store up more treasure in heaven, and, I'm especially mindful of the investments I can make in my family.

I am called to take things "one day at a time." Tomorrow has enough worries of its own.

I need to listen daily … to see what God would have me do to participate in His work. I want to be open to whatever ways God would use my skills, talents and passions for His glory.

He will provide guidance in His time and way.

> *"God, forgive me for being a control freak and not placing my whole trust in You. I put my hope in You and trust You to bring to completion the work I know You have started in my life. I don't have to understand everything, as much as I would love to. I leave my life in Your hands."*
> *Eric*

172

Like everyone's, my days are numbered. None of us knows when our time will draw to a close. I may have a slightly better indication of when, but even that is subject to change at any moment. So I embrace today, rejoice in the progress made so far, and watch for what God has in store. Here's to the ride ahead.

~ *Responses from Family and Friends* ~

I've never met you personally, Eric, but I was one of Tammy's roommates, back in college. I read your posts every day, and I (and folks in my church) have been praying for you all regularly. What you wrote today really touched me. You are walking one tough road, and it makes perfect sense that you would want a few road signs along the way! I will keep praying, as I know many others are. Give Tammy a huge hug for me!

Jenn B., Tammy's college friend

I continue to be amazed at your ability to put into words what you are thinking and feeling. This is a gift the Lord has given to you. Because of your willingness to be transparent, the Lord is being glorified and you are making a difference in the lives of others. I'm being reminded to live my life differently because of the path that you are walking. Thank you my brother. Praise God for all He is doing! Keep talking with Him, reading His Word and know that He holds you in the palm of His hand, and under His wings. I'm praying for your rest, your peace and the grace to give all your thoughts, worries, control to Him. I pray these things for myself as well. Hugs!

JerriLyn K., friend

While I don't write very often, I have read every one of your posts, and have continued to pray for you and your family. I wish I had your attitude, depth of faith, and perspective in this entire matter! Blessings to you and your family!!!

Bonnie H., Village

Thank you once again for sharing from your heart and the lessons God is teaching you (and us thru you). We will continue to pray for your complete healing. We rejoice with you on the good days and prayerful uphold you on the not so good days. Thank you for the reminders, lessons and stretching of your faith. It is a great reminder for all of us (especially those who like to have their world in order). May you have a great week and thanks again for sharing from your heart. as always,

Wanda K., former co-worker of Eric's brother

Thursday, March 15, 2012 – 6:43 p.m.

"Word Cloud" … looking back

Having written 125 journal entries as of yesterday, I thought I'd be a bit retrospective. So, I ran a Word Cloud on all the previous journal entries. Interesting to see what I've been talking about the last nearly six months. I'll let you come to your own conclusions.

(For those who don't know about word clouds … you put in all the words used and the chart makes the most commonly used words biggest and the least used words smallest. Interesting way to see themes emerge.)

Regarding my health, just a few hours ago I took my last dose of steroids this chemo round. Whoo hoo! So very glad to done with those for a few weeks. I won't go back to chemo now until April 9. Then, God willing, we'll have a respite in "maintenance land." The chemo bus has gone easy on me so far. Historically this night is the night things go sideways. So far, so good, though.

Please keep praying. Healing is happening, but total healing hasn't come yet. I am fatigued physically, mentally, emotionally, and spiritually. Tammy is worn out, too. Please join us in asking for renewal. And as always … thanks for your ongoing love and support. We could never do this alone.

~ *Responses from Family and Friends* ~

I know you've been told this before, but you really are a gifted writer! Being transparent is the key to being an effective communicator as well as a testimony to God's ever-present help in your daily life. We continue to read your journal regularly which allows us to pray for you, Tammy, and the kids in specific ways. God loves you, Eric and Tammy. Never forget that. Praying,   *Karen and Lamont R., parents of Eric's best man*

Eric, you write so well. Thanks for sharing your feelings as you are on this journey, always bringing the focus back to our good God – I really appreciate your humility and faith which is evident on each post.
Charlotte H., formerly at Village

Believe ... Believe ... Believe   *Laura B., Intel*

Word cloud: I saw "good God" come before "chemo cancer." You have kept your sights where you want them! I hope this night, and the many others hereafter, are peaceful and ever better for you and yours! xoxo,
Carissa H., Intel

Eric (and Tammy!) I love your word cloud. I want to figure out how to do that!!!! As a calligrapher ... it is very inspiring. I've followed your posts daily and have your photo on my bulletin board with a prayer for you ... and I do pray for you and your family. I'm elated to hear the news of your last tests ... praying for full healing and restored health. Blessings,   *Nancy P., mom of Tammy's friend*

Dear Heerwagens, We are so pleased to be able to continue to pray for all of you! God has certainly gotten our attention to PRAY! We hope you two can get some rest now and prepare for the path to follow. Love to all,   *Chuck and Doris H., Village*

You don't know me, but my husband and I know your dad. We went to high school with him. I have read your story and have been deeply touched, especially by your Christian witness. I want you to know that my 7 a.m. Tuesday early morning ladies' Bible study will be praying for you and your family. It must be comforting to know that the Lord is in charge, but at the same time must be hard to remember that at times. I am sure you have touched so many lives already, and God isn't finished using you yet! Sending prayers your way,
Janet S., Eric's dad's high school friend in Colorado

Sunday, March 18, 2012 – 6:31 p.m.

Delinquent

So, I avoided journaling for a few days. My emotions/thoughts are still off balance. I was hopeful the chemo fog would pass sooner than later. As of this afternoon, it still hasn't passed. Physically I am doing "okay" – better than most chemo weeks – but I am not feeling great. The nausea and fatigue are still faithful companions, and my emotions are just plain "off."

All that said, here's the truth I am forcing myself to remember ... I say forcing, because my emotions are often lousy validators of truth. And if I only look at the cancer mess right in front of me, the bigger truth gets obscured.

The truth comes from Psalm 117, where I just "happened" to be reading last night. Amazing how God's Word speaks right where and when it is needed – with God there are no "chance" encounters.

"God is worthy to be praised
because He is faithful and loving.
Praise God."
(*My paraphrase of Psalm 117.*)

So there it is. May the whole world praise God for He is faithful and loving. Even though I don't feel it today, I bring the sacrifice of praise to my God.

May you be blessed as you head into the work week. Thanks for continued prayer and love. Special thanks to the Korean Fellowship at our church ... an elderly Korean lady came up to me today and let me know in her broken English that she was praying for me.

There are so many I don't even know, and yet they faithfully pray for me. Humbling.

Monday, March 19, 2012 – 6:58 p.m.

My journal gets a helper

"Dear Journal,

"I have oft said that you are cheaper than a counselor. I hope I have not hurt your feelings by implying you are cheap. In fact, you have been an invaluable help to me, and all I've invested is time. As I process through all the issues surrounding my cancer, you have been there, listening ... for free. Thank you so much. I am in your debt.

"That said, a time comes in every relationship where change must happen, and our relationship, has come to just such a place. You see, I need more help than just you alone can give ... Tomorrow I am meeting with a Christian counselor. Thanks to insurance, he should be free to use, just like you.

"Don't worry ... I'll still talk with you regularly. In fact, I expect our time together to be even more helpful in the days to come. "There's a lot of learning ahead of me. Most important is the question of how to truly live in the shadow of cancer.   Yours truly, Eric."

~ Responses from Family and Friends ~

I am a big believer in people seeking help during dark times in their lives. I continue to pray for you, knowing that all that's going on in your life right now has to have some kind of purpose. That purpose we may not know for a very long time, but your posts over the last few months have touched so many people, believers and not-yet-believers. For that I am so grateful and blessed to call you a friend. Praying, praying, praying.
Terri B., Village

Good to hear that you're seeking input from a counselor. We weren't meant to walk this road alone and goodness knows your journey has been a rough one. I will be praying for godly counsel. Continue to seek His face and allow His grace and His mercy to transform you and heal you, physically, spiritually and emotionally. As you have testified so many times, God is with you and will not abandon you.
Becky J., formerly at Village

Tuesday, March 20, 2012 – 11:26pm

Good counsel

Today things are looking up. The chemo effects are lessening. I had a normal dinner – first time on this chemo cycle and, after dinner, I was able to have my first counseling session. All in all, a pretty good day. The counseling will be a long road ahead, but I'm ready. The counselor was encouraging and consoling. With all that I and my family have been through the past five plus months, I'm sure there is plenty for me to unpack with professional help.

♦ A FEW INSIGHTS FROM THE SESSION:

God is still with me and for me – each day that I have breath is another day God has given me to make a difference in this world.

It is not all about me – God is using this to impact lives all around me.

To help me focus beyond myself, I need to sign up for something as simple as owning an ongoing household chore. It will not only help me, but help Tammy, too.

My wife needs time off and help as we go through all this together. (Can you say "spa day?")

Here's to the road ahead. It seems that God is granting me days of better health. I don't know for how long, but I am determined to make the best of them.

As always, thanks to everyone for all the love and support.

~ *Responses from Family and Friends* ~

As so many have said before, Eric, thank you for how your postings touch all of us who read them. In particular: Tammy has made the comment "living in the fishbowl." I thank you for how often you mention Tammy's needs – so those of us around her can be reminded to reach out to her. Thank you Eric, for helping us see your family needs in the "fishbowl." Glad to hear you are finding another avenue of support through counseling.   *Debra F., Tammy's co-worker*

I keep waiting to write on here [on CaringBridge], waiting for big eloquent words, worthwhile thoughts, but I have none. I just know I pray for your family constantly, randomly, and sporadically – as life with three "littles" can only be, but you're never far from my mind. Tammy has to be the most inspirational woman I've encountered; her faith, love, and beauty are astounding. I am truly touched by your faithfulness, openness, and willingness to be so transparent. I am left in awe by your entire family. Constant prayers, love, hugs, and any meager encouragement I can offer are ALL YOURS! You're amazing as is our God!!   *Holly B., Village*

Eric, this is wonderful and there is no shame in allowing a professional who is has training to help lead you through your processing. Allow God to move you through those rough spots through that counselor. We are praying for peace for you and rest for you and your family.   *Kristina W., Eric's college friend*

Eric, I am so glad to hear that you have decided to speak with a counselor. The opportunity to express yourself freely and privately will give you the opportunity to be open and forthright in describing your innermost thoughts and emotions ... without worrying that you will hurt someone. Doing this is so very healing. You are brave, and faithful, and deserve to be YOU. I am proud of you!

Pamela Z., grandma of Ellie's friend

Well, God bless you Eric, I think expressing your thoughts to a flesh and blood human being is a very good move on your part. I just hope that you still feel that need to use your old buddy that journal so that we can continue to share your journey with you. I think seeing a counselor will not only do you some good but it will be helpful to your whole family – and that includes your "family" here too. Thanks for sharing.

Candace L., Village

Thursday, March 22, 2012 – 3:34 p.m.

Disciplined or driven

I am amazed at how much my health has improved over just a month ago. This week, I'm working on the spice cabinet for Tammy. After a short stint in the garage, I came in to hear Tammy say, "It's almost like the old Eric is back."

Also on my to-do list within the next week or two is to review the videos I've made for my family. [See entry for Jan. 15, 2012.] I think I finally have enough reserve to watch the videos. It will feel good to get a few projects completed.

As I am able to "do" more each day, I am reminded of something my brother asked me several months ago – "Are you driven or disciplined?" The answer comes all too easy … I am driven. I am so driven. I think the tombstone for me could easily read, "He even died efficiently." ☺

The problem with "driven" is, I miss the relationships and overindulge in tasks. And … as my counselor pointed out, "drivers" are often narcissistic. At first, I took exception to his suggesting I am too focused on me, but the more I ponder it, the more I realize the need to focus beyond me and my problems.

♦ SO, HERE'S TO ADDING DISCIPLINE TO MY LIFE:

Discipline to grow my prayers beyond just my needs and asking God to heal me.

Discipline to help more around the house … Tammy officially gave me the chore of emptying the dishwasher.

Discipline to use my time well in the days ahead.

Discipline to be thankful each day … recognizing God at work in more than just my life.

Enough for today, though … a nap is calling and then maybe a bit more work on the spice cabinet. Oh … and … being relational with my family too.

Friday, March 23, 2012 – 8:50 p.m.

Day by day

Despite snow being on the ground just yesterday, today's weather here in Oregon is spectacular. The sun is still shining as I type. The weather matches my health … sunny with a few clouds.

It seems that with this chemo round my health is getting better day by day. I almost feel like the old me. Hopefully, with time, my stamina will only get better.

Today was fun as we installed the main part of Tammy's new spice cabinet. It feels great to have a project and to see progress. My brother has been a huge help – doing big parts of the project for and with me. This next week I get to work on paint and doors. Fun to have a few things still to do.

I suppose I could try and write something deep today, but I'm not in a deep mood. Today is a play day. At another time I can focus on BHAGs (big, hairy, audacious goals) and profound questions of purpose. While I know I'll need to wrestle with … how to go back to work, eating better (apologies to Dairy Queen and Long John Silver's), getting regular exercise (beyond frequent trips to the refrigerator, etc.) … today I am enjoying the sun and shallow thoughts. ☺

Keep the notes coming. We love to hear from you. Thanks and blessings!

p.s. If you think you see hair on my head, you are right. It is still thin and feels like duck fuzz, but it is growing back. The hair is a few shades darker than pre-cancer color. I'm curious to see what color it will end up being.

~ *Responses from Family and Friends* ~

Nice job on the spice rack. It looks great. At least the hair isn't coming back in GRAY! Hope you have a great weekend just enjoying your blessings and opportunities. All the best.   *Kris K., friend*

I agree with several others: you sound like your old self. Tammy is going to love that spice rack! (I sure would!!!) So glad that you are able to work on it and that you are feeling better. We need to see you soon. Small interactions via the web just aren't enough! Love,
Dawn R., Tammy's sister

So glad to see the spice cupboard. WOW that is huge. So glad you and Brian got to work on it together. So thankful you are feeling some better and pray that you only continue to get stronger and stronger. Relax and enjoy your day(s). God please continue to bless this family and the lessons and challenges they are experiencing. You are an AWESOME God and we rest totally in your hands.
Wanda K., former co-worker of Eric's brother

I love the spice storage. I guess I'll be needing to bring a dinner over so I can see it in person. Tammy, your spice area and I will want to be friends. I like how she looks! Great post, Eric. Glad to see prayers are being answered.   *Dawn Denice R., friend*

My mind was picturing a spice cabinet about 1/8 that size! That is going to be really nice and very useful! Glad your mind is taking on "project-mode thinking" and your body is supporting it!
Chip M., Tammy's dad

The spice cabinet looks wonderful. As my friends know, I only use about six spices ... so I wouldn't know what to do with something so big!! Absolutely enjoy the sunshine and days where you don't have to think of "big" things. Enjoy the day! I know my spirits have been uplifted with the sunshine!   *Jessie N., Village*

Wow ... now THAT is a spice rack! Looks great. Thankful for shallow thoughts, thankful for feeling better, thankful for sunny skies, thankful for the new growth of Spring (including hair!), thankful for YOU! See you tonight! Praying as always,   *Chick L., Village Life Group*

The spice rack is impressive – it inspires me to search the spice aisle beyond parsley, basil and oregano. :) Thanks for sharing your journey with so many; such a blessing.   *Tara F., Village*

Tuesday, March 27, 2012 – 10:08 p.m.

In search of the right attitude

Spring break ... oddly enough, I am seeing less of the kids than normal. It's been a nice break so far ☺. Thanks to feeling better, I am doing more. Over the last few days, I've attended a family party [Tammy's extended family] in Canby, worked a bit more on the spice cabinet, reviewed my video messages to my family, and I even went with the family to Chuck E Cheese's. All in all, I've been doing way more than in the past months. That said, I'm still needing naps. Monday afternoon's was an especially long and deep nap.

In some ways, I'm back to the old me. In other ways, there is still a lot more healing to be done.

◆ LOTS OF QUESTIONS SWIRL:

When to head back to work?

What happens after the next chemo and maintenance starts?

How long do I have in maintenance?

Will the fatigue lessen?

Will my leg stop hurting?

Can I plan much beyond today?

Do I need to care about retirement planning ...?

The further into this I get, the more I realize I am not alone in having tough circumstances. The world in which we live is fundamentally broken, but I remain convinced that our God is big and good. He will use even the horrible things of this world for good.

I am also growing in my conviction that I need to focus beyond myself. It is altogether too easy to be ungrateful and wallow in self-pity. Lots of people have bad situations; I am not alone in my suffering. It is my choice how I respond – with selfishness or generosity. A coworker of mine sent me a link to a video of an inspirational speaker; the man was born without limbs. His giving spirit is amazing. Instead of bitterness, he shows a great love and joy in life. Humbling.

Here's to a great rest of the week. May you find God's blessings throughout each day.

p.s. Please keep dropping notes on email, Facebook, or the guestbook. I love hearing from everyone. It really does help me in the fight to hear friends and family. Even the simple notes of "Hi" are encouraging.

~ *Responses from Family and Friends* ~

You are a tremendous inspiration to each and every one of us who have the privilege to follow you on this journey. And with over 30,000 visits [on CaringBridge] you have a lot of company. Thank you for your posts. They are both thoughtful and thought provoking. Keep up the good fight. All my best to you and your family. *Greg B., Intel*

Great to hear of days of better health and a lift in your spirits! And the spice rack looks great! I can just imagine Tammy using it. Continuing to PRAY for all of you and I rejoice with you in the positive things you're seeing these days. Have fun emptying the dishwasher.
Bonnie and Kevin O., missionary friends in Burkina Faso

The spice cabinet looks great! Glad to hear (read) you're doing better, but don't worry, it won't stop us praying for complete healing.
Annabelle and John P., Village

Hey Buddy! I appreciate your sharing through this journey ... helpful on this end of the line too. Glad you are feeling better! This year ISMC theme was Carpe Diem ... I think you are certainly displaying that! Here's to more good days!! *Mike L., Intel*

[There were 157 responses in the guestbook
from March 1-31, 2012.]

184

April 2012

~ *The Seventh Month* ~

Sunday, April 1, 2012 – 7:38 p.m.

Smorgasbord

The last few days have been mixed. Highlights include going out with "the guys" on Saturday night. It was fun to have a few hours to reconnect and a blessing to have enough energy to actually be out. Lowlights include bad emotions off and on … more on than off. Today in general has been an "off" day. This morning I was grumpy. After my afternoon nap, I am feeling grumpy and nauseous. Needless to say, I am looking forward to meeting with my counselor tomorrow. I'm hoping with help I can get past the emotions I really don't understand.

Someone close to me recently pointed out that I am getting quite adept at identifying the problems, but the problem solving action is lacking. While I am doing some good things (counseling, praying, journaling, etc.) to help, I really am struggling.

I don't know what of the emotions are "normal" and what emotions are things I should "get over." Either way, I'd love to have a less grumpy, less sad, less confused outlook on life. Living life seems to be the real challenge.

This morning (yes during church) I found my mind wandering to 13 years ago when my roommate, Jared, passed away unexpectedly. We were out for a bike ride and just before we reached the church [Village], Jared suffered a fatal arrhythmia of the heart. A few days later he actually passed away. That was the closest I've been to someone's death. It rocked my world … and a lot of others around us, especially the other person on the bike ride with us.

In thinking of Jared's death, my mind jumped to my own brush with death [experiencing anaphylactic shock during chemo and the immediate ambulance trip to the ER], and to the last five-plus months. It has really taken a toll.

Interestingly enough, dying is hard, but living is proving harder. I am faced with living in the shadow of my own very real mortality. I am no longer invincible. Worse than that, I am aware of how close

I am to death. How now do I live?

Making the choice to live well in some ways is far more valiant than dying well. Living well in a broken world is hard. Lots to ponder and lots of time to ponder. Here's to "sunnier" days ahead.

~ *Responses from Family and Friends* ~

Eric, as a note of encouragement YOU are doing this well. Heard a great quote in a movie tonight. You don't choose a life, you "Live a life" ... Keep on keeping on in the living-life part you are playing. It is a one step at a time kind of life you are living. One day one hour one minute. Think baby steps not huge steps ...   *Becki C., Village*

I am blessed to tears and challenged to live DAILY as I read your "journal honesty" and notes others leave. Thank you for letting God use your life experiences again and again. Feelings are fickle but definitely to be reckoned with. Praying for you and your family.
Karen R., friend of a friend

Monday, April 2, 2012 – 2:49 p.m.

Thanks for good counsel

Thanks to everyone for the notes of encouragement. I just got back from a solid hour of good counseling.

♦ HERE ARE A FEW OF THE THINGS I HEARD:

When I complain about not hearing God, I am forgetting that I have the whole Bible to give me direction already.

I get frustrated and angry when I don't have a big-picture road map of where things are going. The need to know all the steps is flawed, though. God promises to meet our daily needs (Matthew 6:11). He says that as we trust Him, He will give us light for the path ahead – not a search light showing the whole path; just enough for the next step ahead (Psalm 119:105).

I need to focus on baby steps each day. Make one good choice each day to live life abundantly (John 10:10). It is a lot easier to give up and not live than it is to fight and live. I have to keep up the fight and choose to live. (I don't have to figure it all out in one day, but I do have to make progress.)

We are made for fellowship (Hebrews 10:24-25). The more I can make time to get out of the house and engage with friends, the better things will go for me.

(NOTE: I don't pretend to fully understand, but I hope to gain a better real-life understanding of these in the days ahead. Understanding in my brain is one thing; applying all this to action is a totally different and more difficult thing.)

Next week, I skip counseling because I have chemo again. I am not looking forward to Monday, but it is a necessary evil. The good news is this should be my last chemo for some time. After this, we start maintenance. I'll know more of what to expect after our meeting with Dr. Andersen next week.

As a parting thought, I wanted to share a passage from Philippians 4. When I talked about some of these verses for Christmas, I focused on verses 5b-7. Today I was reminded of verses 8-10 as well.

What I find especially informative is the bookend remarks about God being near/with us. As I practice baby steps of abundant life, I hope to experience more of God's presence in my life. Mentally, I know He is good, loving, and powerful, but in the thick of suffering it is easy to doubt His goodness. He can seem almost capricious. So here it is:

"The Lord is near. Do not be anxious about anything, but in every situation, by prayer and petition, with thanksgiving, present your requests to God. And the peace of God, which transcends all understanding, will guard your hearts and your minds in Christ Jesus. Finally, brothers and sisters, whatever is true, whatever is noble, whatever is right, whatever is pure, whatever is lovely, whatever is admirable — if anything is excellent or praiseworthy – think about such things. Whatever you have learned or received or heard from me, or seen in me – put into practice. And the God of peace will **be with you**." *(Philippians 4:5b-10 NIV).*

Here's to living each day given us to the full. May we all feel something of God's presence in our lives.

p.s. If you haven't considered the claims of Jesus, I encourage you to seriously look into it – especially this week as the Church around the world gets ready to celebrate Easter.

He is risen! He is risen indeed!

Wednesday, April 4, 2012 – 4:26 p.m.

"Socks" and averages

Today I actually made it out by myself for a few errands ... pharmacy, grocery, and Long John Silver's. (Don't tell Tammy about my lunch trip ☺.) Yesterday, Tammy and I assembled a dining table and chairs set for our breakfast area. Phew! That was a lot of work, but rewarding.

On another note, thanks to all of you who sent Tammy fun socks. Her drawer truly overflows. For those of you not in the know ... Tammy's sister, Dawn, started a campaign to encourage Tammy. Friends and family were asked to send Tammy pairs of fun socks along with notes to let her know that she, too – like me – is being covered in prayer. Thanks! (And special thanks to Dawn.)

A closing thought for today ... God doesn't Google.

This afternoon, I thought I would research what "maintenance" phase would entail. So I Googled "chemo maintenance lung cancer" – non-small-cell lung cancer to be specific. It was informative but not altogether encouraging. The drug Alimta, which will likely be my maintenance drug of choice, added roughly three months average to the patient survival rate. Hmmmm. Other sites did have stories of patients who far exceed the average and have survived on a much less toxic maintenance-only plan. These people have gone years with their cancer suppressed.

So, what does it mean for me? I don't know. What I do know is that God has His plan for me. I don't believe God is inhibited by averages or Google search results.

188

Next week when I see Dr. Andersen, I will start asking the "what if" questions to better understand maintenance. I don't know about returning to work, starting a real exercise routine with my [continuing] left leg pain, or responsibly dialing back from the 230-plus pounds I weigh now. (We've had great meals delivered.)

My guess is that Dr. Andersen won't have specific answers. He'll probably use vague phrases like "to tolerance" ... sigh. I do have a lead on another resource that might have more of a dialogue with me, but the RN (registered nurse) connection is on vacation this week, so I'll have to wait until she returns next week. Perhaps if I triangulate answers, I can get closer to knowing at least what is in the realm of possible.

Please keep praying for a miracle. Complete healing would be awesome and God for sure can do it. In the meantime, please keep praying that Tammy and I both would have the strength to persevere through all this. Thanks!

p.s. Thanks to my friends who have been pulling me out of my hermitage. It is hard for me to want to be social, but once I am out, I really enjoy the interaction.

~ Responses from Family and Friends ~

I haven't commented in a while. Just want to let you know I'm still tracking and I'm heartened by how "up" the last few posts have been, despite grappling with some difficult questions. It seems that having the counselor to talk to, and a spice rack to work on, does you good. Busy hands and a mental pressure valve ... good things. Hang in there, my friend!
Mike F., Intel

Hey Eric, Just wanted to let you know we continue to pray for you, Tammy and the kids daily. We so appreciate all your updates so we can know specifically how to pray - in addition to the prayers for a miracle!
Tana K., friend

You know, when we got some crazy health news, I would run to the computer to research. I always wanted to know what to expect. I realized that God is not a God of statistics, but a loving and healing Father. ANYTHING is possible through him. Fight on my friend. God is listening and wants you to trust him every step of the way. Lifting you and your beautiful family up in prayer,
Dorothy G., formerly at Village

Friday, April 6, 2012 – 10:51 a.m.

Good Friday

I love it when I read the Bible and new insights pop off the page. The Word of God is like that – it speaks to me right where I am … some days more than others.

Last night as I was thinking about Easter weekend, I turned to Mark 15. Two things popped off the page for me – encouragement to be a great father, and perspective on my suffering.

First, I smiled as I read, "There was a man walking by, coming from work, Simon of Cyrene, the father of Alexander and Rufus …" Granted, smiling while reading the crucifixion account is not the norm, but here is what made me smile … Wouldn't it be so cool if some day in the distant future someone wrote about me and they said, "A certain man from Beaverton, Eric, the father of Ellie and Timmy …"

I want to be known as a good father with great kids. Alexander and Rufus were likely known to the early church. I imagine them as being integral parts of the fledgling church. How cool would it be for my kids to be known as outstanding followers of Jesus. How neat to know, even decades later, that how Tammy and I parented our children helped form them into the man and woman of God that they became.

The other thing – I couldn't help but draw parallels between Jesus Christ's suffering and my own. I know that the betrayal, beatings, whippings, mocking, rejection, crucifixion, and worst of all taking the weight of the world's sin upon Himself is more suffering than I will ever know. But, I let my mind wander a bit last night.

♦ HERE ARE THE COMPARISONS I DREW
(AND THE CONTRASTS):

Jesus knew his days were numbered, and yet He willed Himself to press onward toward the cross. Jesus didn't wallow in pity, but loved His disciples deeply in the last days. He knew with much more certainty than I do when His time was to end. The cancer for me has given me a higher probability of passing sooner than later, and even with that … I have to choose to follow Jesus' leading each day and live an abundant life.

Jesus prayed in the Garden of Gethsemane and asked God to "take this cup" from Him. He knew the suffering ahead and asked for a reprieve. I, too, ask God to spare me the suffering.

This suffering is to be expected. The world in which I live is broken because of sin and, in a broken world, bad things like cancer happen. Jesus, on the other hand, didn't deserve the suffering of the cross, but He willingly entered into it so all who believe in Him could be saved.

Suffering is useful and will be used by God to shape and mold me more to His image (James 1). On a much, much larger scale, Jesus' suffering was meant for ultimate evil, but God used it for ultimate good. Through Jesus' suffering on the cross, we have received the way to be forgiven our sin and the promise of eternity with God.

At times, God feels distant from me. I cry out and I don't hear an answer. While on the cross, Jesus cried out, "My God, My God. Why have you forsaken me?" While Jesus, blameless, bore upon Himself the weight of our sin, He was separated from Father God. Here there is no comparison to my situation. In fact, the Bible assures me that as a follower of Jesus, I will never be separated from the love of God. Never will He leave me or forsake me.

Jesus' account doesn't end with the cross. Three days later He rose from the grave and now sits enthroned at the right hand of God. Through His resurrection power, we as Christ followers can live fully today and know that we too will see eternity because of what Christ did for us.

It humbles me to see Jesus' example. His example of the cross puts my suffering in perspective. Cancer sucks and my battle is hard, but Jesus has already been through so much worse, and He has promised to walk this path with me.

Happy Easter!

(And as always – thanks. I am amazed by how many are following my story. To God be the glory.)

~ *Responses from Family and Friends* ~

I don't think you realize the gift the Lord has given to you ... to be able to articulate your journey as you speak the Truth of His Word, His Mercy and Grace.... wow, it's incredible. Even through your pain and struggles, God is being glorified. You are having a great impact in the lives of others Eric. Yes, I am sure there have been and continue to be numerous times where you would rather NOT to have been put on this path, but I'm hoping you see and know that in your obedience to follow Christ in all things, others are being challenged to do the same. Hugs to you my brother. Praying for His strength, grace and joy to overflow in your heart/mind/soul!   *JerriLyn K., friend*

You won't remember us, but we remember when we visited your family last in the summer of 1986 [when Eric was 10]. God has allowed our family various health (and other) trials, over the last quarter century, but nothing of the magnitude you are undergoing. I thank God for your faith and willingness to share His goodness to your family. God is always good and this life is but a vapor for us all. Here's to eternity!!
Michael and Laurie K., college friends of Eric's brother

It was great seeing you guys last week weekend. Now the boys know who they are praying for :) I had a great time hanging out, catching up and look forward to many more years of good times with you guys. Glad I could assist in getting out for a couple hours too :)
Kyle R., best man at Eric's and Tammy's wedding

Monday, April 9, 2012 – 12:55 p.m.

Sixth and last?

I'm writing this from the chemo room. This is Round 6 ...the last chemo on this recipe of drugs. Two-and-a-half weeks out, I get another PET scan which should lead to maintenance chemo (Alimta every two to three months).

Last night was emotional. I really was sad/upset with the thought of yet another chemo (and an optional one at that). Thanks to a suggestion from a physical therapist friend of ours, we have doctor's orders to visit an oncology physical therapist. With their help, I can unpack what "to tolerance" means and hopefully build up my strength and endurance. At this point, I tire so easily and have put on a bunch of weight. Hopefully PT (physical therapy) will help on all fronts.

Thank you for helping, praying, and dropping notes. We are amazed at how far our story has spread. Please keep us in your prayers. The steroids are especially hideous this week. Time to log off – I am falling asleep. Hope everyone had a phenomenal Easter weekend.

It's still Monday – 2:19 p.m.

Oops, allergic reaction … again

(Still in the chemo chair.) Shortly after writing the last post, earlier this morning, I had the start of an allergic reaction to the chemo drug (Cisplatin). At least I am not riding in an ambulance to the hospital now – just taking a "time out" while the Benadryl and one other drug (Famotidine) take hold. If my body doesn't stop the itching, I'll get more steroids – whoo hoo.

Once everything is under control, we'll try again with the Cisplatin. With this being Round 6 on this chemo mix, it makes sense for my body to react against it. I'm thankful the reaction appears minor so far.

The last month-plus has been almost normal for a chemo patient. My regular nurse, Rob, smiled and chuckled a bit today when he heard I was reacting. He also gave the attending nurse guff about her patient count. She said she only had two patients at the time. Rob corrected her and raised the total to 2.5, and stared at me with a grin. "Mr. Atypical" has made a bit of a comeback … though this is within the range of normal. Harrumph!

At least this should be the last chemo for a while.

~ *Responses from Family and Friends* ~

Thank you for sharing your heart with us. Our prayers continue to be with you and your family daily. It was so good to see you yesterday at church picking up Ellie. Lynda F. surprised me and came Saturday morning to make balloon animals for the children using the skills that you taught her in your balloon animal making class. You taught her well!

Donna T., Village

Tuesday, April 10, 2012 – 8:16 p.m.

Decent day

Steroids! Ick. With yesterday's allergic reaction to the Cisplatin, I got an extra dose of steroids yesterday. Then today I had the normal steroid regimen. Only two more days of steroids though. I can do this ... I can do this ...

In between lots of naps today, I was able to run a few errands (birthday shopping at one store, white blood cell booster shot at the oncology clinic, and a pharmacy pit stop). My parents were a huge help today, getting me all around town.

Next week, God willing, I will start in with physical therapy. I've got appointments on Wednesday and Friday. It should be interesting to see how much improvement I can see with professional help. Short of God's hand of full healing, I may have a certain measure of fatigue that is just permanent (if I believe the websites). It is near impossible to tell at this stage how things will shake out. Will I always need lots of naps? Will I be able to return to work 20-plus hours a week? What is my "tolerance" level? Is 4 p.m. to 8 p.m. a permanent energy trough? I just don't know.

As I was preparing (Easter) Sunday night to head in to another chemo session, I found it very hard to psych myself up for Monday's "optional" chemo session. To screw up the courage to willingly suffer again was very hard. It somewhat defied logic. I could tell myself the wisdom of running another round to make sure maintenance phase is as long as possible, but ... willingly entering extreme nausea, possibly more hair falling out, fatigue galore, steroids and all their side effects for days, etc. ... Wow. No fun.

I found it ... and still do find it ... hard to willingly suffer just for my own chance to improve my health. As a parent (and as my parents have even said to me), I would trade with my kids if they had to suffer like I am. I'd like to think I would trade with Tammy and take her suffering. I might trade with a good friend. Certainly, I wouldn't want to take on the suffering of my enemies.

All those thoughts of suffering took me beyond the Easter eggs, the Easter bunny, and eating myself into oblivion.

♦ I STARTED TO PONDER
THE TRUE MEANING OF EASTER:

Jesus said, "Greater love has no one than this: to lay down one's life for one's friends" (John 15:13). I can get the friend part ... sort of ... I'm not sure if I'd go that far ... but I get it.

Paul, inspired by the Holy Spirit, said "But God demonstrates his own love for us in this: While we were still sinners, Christ died for us" (Romans 5:8).

This is beyond me. While we were enemies of God, He sent Jesus to take our punishment and provide a way for us to be part of God's forever family. It blows my mind that Jesus would willing suffer as He did – humiliation, scourging, death on the cross, separation from His Father, and the weight of the sin of the world ... past, present, and future. Is it any wonder that in the garden, just before His arrest, Christ prayed multiple times:

"Going a little farther, he fell with his face to the ground and prayed, 'My Father, if it is possible, may this cup be taken from me. Yet not as I will, but as you will.'" (Matthew 26:39)

I am so thankful that Jesus suffered for me and for you. Happy belated Easter.

"For the wages of sin is death, but the gift of God is eternal life in Christ Jesus our Lord." (Romans 6:23)

As always ... thanks! Knowing so many are with me and my family through this battle is such a huge help. Thank you, thank you, thank you!!!

~ *Responses from Family and Friends* ~

I am so amazed that Jesus willingly died for me despite my great flaws. But what is even more amazing is that he didn't die a quick, quiet, relatively painless death. He willingly suffered humiliation and torture on our behalf. That's a degree of grace I find simply unbelievable! Thank you for adding your unique perspective of God's grace as well! I pray that these side effects would quickly pass for you.

Lori H., Village

195

Thursday, April 12, 2012 – 7:44 p.m.

Steroids be gone

Last dose of steroids today! Took the last half pill today at 1 p.m. and then hit dreamland until 5 p.m. The steroid effects will be with me for some time yet, but I'm at least done actively pumping them into my body. Huzzah!

When maintenance phase starts (assuming everything continues as planned), I'll have steroids too, but just on the day of the Alimta dosing. Better yet, the frequency of maintenance dosing should be every two to three months or so … if I remember correctly what Dr. Andersen said.

As for the rest of the family – Ellie has a fever, Tammy is in the thick of taxes (final pen strokes), and Timmy is just plain verbose … he'll even tell you with great discourse why he will be quiet next. Can you guess which of the three things get my goat the most? (I love my dear boy.)

Life goes on … day by day. We still have lots of helpers … lawn mowing, cleaning, meals ... Wow! We are so blessed. Others around us are surrounded by life (and death) as well. My thoughts turn to a friend who is wrestling with cancer spreading – not retreating. Siblings, on both sides [Heerwagens and Morrises], have their challenges too. Some of the challenges seem almost insurmountable.

In all of the life that surrounds, we continue to hold on to our faith – anchored in who God is and what He has done as revealed in His Word. We bring our requests to His throne and seek His hand of provision. And in all this, we remember that life is so much more than the troubles we can so easily see.

Here's to seeing God at work each day – one day at a time.

Saturday, April 14, 2012 – 3:26 p.m.

Music and emotions

After being cooped up in the house most of the morning, at my dad's suggestion, I went for a walk through the neighborhood and took in a little sun. On went the noise-cancelling headphones and

Tammy's iPod ... which has a radio setting and better music selection than my older iPod. Walking at a shuffle, my heart rate jumped to well over 100 and stayed fast the whole two laps.

At the start of the walk, I was listening to top songs on 104.1 The Fish – "Strong Enough to Save" (Tenth Avenue North), "Where I Belong" (Building 429), and "My Hope is in You" (Aaron Shust).

Each song had lyrics that brought me to tears. Then came "Cinderella" (Steven Curtis Chapman). Look up the lyrics if you don't know them and you'll know why I quickly changed over to Tammy's playlist of songs.

Out of the frying pan and into the fire – Tammy's first song on her workout playlist was "I'm Gonna' Be (500 Miles)" by the Proclaimers. A song Tammy and I really enjoy. (We like Steven Curtis Chapman's version even better; he rewrites the "havering" (a Scottish term I believe) line.

I kept listening ... "I would walk 500 miles and I would walk 500 more just to be the man who would walk a thousand miles just to fall down at your door."

Today I was the man who walked two shuffling laps through the neighborhood ... not quite 1,000 thousand miles. But as my neighbor reminded me as I was almost to our driveway and home – we take the days we can get and enjoy each precious moment. I was glad not to have run across any neighbors on the rest of the walk. I was a bit of a blubbering mess. Between the songs, steroids, kid stress, and just being wiped out this week from chemo, I guess I had a good reason to have waterworks.

Hopefully each day forward will be on the upswing. A part of me is waiting for the other shoe to drop, but that is a horrible way to live –and not honoring to God. So, here's to sunshine and improving health.

Monday is my counseling session – work out my mind/emotions. Wednesday and Friday I get a physical therapist to work me over. Thursday is the brain MRI, which should be "much ado about nothing." Hope everyone has a great weekend. The sun is out ... at least here in Oregon. I think my webbed feet are drying out. ☺

~ *Responses from Family and Friends* ~

Praying for peace, patience, healing, perseverance ... ALL you need! Sure hope Ellie feels better soon. Music has a way of getting right into our hearts, doesn't it? I'm sure glad that you were able to get out and walk today, Eric! I love that "500 Miles" song, too, and will pray that God upholds you all on each step on this journey ... whether two blocks or 500 miles! As others have said, you are an inspiration ... to be thankful each day and press on, regardless of circumstances. Love in Christ.

Laurie G., Village

I believe that when words fail and we express ourselves through tears – even us men who are not allowed to cry – that the Holy Spirit is really able to communicate to our Heavenly Father for us. "In the same way, the Spirit helps us in our weakness. We do not know what we ought to pray for, but the Spirit himself intercedes for us through wordless groans" (Romans 8:26). You are in my prayers daily – your wife and children too. God Bless.

Rex B., friend of a friend

Monday, April 16, 2012 – 2:58 p.m.

Losses

Today, more than other days, it hit me. In these last months, I have lost much and my future days have lost much, too. All this loss is hard to process. Fortunately, I have a patient family, a good counselor, and a very good God.

Before cancer, I would take a project ...either at work or home ... and once I started, I'd race to complete it with the best possible outcome. Those who have seen me at work, or at "play," know that I was focused and fast. Each annual work review made some remark about my "results orientation" (a big Intel value). Tammy can attest to how enmeshed I can be with projects. My personal "brand" was all about getting things done fast and well. [Ed. note: This was Eric's life pattern from early childhood.]

Now with cancer, I don't have the same abilities. I have to pace myself much more. Walking around the block is now a great accomplishment vs. last year's big accomplishment of producing [Intel's] rocking, integrated, marketing strategy.

198

Today I'm not even sure yet how much capacity I have for working with Intel. This week I'm actively working through my medical leave timing ... there are just so many things I don't know. Wow! What a head bender. (Last night I spent some time looking through an old photo album of my Mexico trip ... another lifetime ago. I miss being well.)

With one disease everything gets upended. Going forward, I am in large part always going to be defined by this cancer. Barring immediate healing, and even with a really long maintenance phase, I still will have labs, scans, MRIs, physical limitations, etc. Isn't that cheery?

I know it is not all about what is lost. There has been gain in this too ... and not just my weight. Today though, I am choosing to process the loss, process the grief. In the days ahead, I may get more function back ... even more than I expect. Even with that though, a huge part of me grieves. I want to say, "It isn't fair. Can someone else please take a turn?" So, today I'm going to stay away from the pat answers and mourn.

In the coming week plus I should get lots more clarity around my limitations. The PET scan, brain MRI, recovery from last chemo, physical therapy, and first maintenance dose will all shape/define the days ahead. As I process the loss, I can accept it better and move forward under the new rules of engagement.

Thanks for your ongoing prayers. Please keep us in your prayers as we adjust to this new norm. I want to graciously accept what God gives/allows. (Please also pray for Tammy and Ellie this week as they both are under the weather.) Thanks!

~ *Responses from Family and Friends* ~

Praying for you and your family. Loss and change are complicated. Keep the faith ... God is with you.   *Laura B., Intel*

What I love about your posts is your honesty. Your pain and discouragement is so apparent and yet your awareness of what is difficult, painful, frustrating doesn't overcome your awareness of God's grace and the love of your family and friends. Thank you for the reminder that even in the valleys of life, God's grace is evident.   *Candace L., Village*

Tuesday, April 17, 2012 – 6:26 p.m.

I'm going on a picnic

Monday, we started the day with Tammy and Ellie being the sick ones in the house. We closed the day by adding Timmy to the list of fallen. I am bracing for my turn (fever and nasty cold symptoms), but hopefully the white blood cell booster shot I got a week ago will keep me in the clear. (Side note ... a piece of me would welcome another hospital stay. The peace and quiet would be nice ☺. Apologies to my loving family.)

Since yesterday was a heavy topic and today, aside from routine illness, is normal, I was thinking I might play a bit with this post. I know there are a lot of people reading/following our story. I also know I love to see guestbook entries. So at the risk of taking a census when I shouldn't (a la King David, 2 Samuel 24) ...here's what I would propose:

We're going on a picnic. I am tired of this cancer and would love diversion. I'm inviting everyone to come. Let me know via the guestbook what you are going to bring. We'll do this "pot luck" style (just like the Baptist picnics I grew up with). Bonus points if what you bring has something to do with where you live now, where you would say you're from, or something that connects the two of us.

Just write in the guestbook what you are bringing. Feel free to explain or just list your food. Thanks in advance for playing along with me. (Tammy will thank you too; this is way less expensive than me going out and getting a midlife-crisis car.) Have a blessed week!

~ *Picnic Responses from Family and Friends* ~

I will bring New England clam chowder (Boston's finest) and will have the Blue Men Group as my side "dish" ... providing us entertainment and a little "Intel Blue" fun!!   *Laura B., Intel*

I'll bring some perfect-for-a-picnic Southwest guacamole. Hoping it reminds you of your friend in Arizona whose favorite lunch place is Chipotle. Miss you Bro!   *Fred J., Intel*

~ *Picnic Responses (continued)* ~

I'm bringing some Kansas City slow smoked ribs and burnt ends.
Rich C., Eric's high school friend

Prickly pear (cactus) jam from Arizona, and sunshine to go with it!
Sandy G., formerly at Village

I'll bring Ella's Incredible Lemon Cake, simply because it's the one thing I make that continually goes over well. And in the spirit of the game I will also include fried rainbow trout because I grew up with the Rogue River as my backyard and spent many happy hours fishing and swimming.
Ella B., Village

One morning at breakfast in Walker's cafeteria [at Illinois State University], you held Frosted Mini-Wheats up to your eyes, saying, "Look! Fiber optics!" So my contribution would be that cereal.
Sara P., Eric's college friend

I grew up, mostly, in Forest Grove right near Verboort. So I will bring the Verboort sausage and fresh made sauerkraut!   *Shelley J., Village*

I'll order from Taste of Chicago and have it sent there to meet us ... Beef from Portillo's and Deep Dish Pizza from Lou Malnati's. :)
Valerie H., Eric's high school friend

I'll bring Grandma Goldsmith's [Eric's mom's mother] orange ice and several batches of her Lebkuchen cookies to share. Love to you and your family,   *Ruthie K., Eric's aunt in Colorado*

A picnic sounds terrific! I'll bring Grandma Goldsmith's fried chicken and baked beans. Sure hope we have blue sky and sunshine!!
Marty L., Eric's aunt in Colorado

We'll bring salmon and crab! The sun is shining right now, so hope the weather stays nice for our picnic. Love,
Deb and Steve E., Eric's aunt and uncle in Seattle

What a great combination of foods! I'm going to add a couple of authentic Italian pasta dishes and some great vegetables cooked Italian-style. And then ... to top it all off... I'm going to arrange for some music, and maybe we need some "Silly Songs with Larry" for the kids. Now, we have great friends, lots of awesome food, and MUSIC. This picnic is turning into quite a DEAL!!!! Love you guys! *Brian H., Eric's brother*

A picnic sounds like fun ... when the sun is shining more than 15 minutes at a time ... I would bring my favorite Potato Salad ... my mom the pastor's wife always brought it to church potlucks and picnics
Becki C., Village

~ *Picnic Responses (continued)* ~

Being from "Farm...ington," I will bring the Roast, so we can tell jokes on each other ...   *Chip M., Tammy's dad*

Well, I grew up near Crow, Oregon (in the country outside of Eugene), so I will bring some fresh corn-on-the-cob, from the country corn field. Great idea, Eric - I'll be there. God bless you, my friend – prayers always, you know.   *Terri B., Village*

So ... I'm bringing Chicken Tikka Masala (picked up to go just before we all leave so it is still warm!). Why... because I fell in love with Indian food while living in Beaverton and attending Village – and I know the Heerwagens enjoy it as well. Still praying for you all daily!
                                                       Tana K., friend

I spent many years in Hawaii. My potluck would be sweet pineapple (juice and chunks). For the kids, I would introduce Mango Tag. We played it at night using the fallen mangoes (read rotten) and throwing them at each other to tag the next person who would be it. It's all about building memories.   *Dawn Denice R., friend*

Hi All, I'll be coming in from Salt Lake City where I'm staying with grandkids. I'll bring some Dunford doughnuts and perhaps a few Osmonds for some music! Sure hope there's lots of sunshine for this shindig! God bless you.   *Kathy P., Tammy's former co-worker*

Hi Eric, Thanks for the invite to the picnic! When I grew up in Wyoming, our picnic destinations were usually to a nearby lake or up the mountain to a fun, 100-year-old family cabin overlooking my hometown. There were always two requirements – food and games. :) Watermelon and soda got thrown in the creek to cool down. And then ... let the games begin! Volleyball or football or whiffle ball or frisbee, or hearts or spades, gin rummy ... or water balloon toss (fight?). Or croquet, etc., etc., etc.
                                                   Melissa L., close friend

I'll be there! I am bringing oranges from Orangevale, CA, and brownies cause well why not. =)   *Heidi L., friend*

Since we live in the land of Garrison Keillor and Lake Wobegone, we would have to bring hot dish and jello salad to the picnic!
                                           Charlotte H., formerly at Village

In the style of a true Baptist potluck, I'll bring some carrot and raisin salad! (Which no one will eat, but everyone will feel better having it near, sort of like fruitcake at Christmas.)   *Jennie P., Village*

~ *Picnic Responses (continued)* ~

Since Laura B. is actually bringing two things – maybe I could just show up empty handed and walk close to Laura.   *Kathleen M., Intel*

I'm bringing fresh picked raspberries from the berry farm down the street from me.   *Candace L., Village*

I am bringing fried chicken, because my parents were from Missouri, and we never went on a picnic without first frying the chicken! Yum.   *Kathy B., Village*

Grilled Canby asparagus with cream cheese and ham wrapped around it.   *Renee S., mother of Tammy's sister-in-law*

I grew up in McMinnville ... home of Turkey Rama each summer, or as the locals call it: Turkey Trauma! I'll pack up some wonderful BBQ turkey for the picnic, and we'll watch and see who will be crowned "Biggest Turkey" this year!   *Laurie G., Village*

I'd bring a cornbread salad cause it's different than most other picnic salads. It actually tastes much better than it sounds – probably in need of a serious marketing campaign :)   *Kris K., friend*

Eric, So, if you have a picnic you have to have potato salad!! I don't know why some foods are just for certain times of the year! Like Pumpkin pie! I could eat that all year long but it is only a Thanksgiving desert! What is up with that!!!!   *Jane E., Village*

Okay ... Now that I'm done giggling about Jennie's post of raisin/carrot salad ... (gosh that is so true) :) ummm I think I will bring Arizona Green Tea!   *Corinna T., Tammy's cousin*

Chuck and I would like to bring chocolate coated macadamia nuts. Guess you could say your trip to Hawaii brought lots of memories for us too. Love,   *Chuck and Doris H., Village*

I can bring some In-N-Out burgers, a bottle of Amador County wine and some grapes. California style :) It was GREAT to see you a couple weeks ago. Hope to see you soon again.   *Kyle R., best man at Eric's and Tammy's wedding*

I'll bring that pizza Dad always made for birthday parties at our house. You know, the one that used dough for an entire loaf of French bread for the crust, copious amounts of tomato sauce, and about a pound of mozzarella cheese.   *Betty T., Eric's high school friend*

~ *Picnic Responses (continued)* ~

Great idea Eric! So many things I would like to bring .... I grew up in southern California, I might bring chile relleno casserole since we cooked and ate a lot of Mexican food. I would also bring some amazing stuffed Chicago pizza (spinach and sausage), since I lived there for about nine months. This picnic has the added advantage of being much kinder to my waistline than most picnics! *Lori O., Village*

Ooooo! A picnic! Count me in! Let's see...what shall I bring? Well, since I am an overachiever I think I will plan three items! First, for the main dish, I will bring Korean Beef because you and I enjoyed this together at the Holt picnic. (And, I guess there is that small little tie of us both having Korean sons ...) I would also bring a beverage that comes from my location. Dundee/Newberg is known for wine and hazelnuts. So, I'm thinking hazelnut cocoa is a good fit? And for dessert I'll bring cookies, just because cookies are what I do! *Dawn R., Tammy's sister*

Picnic! Well, I'm not old enough to bring you wine from Newberg, and Dawn already took the hazelnuts ;) So I'll bring grape juice, to substitute for the wine. I will also bring marshmallows and chocolate chips, to make up for all the times I snuck a few out of your pantry while I was babysitting Ellie (Shhh! it's a secret.) *Shellie M., Tammy's sister*

I'll bring the ribs, Montgomery Inn style so that you get some of that Midwest flavor. *Dave I., Intel*

I'd like all your Cali friends to bring the sun. I'll bring this great blanket that is waterproof for the dewy grass. (Ever practical, I know.) As for food, I'd ask my hubby to make his mom's famous potato salad recipe and I would make dessert. The hard part is picking which dessert! If I fast forward a few months, I think something with berries would really show off my Oregon roots. Or an apple crisp made with apples from our yard. But then again, I'm always a sucker for chocolate. Ugh, how to choose! Ok, I'd go with a chocolate strawberry shortcake.

Lori H., Village

A picnic with ALL your friends, AWESOME! In honor of the Boy Scout bike tour (including the bicycle hill race you won) and your awesome camping trip with Dad and friends in the U.P., Dad and I decided to bring an "Upper Great Lakes Fish Boil." We'll serve it along with coleslaw, rolls and butter, along with lemon wedges for the fish. (And, like Grandma Goldsmith always did, we'll bring extra rolls and butter for the little kids.) Oh, yeah, I won't forget to bring a couple of my world-famous apple pies! See you all there!

Sally H., Eric's mom

204

Wednesday, April 18, 2012 – 6:43 p.m.

Physical therapy

Wow, am I tired! This morning marked the start of my physical therapy torture … er … training. My physical therapist dove right in and worked me through six exercises (three stretches and three core-strength builders). Had you shown me the exercises a year ago and told me doing these six would be a workout that would get my heart rate to 120, I would have laughed. On top of the exercises, I "get" to walk 20 minutes a day. I'll gradually build up the time walking … adding five minutes a day each week.

I guess we have to start somewhere, but it is quite frustrating to physically be in the weeds as much as I am. I do recognize how far I've come in the last few months though. Just a few months ago, I was winded walking to the bathroom, and taking a shower meant major exertion.

On a separate topic – thanks for the great picnic. If you haven't shared in the guestbook, please do. I smile a lot as I read through the entries. One of my favorites so far is from my college friend Sara Powell ["Look! Fiber optics!"]. I honestly don't remember saying that, but I laughed hard at my joke from way back. My wife said, "That is so you! (eye roll)."

On the good news front … the family is on the mend. Timmy hasn't slowed much. Ellie and Tammy are still a bit ill, but able to function through the day just fine. And I have not yet caught anything, thank God. Here's to taking life as it comes – one day at a time.

~ (More) *Picnic Responses* ~

Eric, I would show up with Long John Silver's fish and chips. One for me and one for you. Keep fighting the fight brother.
Chris McD., former co-worker of Eric's brother

I've been keeping up with your posts and praying as always, just haven't had time to write back in a while ... I'm missing the wild salmon from the Pacific Northwest. Is it Copper River Salmon time yet? I would spring for that. *Becky J., formerly at Village*

Continuing to pray as PT starts and you adjust to the new movements of exercise! Oh that dreaded word! Picnic sounds wonderful by the way ... I'll bring Laine's favorite enchiladas!!!! *Colleen H., Tammy's friend*

Think we'll be bringing some traditional Boston baked beans (the real stuff, not the candy!). Only just now getting around to learning to make beans. Praying for you all,
Chris and Beth M., Tammy's brother and wife

Hi! We're arriving a bit late ... but ... will bring some cactus jelly! Don't forget Great-granddaddy's eggnog. Loving music as we all do, how about some karaoke, too? Love you all so much and thank you for this special invite to this spectacular picnic! Prayers always!
Bonnie and George J., Tammy's aunt and uncle in Arizona

I would bring, if I had the recipe, the garlic potatoes you guys bring for family Christmas. Love you, and am extremely proud of you. Tammy, you are showing the Lord's grace and love in the way you are caring for Eric and your children. I am so thankful for the way you guys whole heartedly depend on the Lord. I love you guys deeply.
Ashley M., Tammy's brother's wife

I would bring macaroni and cheese and cupcakes for the (having four young kids myself) the kids and little boxes of juice. I went to college with Tammy, I was on her dorm floor. Tammy might remember me if you say I have a twin sister, Cindy who was on Tammy's dorm floor as well. I heard about you and your site from Jaymi F. who was also on our dorm floor. My husband is sick with MS, so I know a little bit about living with a sick family member and having young kids. My boys are 5 (twins) and my girls are 3 (twins as well). I will keep all of you in my prayers!
Christie W., Tammy's college friend

~ *Picnic Responses (continued)* ~

I live near Napa – so count me in for some amazing red wine!! Straight from the Napa and Sonoma vineyards :). Picnics are fun!!

Pam M., Intel

A loaf of bread and a jug of ice cold grape juice.

Rex B., friend of a friend

I'm bringing mangoes (straight off the tree and really sweet).

Mythraie G., Village

Hi Eric, I'm late to the picnic. My only excuses are that I forgot what day it was again, and then I discovered that the fridge was empty. To make up for it, I flew to Chicago and got you my favorite childhood pizza from Aurelio's. Hope you, Tammy and the kids are well enough to enjoy this beautiful weekend in the NW!

Carissa H., Intel

The picnic food sounds delicious! Cooking is not my strong suit. How about I bring all the napkins and straws we can eat ...er, use!

Jim and Jessie N., Village

I'll bring Korean BBQ and watermelon. Eric, I thank God for miracles in your life and your progress so far. Keep lifting you, Tammy, and your family up in prayers. Love you, Tammy. May God give you extra strength and peace in taking care of yourself and your family.

Lynda F., Village

Dear Eric, I started to read what everyone else was bringing to the picnic and started to get a little flushed and my heart was racing. Too much good food. So I decided that I would need to bring something different. So we will bring some children and we will bring some fun games and hot weather. The forecast here is for 100F with clear skies today. I think I can Skype this to you all. Thank you for including us all on your spiritual journey with God. Prayerfully,

John and Sarah S., missionary friends in India

Sunday, April 22, 2012 – 10:50 p.m.

The week ahead

Sunday night ... I am worn out. My muscles ache from the PT exercises and 20 minutes of walking each day. Family and friends that see me, though, have all remarked at how much I look like the "old" Eric. My hair is growing back well (though still baby fine) and my overall energy/focus is coming back.

Monday, April 30, is the next appointment with Dr. Andersen. During that appointment, I'll get results from the Wednesday PET scan, and I fully expect to be put on maintenance meds. Also this coming week, I get results from last week's MRI. Based on how I am feeling, I don't expect any surprises. Keep praying for NED (no evidence of disease) or better. ☺

Next weekend, Tammy gets time away with some women she's known since well before we were married. The yearly retreat should be a much needed reboot for her. In the days ahead, we'll be even more intentional about getting breaks for Tammy; she really needs them for her health/sanity.

In all of this, Tammy and I are working through what the new norm is. Fortunately, we have one more month of planned absence from work to allow me to focus on counseling, PT, and starting maintenance. While nothing is a done deal, I think we have a fairly high confidence for how things will play out in the next few weeks. (Granted, the "atypical patient" is the guy saying this.)

So ... day by day. I'm doing my best to take each day for what it is. I am working hard to choose life each day. Not easy to do – especially when I am faced with having to do really hard PT exercises or needing to do a 20-minute walk I'd rather skip. Somehow God has seen fit to give me more time ... I'll do my best to honor the gift.

Monday, April 23, 2012 – 9:35 p.m.

Mice and men

I should know better. Just yesterday I was feeling like we had a lock on how things would progress – at least for the next week. Well, as they say, "The best laid plans of mice and men often go astray," or as the Bible says, "Many are the plans in a man's heart, but it is the LORD's purpose that prevails" (Proverbs 19:21).

Last night I noticed my lower-left leg was swollen. After consulting with my oncology clinic today, I now have a 2 p.m. appointment tomorrow at St. Vincent's [Hospital]. They will ultrasound my leg and see if new clots have formed. If new clots are present, I am not sure what treatment would look like. I'm already on the last option for clot prevention. I'm hopeful that the leg is just swollen from overuse ... all the PT and walking of late. We're praying and trusting that God knows what He is doing.

On a happier note, I had my midlife crisis ☺. With Tammy's full blessing, we traded our RAV4 in for a PriusV. Sweet ride! I feel like such an Oregonian driving my hybrid now ☺. We picked up the car earlier tonight, and even Ellie was okay with the change.

And ... on the really good news front, the brain MRI results came back and the brain tumor is reducing as expected. We'll get the full lowdown on Thursday, but the nurse called earlier today to let us know we had nothing to worry about in this scan. More to come as we know it.

~ *Responses from Family and Friends* ~

Umm ... a Prius is NOT a midlife crisis. Just for the record, a Lamborghini is a midlife crisis. (Though, I can certainly see why Tammy would not have blessed THAT). Praying all goes well with your leg check tomorrow and you can continue with your PT and adjusting to the new normal. All the best.
Kris K., friend

Good to hear ... both for the new car and the MRI results!
Chris and Beth M., Tammy's brother and wife

Great news on the brain scan and sweet ride man! *Tim W., Intel*

Nice RED Prius! Praying for you as always. Love you.
Shellie M., Tammy's sister

You know you're a full-blooded Oregonian when your mid-life crisis car is a Prius, not a Viper! Have fun with the new toy, and I hope the leg turns out to be no big deal.
Mike F., Intel

Tuesday, April 24, 2012 – 5:59 p.m.

No clots

Thanks for praying. The vascular ultrasound tech didn't see any deep vein clots. She couldn't share the results, technically, but she didn't go running out the door to call my doc either. So ... now I wait to find out next steps from Dr. Andersen. Fun times.

~ *Responses from Family and Friends* ~

Be sure to get some spinners on that Prius!   *Andy T., Intel*

Nice wheels! Love the rebellious red on the otherwise quite sensible hybrid. I think you may need to get some custom pinstripes or maybe flames to truly qualify for a midlife crisis car though!   *Lori H., Village*

That's great news! Maybe it's just a reaction from increasing your activity/walking. Nice new ride you got there! Can I just come over and sit in it so I can get a whiff of that new car smell ... I can kind of recall what a new car smells like, but it was so very long ago. Hugs!
JerriLyn K., friend

Thursday, April 26, 2012 – 7:10 p.m.

Headed to maintenance

(A word of advice – if ever you have a chance to get a report before the doctor sees it, think twice. Monday is my doctor's appointment –when I usually get test results, but I knew the PET scan results were available at the hospital today. I've seen PET reports before and figured I would have no problem reading this report. Think again.)

This morning I descended into the bowels of St. Vincent. After completing a lengthy request form (thanks HIPAA), and waiting longer than I wanted inside a small windowless room, I emerged with a manila envelope containing a three-page report. I debated if I would even open the envelope before getting home, but curiosity won out.

As I read through the medical jargon, I grew more and more concerned. Between indiscernible anatomy words, I saw things like, "worsening of activity (in the chest) ... early disease (in the spine) ... overall worsening ... malignant." Yikes.

Before you ask ... I called my doctor [Dr. Andersen], and he was confused by the report as well. He said I should plan for maintenance on Monday despite the ominous report. I'll trust my doctor to confer with the radiologist and get a clearer view of what the PET scan revealed. So until Monday, we sit tight – the radiologist also wrote in the middle of the report, "These finding are questionable in nature." ... Hmmmm.

Good news ... This afternoon I met with Dr. Patton, who is overseeing my brain tumor treatment. My dad and I drove to the Rose Quarter offices and had a great consult with the doctor. Together, with Dr. Patton, we reviewed the brain MRI imaging. The gamma knife images from January clearly showed the tumor. The images from last week showed no signs of the tumor – except for some faint echoes that only a brain doc would see. Thank God!

In all of this, I try to remember that God is in control ... not me. He is also infinitely good. Even if I have to go through chemo again next week, God still loves me deeply and will care for me and my family. That said, I feel like I am on a merry-go-round that won't stop. Both Tammy and I would love to escape from the drama of cancer. The reality of our situation though is that we don't really get a break. We just have to take each day as it comes.

Please pray that God would replenish our reserves. It is hard to keep a good/right attitude through all of this. As always... thanks! And, regarding some of the posts on my new car – thanks for the laughs.

~ Responses from Family and Friends ~

Sorry you had to deal with all the medical release paperwork, only to get a confusing report. Praying for you and your family, and praying that you would be filled with His peace as you wait to talk to the doctor Monday. Hopefully there will be some nice weekend weather where you can take your Prius out for a spin! Blessings,

Melissa and Brian L., close friends

Sunday, April 29, 2012 – 8:26 p.m.

Life isn't fair

What does success look like? I've given it some thought these days as I wrestle with my "new norm."

◆ I BELIEVE CULTURE TELLS US WE ARE
TO STRIVE FOR PERFECTION IN OUR:

Appearance: Just look at the plethora of diets and diet pills on the market. Plastic surgery abounds. Only the glamorous survive in Hollywood.

Finances: How many commercials have I heard with some get rich quick scheme? Isn't it the poorest of poor who most often play the lottery?

Intelligence: Do you believe Ellie [at age 8] already has a college readiness plan? I have coworkers who have stress over what Pre-K school their kids will go to, as if that one choice would make or break the kids' Harvard chances.

Behavior: I've often heard remarks about "karma" and "pay it forward." We do good to get good. It is often about what we look like. (The Pharisees were a great example of such a focus on the outward behavior, carefully covering over any imperfections.)

Relationships: I think a lot of people ... even those in the church ... view marriage as a contract and not a covenant. Said another way, at the first signs of trouble many people bolt.

Children: Our kids reflect on us, thus they should be the best they can be. I remember not too long ago reading about an Oregon couple who sued their doctor because their newborn had Down Syndrome. Had they known, they would have ended the pregnancy. Even sadder than the couple's suit is the fact they won.

On to this list, we layer an expectation ... no, an entitlement ...

to have perfection in all these areas. If life deals us a bad hand, we feel wronged. Life is not fair – never mind the truism that we reap what we sow.

♦ THERE IS NO ROOM FOR THE IMPERFECT; LIFE ITSELF BECOMES DEVALUED:

My child has a disability;

I am only 36 and I have Stage IV lung cancer;

I have kids and now my free time is gone;

As long as I have credit, why not go shopping;

My little brother won't share his toy with me;

... and the list goes on.

We have built in a fundamental assumption that in this life we should have only the best. Suffering is to be shunned. As Francis Schaeffer said, we seek our own "personal peace and affluence."

We are (I am) naturally selfish. And if this world were all there was, I could somewhat understand. If we just end up as worm food, why not push to live for ourselves – why not just be selfish.

It is hard for me in the middle of this sickness to think of others first. I do it very poorly. Most of my prayers are, "God help me." I fail to look to my good and faithful God for what He has for me each day. When things go poorly I get mad. I am owed better, aren't I?

I think the answer goes both ways as I read through Scripture. First, we all are owed death – eternal separation from God. If it were not for Jesus' unfair suffering, we would not be saved. Thankfully God's grace protects us from His ultimate fairness. On the other hand, for those who claim Jesus as Lord and Savior, we have the assurance of an eternity of perfection. This life of suffering is just a blip against the expanse of eternity that awaits.

This side of Heaven, we are guaranteed suffering. Conversely, we are guaranteed no more tears, death, crying, or pain in Heaven. The stain of sin will be forever removed from our lives and the world around us (Revelation 21).

So, as I grumble and groan at how much I have lost, as I worry about how many more days I have ... I have to remember to humble myself before God and embrace His plan for my life. I fix my eyes on the unseen that lasts forever (2 Corinthians 4:16-18). This life is less about me and much more about God and others. It is up to Him what role my life will have. He is the potter and I am the clay. He chooses what to make with my life. Then out of gratitude for my salvation and life, I am called to live a life following Jesus.

Here's to living a life of grace in the days ahead, living for God and not just for myself. Easier said than done, but thankfully – as a believer – I have the help of the Holy Spirit to empower my journey.

Tomorrow is the next step in my journey. Tomorrow we go to the oncology clinic for maintenance ... hopefully. I'll post more as I know more. Likely I can post from the infusion room around the middle of the day. Thanks for your prayers, love and support

> p.s. I made it through the weekend without Tammy. My folks were a great help. Tammy is safely home from her retreat and I am so thankful to have her back.

~ *Responses from Family and Friends* ~

Well said, Eric. Here is to living one day at a time for others and God the best we can, placing our lives in the hand of our Creator, and thanking Jesus that He made a way for us to be with Him forever. We are blessed beyond compare! Praying for a good report and God's very presence with you as you face the new day. Blessings,   *Kathy B., Village*

We are praying for you. We pray that tomorrow goes well and that peace will fill both you and Tammy no matter what comes. So glad to hear that Tammy was able to go on her retreat, and that you and the kids are glad to have her home. Love you,   *Dawn R., Tammy's sister*

Really liked your post tonight, Eric! I was grappling with some of those ideas this weekend, but could not articulate it. Thank you for your posts, your honesty and letting us follow your journey. I hope that I learn and apply some of your lessons to my own life. I am so glad that Tammy was able to go to the retreat. I really missed it this year. We continue to hold you, Tammy, and the kids up in prayer daily.   *Lori O., Village*

Monday, April 30, 2012 – 1:05 p.m.

Maintenance deferred

I am writing to you from the infusion room at Compass Oncology.

First ... the optimist ... Dr. Andersen is much encouraged by how good I look. His physical exam couldn't find many of the swollen glands that he had felt in previous exams. A number of the active sites of cancer show fairly low levels of activity, and the difference from PET scan to PET scan could be statistically insignificant.

(If you remember ... cancer activity measure of 2.0 or lower is what we needed across all the cancer sites for maintenance to start.) Since there is an area of new growth in the left chest lining, and the activity level is concerning, Dr. Andersen encouraged us to move to the third-line drug called Adriamycin. Initial lab tests on my cancer showed the cancer could respond well to Adriamycin. Fortunately the side effects of the Adriamycin should be less strong than my last chemo drug (Cisplatin).

Now ... the "realist" ... I have three cycles of the Adriamycin to gut through – nausea, steroids, hair loss ... starting mid-May, bad nails, etc. Then, in mid-July, we'll have our next PET scan with results shared on July 23 ... 12 weeks from now.

As mentioned above, this is the third-line of defense against the lung cancer. Medically, after this drug, we don't have any more "proven" treatments. There are other things Dr. Andersen can do, but it will be more of an art than a science. Like other drugs, I assume we'll have a six-treatment max on the Adriamycin. God willing, we will beat down the cancer enough to enter maintenance. Better yet, God will choose to answer in the affirmative the many prayers for my complete healing ...this side of Heaven.

Please keep praying for total healing. Pray also for us to not lose heart. As I type, it is all but too easy to jump to conclusions. I am disheartened (probably too weak a word) to not be moving to maintenance.

On one level – I know God is good and in control. I know He has a plan and knows how my days are numbered. It does me no good to borrow trouble from tomorrow – today has enough troubles of its own. That said, I need God's help to put my little faith to work. It is hard to not view this as a setback, and we are already worn out.

(Side note: I still have swelling in the left leg and new pain in the left upper back/chest. These could be cancer related or physical therapy related. There is no way to know for sure. For now we will approach them from a PT perspective and treat for the pain. Hopefully this is just a side effect of being a whole lot more active.)

As always ... thanks.

~ *Responses from Family and Friends* ~

I know I'll re-read your post many times as it's filled with such wisdom and perspective! A friend and I were talking this weekend about how we are wired to be selfish. It's such work to choose to live as a humble servant because it's so contrary to our wiring. I have been thinking a lot about what Pastor John said about Paul never getting over the gift of grace. I hope I can feel that indebtedness too! That is the cure for self-ishness. The knowledge that all I have, my very life, my eternal salvation, are gifts I am so unworthy of receiving. Thank you for shining your light and for making me think! Have a great day today, I'm praying for all of you.   *Lori H., Village*

Thanks for the update. I imagine that's a hard one to write. Sometimes battling cancer seems like a roller coaster! Just when you get used to the idea of maintenance, you are in to more treatment. Praying for you all.   *Mythraie G., Village*

[There were 163 responses in the guestbook
from April 1-30, 2012.]

May 2012

~ *The Eighth Month* ~

Wednesday, May 2, 2012 – 6:02 p.m.

Angry

It's Wednesday after chemo, and things are going better than expected. I am sleeping a ton, but so far the nausea and other symptoms have been held at bay. I do find myself a bit over emotional, and I am tracking down the source of an ache in my lower left chest. I'm hoping it is just painful muscles from sawing the spice cabinet that is still a work in process, and not new cancer-related pain.

Yesterday I had a trusted friend over. Real friends aren't afraid to speak the truth and ask the tough questions. Through the course of the conversation, I realized a few things ... I am angry with God. I know that has not played well with Bible personalities (just think of Job), but hang with me for a moment.

♦ MY THOUGHT PROCESS GOES SOMETHING LIKE:

I don't deserve this. We were just on the brink of a break ... with maintenance mode that was going to last for a very long time, and now I am back into chemo space for at least two more cycles – not counting this last Monday. I want a break and You won't give it to me. I hate suffering.

I see the impact of my illness on those around me, especially my children. Telling Ellie that I have to lose my hair again is hard. She knows what this means. More than just hair loss, we are one step closer to the end game. Timmy, though he could never articulate it ... he's just 4 ... knows things are off. His behavior at home is full-on anger and frustration. And, I've not even begun to write about the impact on Tammy ...

My pride really doesn't like the idea that God would choose to allow my body to go through such an illness. I could understand if I were a smoke-a-pack-a-day person and I got lung cancer, or if I were a very elderly person with just a few years left of life anyway. And yet ... here I am at 36 with aggressive lung cancer. These last seven-plus months have been more than a roller coaster. I don't like being the Potter's creation that is destined for cancer and suffering.

> "Yet you Lord, are our Father. We are the clay, you are the potter; we are all the work of your hand."   *Isaiah 64:8*

> "Does not the potter have the right to make out of the same lump of clay some pottery for special purposes and some for common use?"
> *Romans 9:21*

Add on to that the many people praying fervently for my healing. You are a God who wants to give good gifts, so why not grant the prayers of Your people?

Now ... before lightning strikes, here is the other part of the thought process that I have to embrace. At first I didn't like what I'm about to write, but it is growing on me and giving me some measure of freedom that I didn't have before.

♦ SO HERE IT IS ...

This is NOT all about me. The Lord's prayer starts with, "Our Father, who is in heaven. Holy be your name. Your kingdom come. Your will be done." Not a single "I" or "me" in the intro is there? Jesus in the Garden of Gethsemane asked for the cup to pass, but was resolved to follow His Father regardless of the suffering ahead. The Messiah didn't have a need to suffer – He was the only living man to be truly without sin.

God knows the bigger plan. He sees way more than I do. Somehow in His infinite wisdom, by allowing me to have cancer, He is adding to His glory – in lives around me – perhaps in my children, Tammy, or even some of you who are reading this will find that because of my suffering you have been drawn closer to God and He gets more glory.

These last seven months have allowed me to be an ambassador for Jesus in ways I've never had before. Though costly, I believe my life has mattered in a much more profound way these last months.

I am called to follow, regardless of the cost. My Christianity is not just a weekend-fan thing that I use when it suits me. It must be the core of who I am. Jesus doesn't ask me to only follow when the cost is low. He asks me to daily pick up my cross and follow Him (Luke 9:23b). So I have to put my faith first and foremost in the God who has saved me from death already and has promised me an eternity with Him in the new Heaven and new Earth. In the meantime, I do my best to follow Him daily.

Do I have it all figured out? Not in the least. That said, my faith is growing ... in ways that I believe it never would have if I skipped the suffering. I fix my eyes on the things unseen (2 Cor. 4) – the impact I know God is having, the glory He is receiving, the treasures of Heaven He has for me.

Thanks for your continued prayers and love! We couldn't do this alone.

One specific prayer is that in the midst of all the mess, we would find times of refreshing. Also, pray that as we invite a play therapist to spend time with Timmy in the next few weeks we would gain valuable insights into how we can help him through all this.

Here's to the freedom of not being the center of the universe ... and to allowing Him who made all things by just speaking to be in control.

[Ed. Note: Yesterday a post was sent out via Facebook and copied onto CaringBridge inviting anyone who has been praying for Eric and his family to be a part of a "prayer tree poster." Each person/family was invited to send a green ink/paint fingerprint on plain white paper with their name(s) printed around the print. Each finger-print then will be a "leaf on the prayer tree."]

~ *Responses from Family and Friends* ~

Thanks for sharing openly and honestly about even the darker times on this journey. I will certainly ratchet up the prayers for you guys and especially the kids in the weeks ahead. I will specifically pray for God's peace to speak perfectly to their hearts so even in the uncertainty of their dad's illness, they are certain of the fact they are loved by their family, by their community and by a great God.   *Kim G., Village*

How can I ever express to you the importance of what you have just written. As I pray for your recovery, I gain so much from your journey. I have been sharing your thoughts and struggles with a close friend who is on the same journey. She has gained so much strength and understanding from all you write as she knows you are where she is. But your current words came at exactly the right time. I was faced with the same questions from her just this week and was able to read to her your feelings and insight this morning. Words can never tell you the relief she felt as she listened to your words express exactly what she has been feeling but could never express the way you can. I am saying "thank you" from her and from me for the courageous way you are able to share so much, and continue to help so many while you face such a difficult journey.
Sue B., friend

Thanks for being willing to share from the depths of your soul, Eric. Know that you are making an impact in the lives of those who read your words, in ways that you may never know. Will be praying especially for Timmy these weeks and that you and Tammy will know best how to help him. May God meet each of you exactly where you need to be met!
Bonnie and Kevin O., missionary friends in Burkina Faso

I thank God for the people he has given you as a support network, to care for your physical and emotional needs. I thank God that He has given you a wife and two children to pour out your love to. I praise Him that he prepared you your whole life, even though you did not know it, for this very time, so you could stand up to the test. And I give Him glory, that we will be healed, and when we see His face, the pain will all be forgotten and the tears will be wiped away.   *Betty T., Eric's high school friend*

~ *Responses from Family and Friends (cont.)* ~

Wow Eric ... your ability to put all your thoughts into words ... amazing! You are growing and learning so very much ... about God, about His Love, Mercy, Grace... about yourself and the humanity that constrains not only you, but all of us. Through you, we are also learning About God, About His Love, Mercy and Grace. To God Be the Glory Great Things He Has Done, and I will add ... Will Also DO!!! Prayers and Hugs!

JerriLyn K., friend

Eric and Tammy, You know my heart, my tears, my prayers for you. You are human, but you are way above "normal" when it comes to this disease. You, by faith, are placing your will into the Father's hands. That takes fortitude and lots of faith. I for one am very proud to be your friend and your sister in Christ, that, no matter what, will never change, not even for eternity.

Kathy B., Village

Wow ... I am honored to call you friend, brother in Christ and life-groupie. Your heartfelt words of wisdom are reaching so many and are a blessing and truth. Thank you for your honesty and wisdom. Praying praying! Love,

Chick L., Village Live Group

Eric, Tammy, Ellie and Timmy – Frustration ... is going thru the cancer process the last seven-plus months and it's not fair! My heart goes out to your family as you still have so many "unknowns" in your future. I continue to pray for your lovely family and will help in any way I can. May you be able to focus on each moment, hour, and day on your lovely family ... because each moment is so precious! Love and prayers for each of you.

Colleen H., Tammy's friend

Saturday, May 5, 2012, 10:53 a.m.

Tammy here ...

We're back in the hospital. Most of yesterday afternoon was spent in the ER, and then Eric was admitted. He's in a lot of pain due to fluid buildup around his left lung and his heart. Around 11 a.m. today they'll drain it – he's had to wait for his blood thinners to wear off enough for them to do the procedure. Then the fluid will be analyzed to see if it's a result of cancer or an infection. Please pray for a safe procedure, good and quick answers, and a safe return home soon. Thanks.

~ *Responses from Family and Friends* ~

Tammy, thank you for letting all of us know. All of us on Team Heerwagen have you in our thoughts.   *Mike F., Intel*

Holding you all close to my heart today ... praying.
Dorothy G., formerly at Village

Tammy and Eric, We're praying for you. Hang in there.
Jeff H., Village

We continue to pray for your complete healing, Eric. And for your family for endurance.   *Annabelle and John P., Village*

Hi, Heerwagens. We just wanted to let you know that we are continuing to hold you all up in prayer. It must be scary to have Eric back in the hospital. We are specifically praying for lessening of pain and comfort during this time. Thank you for so honestly sharing your journey with us,
Heather S., and family, Village

Eric, Tammy, Ellie, and Timmy, Love to your family. Thank you for your beautiful writing. You do bring glory to God. Your lives do touch ours and you do humble me. Thank you! Love,   *Jenny R., Village*

Tammy and Eric, we are fervently praying and I have posted this on Facebook and have many who have never met Eric praying as well. Praying you all feel God's presence with you today. From Wisconsin,
Kristina W., Eric's college friend

Sunday, May 6, 2012, 12:27 p.m.

Tammy again ...

Just met with the doctor this morning. The lung draw took nearly a liter of fluid [about one quart] out of Eric's lung lining. The procedure caused more pain in the process, and now we're working to get that pain under control. Eric will spend at least one more night in the hospital. Finding the exact source of pain is not easy – it could be residual from the fluid, or tumors, or ???

At this point the plan is to medicate and hope for improvement as we continue on chemo and his body adjusts after yesterday's procedure. Thanks as always for the prayers and notes.

~ *Responses from Family and Friends* ~

I don't write to you every day but I do think of you and admire your courage, honesty, and your strong faith thru this. I will continue to pray for you and Tammy and the kids. Hang in there and know we are all surrounding you in HIS love.
Pam M., Intel

Morning, Eric, Love you and your precious family so much. I am so thankful they were able to remove the fluid and offer relief in that way. Thankful for pain meds too :). Your commitment to being real in your journal entries and for doing all you can do to fight this is a true inspiration to me and to countless others. I am praying that God will BE your strength and your joy and your hope for the future
Lorraine. H., Eric's brother's wife

Gave Tammy a hug yesterday. Also saw Ellie and Timmy ... they had just gotten home from a fun time with Grandma at McDonalds:-) So glad to hear you got some sleep last night and have routine pain meds. Looking forward to your arrival back home and seeing you. God is with you and your family.
Laura D., neighbor

We are praying so hard for you and Tammy. God IS doing something, I have had people here that are following you that have been challenged in their walk by your honest posts. Your posts gave me a better perspective on trials. We love you!
Keith, K. and family, friends

Monday, May 7, 2012, 7:41 a.m.

Waiting ...

[Eric writing] I really do like the St. Vincent staff. Very competent. Last night felt like I went from one pain med to another with "sleep" in between. Should know more about plans for treatment around 8:30 a.m.

Thanks for the prayers. We really need them. I am feeling especially discouraged. The kids need help too ... lots to take in for them as well. Happy Monday. Here's to a better post to come.

It's still Monday, 1:39 p.m.

Good medicine

Hey friends and family! It is almost time for lunch on Monday. My mom and dad are bringing lunch to me. Huge thanks!

Earlier today, I had a number of positive things happen, in spite of the overall ugly picture for the day. First, my counselor called me and we met telephonically for 50 minutes. I so needed that. Then, my doctor arranged for my pain meds to be administered on demand, via the port in my chest. I'll carry a small portable [pain med] pump everywhere with me so I can up the dosing as needed (within reason). This way, I get a "constant" drip of meds – so naps shouldn't put me at deficit for pain management. And finally, after we got the pain options on the way to figured out, Dave and Renee showed up at my room. What a blessing to have good friends visit and share laughter. Thanks!

While I'm at the hospital today, the nurse is also going to work with me to figure out an ongoing bladder challenge that is "likely a side effect of all the heavy pain meds." I won't share any deeper on that topic, but know that if we can determine how to help on that front, my night times will be so much improved.

So ... what does all this mean? Not a clue as yet.

I'm going to take this one day at a time. This could be one step closer to the end game – this chemo recipe is the last "proven" recipe. It could also just be a step closer to maintenance. Or, it could be

224

something I haven't even thought of yet.

The one thing I do hold as true is this – God is in control and His power and love are so strong for me that I can put my faith in Him.

May God receive the glory, honor and praise. (By the way, I am somewhat grumpy on this whole cancer front ... but I am working hard to get a right point of view.)

Tuesday, May 8, 2012, 11:15 p.m.

"Leeks and onions"

(I'm tired and on lots of pain meds ☺.) Earlier tonight Pastor Jim came to my hospital room to visit and encourage. These days of hospitalization have been hard on me. They serve as a reminder of just how painful and taxing cancer can be. They also remind me that I am not in control … God is.

Jim was reading from Hebrews 11 (the faith hall of fame) and he wanted me to remember the cloud of witnesses in heaven – and here on this earth, who are cheering me on. God calls me (us) to be faithful in following Him daily. As we make the tough calls, lean on Him, and follow Him by faith, He honors and rewards that. He does that for me, and He does that for Tammy, the kids, etc. All believers have the promise of God being on their side and working "all things together for good." (Romans 8:28)

So here, though, is the tangential thought I had while listening to Hebrews 11 read aloud ... "leeks and onions."

Do you remember how scared the Hebrews were as they emerged from Egypt? God was meeting their daily needs. He had freed them from slavery. He was even going to give them victory over the lands around them – if they just believed. And yet, in Numbers 11, we read how totally mixed up the Hebrews got. In effect they said, "God please send us back to Egypt. The fruit and veggies were 'sooo' good." Really? I guess they kind of edit out the whole slavery thing and all the other negatives that had them calling out for God to rescue them.

I find myself in a bit of the same situation. God, why don't you send me back to how things were before cancer? I had it "so good."

What I forget is that God has appointed each day of my life (each day of my family's lives) to matter for His Kingdom. He will use the good and the bad alike to glorify His name and show His children His unending love.

Some time ago, I had the audacity to ask God to show me what He meant by the "gospel of suffering." I believe He is teaching me that in spades right now. In the hours and days ahead, I just need to trust Him and listen for the cheering section as so many of you and the heavenly host cheer me on to finish strong.

Please keep us in your prayers. We need God's daily infusion of strength so we can make the choices to glorify Him daily. Thanks.

~ *Responses from Family and Friends* ~

I love your heart in all this – you may be discouraged but you always come around to what is true. Jesus is right there riding the yo-yo along with you. Hang in there my friend. Praying for you and your family.
Tara F., Village

I just discovered your post. Words cannot begin to express how sad I am to hear of your battle. I can't imagine the shock and disappointment with such a diagnosis. I'd like to share what my mom said the day they discovered her Stage 4 colon cancer after a routine gall bladder surgery. "This does not change the number of days God has ordained for my life." Over the time she battled cancer, my dad was sick and passed away. She joined him in Glory 15 months later. Her words have brought me such comfort in my own questions of "why." I pray that you will take peace in knowing that He numbered our days, and that your precious family is in the grasp of His hands. In Him, *Cheri C., Eric's childhood friend*

What a roller coaster ride! Good news, bad news, good days, bad days! We still pray for complete healing. Grace and peace to you through our Lord Jesus,
Nancy W., mother of groomsman at Eric's and Tammy's wedding

What a blessing you are!! May God continue to watch over you and the family. Your struggles and your faith in dealing with so much of life out of "your" control are humbling to me.
Wanda K, former co-worker of Eric's brother

Thursday, May 10, 2012, 5:04 p.m.

From home

We made it home … yesterday late. I have a "pain pump" that delivers 4mg of Dilaudid/hour, (*a synthetic derivative of Morphine, with potency about 10 times that of Morphine*), with up to six incremental 6mg doses [per day]. I also have a 24-hour companion by way of oxygen. (*The source is an oxygen concentrator – stationary device that provides oxygen in higher concentrations than available in ambient air; it runs continuously; and is delivered through a tube into a nasal cannula – two small nozzles that protrude into the patient's nostrils.*) We're all pretty fried.

The Dilaudid has me saying/doing/dreaming some pretty odd things. For example, last night I fell/leapt out of bed in response to a dream I was having. After pressing my "dose" button to get 6mg more Dilaudid, I went back to sleep. I honestly could sell tickets for my comedy show.

The oxygen concentrator we have sounds like a diesel sub. But, by 7 p.m. tonight we should have a quieter one delivered. On a happy note, I am super pleased that the concentrator can stay in one spot downstairs and, with the 50-foot cord, I can get around most of the house – the best thing is I can sleep [upstairs] in my own bed next to my lovely wife. Thank you God for simple blessings.

Physical therapy tomorrow is cancelled – there are bigger fish to fry. I am hopeful about restarting PT when we get closer to maintenance. Maintenance is still a possibility.

May have to type this last part standing ... I just can't focus/stay awake. We're taking things one day at a time. Improvement is in the realm of possible ... both on the O^2 and pain fronts. God has a plan and His plan is the best. We, with you, pray that healing me here and now is in that plan. Regardless, God will be glorified. He alone deserves all the praise and glory.

Friday, May 11, 2012, 10:01 p.m.

Heavy thoughts

My mind is awhirl with heavy thoughts today. Great to do on heavy pain meds. ☺

◆ SHORT-FORM MUSINGS:

How much do I need to change my eating habits?

How much should I push to exercise?

How far do I go with all the medical treatments/options?

The short answer on all this is ... I am still confused, but convinced of my need to rely on God's daily revelation and grace.

◆ MY LONGER FORM MUSINGS:

Misconception: It is all my fault; all mine to fix. As the head of the house, I see the pain and suffering endured by Tammy and the kids, caused by my cancer. It grieves me to see how much upheaval this lung cancer has brought. It seems, too, just as we dial in on a new norm, we get thrown a curve ball – like the last week in the hospital. I can all too easily assume responsibility for all of this. "I'm sorry," I want to say to my family. "I wish I could fix this." And so I spiral downward in guilt and shame. I seek for ways in which I can control this cancer, ways I can ease my family's pain. Yet nothing simple presents itself.

Truth: God is in control. This cancer didn't surprise God. And chances are really good that I didn't do anything to earn this cancer curse ... non-smoker, clean living. Sometimes God allows trials in this life because in His plan that is what is best. There is likely something (or lots of somethings) for me to learn in this, but God may be doing this for reasons totally apart from me – totally apart from my family. I may never know His reasons. His Word teaches, though, that He loves each of His children and will be faithful to bring to completion the work He started in us.

228

Application: God loves my family just like I have learned He loves me. As much as I want to be the know-it-all, helicopter-parent with regard to this cancer and my family, I can't do it. I have to turn Tammy, Timmy, and Ellie over to God. He will love them deeply and care for them way better than I could ever care for them. His path for them includes suffering (where my path for them would be a bed of roses), but that is okay, because we/I put our/my trust in God who is good and big.

Misconception: "Missed it by that much ..." There is a predetermined path for me to follow (A, then B, then C, then D, then E ...). If I miss a step along the way, I will have ruined God's plan for my life. I can only reap what I sow. My missing a step totally threw God off His game.

Truth: A blessed path. God's plan for my life is much more generous and forgiving in scope. At the present, I can choose to live an obedient life, aligned with the truth of God's Word, or, I can choose to sin/disobey. The more I sin, the further out of alignment with God's plan for my life I get. The way to get back on track is to confess my sin, turn from the bad choices, and follow God. So long as I make choices of obedience, I can know that I am in the will of God. God's will is not that easily foiled.

Application: My actions will not seal my cancer fate. God's blessing of healing is not contingent on my following a predetermined set of personal health choices. It's tempting to think that if I misstep somehow, I do so only to sign my own death warrant, that every stray French fry or skipped lap around the neighborhood pulls God off His game. This smacks of how the Pharisees lived in Jesus' day. This level of perfection is unattainable, this side of eternity. This weight of "must do" is crushing and leads to great acts of hypocrisy and deceit. It forces a graceless life.

I can err the other direction too though, as I say, "I am free in Christ." For example, all food is blessed, right? There is no distinction between clean and unclean; bring on the bacon! Yet at some point, my bad choices with food and exercise become acts of idolatrous worship. I bow down to the stainless-steel god of Kenmore. My abs melt before the mighty lord TiVo. And here I sit well over my goal weight with no slowing in sight. (I am currently 240-plus pounds.)

♦ SO, WHERE DOES THIS LEAVE ME? CONFUSED AT THE MOMENT.

On one hand, God already has my days numbered. The more legalistic I get about my cancer care, the worse life becomes. I live life looking over my shoulder ... living in guilt over the Hershey's Kiss I just ate. On the other hand, I can still make better choices and help myself feel better. Unfortunately, the cancer battle has me so tired that I don't want to take the energy or time to introduce more disciplines in my life right now – even if they would help. (Just ask Tammy how I react to her tinkering with the menu.)

This is where I am reminded again that Christianity is not a list of do's and don'ts. It is a relationship with our Risen Savior. I wake each day and seek His guidance, His presence, His blessing. Along each step of the day I try to follow Him. When I succeed, I celebrate. When I fail, I seek forgiveness and revel in His unending grace.

I am back to living life – one day at a time. There is no secret code, no quick fix to get me out of this cancer. I don't know how many days God has given me. This round of chemo could work great and maintenance is just around the corner. Or, the pain meds/oxygen could be a new regular fixture, and more days of nasty cancer-killing (body-killing) drugs are ahead of me. Only God knows.

It is altogether too easy for me to borrow trouble from tomorrow. Way too easy.

"Eric's areas for help needed" ... shout if you are local and have desire to help: Reclaim garage (spice cabinet job is almost done). Weeding (way behind). Swap out our failing wireless router. As always ... Thanks!!!!

~ *Responses from Family and Friends* ~

Once again God uses you, Eric, to reach out to me (and countless others I am certain). The whole battle of eating healthy and maintaining a healthy weight is one I have done my best to ignore for most of my life. Thanks be to our Lord on high who makes all things possible no matter how impossible they seem. I will continue to pray for God's strength as you navigate through diet and exercise choices (and as I follow my program). Thank you for publicizing your musings ... they mean so much to so many. God's blessings to you and your family.

Ella B., Village

Eric – I hope you don't mind if I share this post (or rather part of it) with a group of hurting woman that I moderate on-line. This is so helpful to a different type of "painful" situation than yours but it so applies. Thank you for sharing.

Candace L., Village

So glad you are home! Praying for pain relief and peaceful hearts. I just sent you an email regarding similarities between your post and another CaringBridge post I read today. I hope it encourages you like it did me. God's Word is truly alive!

Dawn R., Tammy's sister

So glad that you are home. So much more comfortable than the hospital. You've got a great attitude about the O² and pain meds. Way to stay focused on the positive! Love to you and your family. Praying for you all.

Mythraie G., Village

Eric, it's been a while since I've last posted. The silence does not mean you are not in my thoughts and prayers on a daily basis. We all continue to think about you. Hang in there ...keep your faith!

Frank P., Intel

I will do some weeding for you towards the end of next week.

Laura D., neighbor

Wow! You sure have a gift that touches people deep. You are an incredible person and a great friend. I admire you for your love of the Lord, determined personality to accomplish what you set your mind to,and all of your incredible talents just to name a few. Your friendship is precious to us and I just want to tell you that we love all of you and pray for you every day. Hugs!

Pat and Melanie D., close friends

Saturday, May 12, 2012, 10:22 p.m.

Highlights

Slowly but surely I am clawing my way back out of the chemo/hospital hole. This morning, I had the pleasure of watching Ellie play basketball with her YMCA team. I'm thankful that my dad helped make it possible for me to watch her play. Later, a friend came over and helped me reclaim the garage space.

My mid-life crisis – our beautiful new, red Prius V – is now happily parked where no bird can sully it. The spice cabinet project is just missing a lick of paint ... spices are put away, doors on, and in use. Then, my brother-in-law and his family came over and switched out our wireless router. I was so thankful that he took on the whole project ... gremlins included. There was no way I could have done these projects on my own.

Thank you to everyone who has offered to help. (Side note: Weeds in my backyard ... you are on notice. ☺)

♦ AS FAR AS MY HEALTH GOES:

I'm still on oxygen 24/7 and making full use of the pain pump (ongoing dose of 4mg/hour plus multiple hits of 6mg any given hour). The Dilaudid makes for some very funny, less than lucid moments. Sorry Tammy.

My walking is s-l-o-w, and I get winded so easily. An old "friend" from worse health days is back, too. I'm having a hard time swallowing. Just a normal swallow and I can be thrown into coughing spasms from having what little was in my mouth go down the wrong pipe.

Sleep is rough ... I'm hopeful tonight will be smoother. And with the steep increase in pain meds, I have some pretty strong "twitches" back as well. Please pray that we would have endurance and, God willing, some health improvement very soon.

This is hard. Super hard. Like I have often said though, we continue to trust God. We know He is in control and He will be glorified. Until we know more for sure, we keep praying, waiting, and trusting.

One last note – Happy Mother's Day! (a slight bit early). Tammy you are a great mom and loving wife. I am blessed to have you as my partner through this "Mr. Toad's Wild Ride." Even in the toughest days when our relationship is stretched thin, I know I can count on you. You love God and you love me.

Thank you! Moms [both Tammy's and Eric's] ... thanks for the way you have stepped up these last months. You have shown me and my family so much love. You've played so many kids games, been there for us through so many tears, and made so much possible. Thanks!

Tuesday, May 15, 2012, 11:37 a.m.
Fuzzy wuzzy ... again

As predicted, on day 14 after this chemo round, my hair started to come out in clumps. I still have quite a bit, but a lot has come out over the last 48 hours or so, too. Maybe this time Ellie will be okay with my shaving off the hair and being done with it.

The pain in my left chest and the fatigue are still quite strong. I've backed down ever so slightly from the self-administered pain pump meds. The Providence Home Services respiratory nurse just left our home – I'm now approved for a mobile oxygen cylinder [oxygen concentrator still in use]. They did have to make a compromise on the O^2 sat scores. My clinic wanted 96 as a consistent score, but they had to back it down to 90 so I could qualify for the smaller portable tanks. The ongoing trick will be to breathe through my nose and talk less. Tammy will appreciate that. ☺ (Side note: I'm somewhat disappointed in the testing outcome. I had hoped the O^2 issues were much more minor and on their way to greatly improving.)

Thanks to great friends, we've been given two nights (this coming Thursday and Friday) on the Coast. I am hopeful that the time away will be healing to Tammy and me. I've noticed (in myself mainly) that as the stress levels go up, the more prone I am to snap at Tammy. It is altogether too unfortunate that I strike out against her ... my biggest ally in all of this. Here's to showing better love to Tammy in the days ahead.

As I have said before, we keep trusting God. None of this is catching Him by surprise. So ... one day at a time.

Wednesday, May 16, 2012, 8:26 p.m.

Twitchy and tired

All in all, today has been pretty good. Timmy got special time with a play therapist – more to report as we know more, today was just a meet and greet. Ellie keeps learning/ growing. She's super close to losing her second tooth. Last night, the family took special "craft" time and shaved my head. The chemo had really started to work against my freshly acquired hair.

On the whole, I have been super tired, twitchy, and not very hungry today. On the plus side, my dad and I hit Lowe's. The new portable oxygen tanks are working well. Beyond Lowe's I was able to shuffle through the neighborhood for one loop.

Please join us in asking God to sustain us in all of this. God's timing is perfect Logging off for now. Hopefully tomorrow I will be more awake.

Saturday, May 19, 2012, 11:35 p.m.

Beach and ER

Quick update. Canon Beach was great – minus the oxygen concentrator debacle yesterday. A huge thanks to all the "elves" that made our stay at the beach possible.

Regarding the O^2 debacle and the less-than-helpful Providence Home Services Oxygen folks – even when they knew I had a down oxygen concentrator needing an urgent swap, they dinked around and made the swap extra hard. Huge thanks to my parents for making the drive to the Portland warehouse and then to Cannon Beach ... "speedy delivery." We are blessed to have so many generous people around us. The kids also enjoyed their time without mom and dad. It was great to get home and hug them.

Today, though, was marked with an increase in shortness of breath. Any activity sent me gasping for more air. The doc suggested I "gut it out" until Monday, but I wasn't at ease waiting. So, here I lie in the hospital, waiting for a battery of tests. More as we know it. Thanks in advance for your prayers, notes, etc. we are so loved, even in the midst of this big storm.

~ *Responses from Family and Friends* ~

You and your family are so loved. Praying for you and Tammy and the kids during this difficult time. Praying the doctors will be given divine wisdom to figure out what is going on with you and your lungs right now. Praying, praying, like so many people.   *Terri B., Village*

Lifting you and your family up to the Lord for healing, strength, endurance, and peace. Love to all of you!   *Dan and Jane E., Village*

Praying for you, Tammy, Ellie, Timmy, and your extended family. Remember the footprint in the sand. God is carrying you through this storm in His loving arms. Love to you from our family.
Lynda F., Village

Hang in there! Praying for continued healing, return of energy, and ability to not require the O^2 assist. Keep shining!   *Fred J., Intel*

Sitting on my deck praying for you. May God give you His peace and miraculous healing. So sorry you had to come home to go yet again to the ER. A big big hug to you, Tammy, Ellie, and Timmy.
Chick L., Village Life Group

Thoughts with you Eric. Too bad you had to feel like you were in Mexico City while in Canon Beach ... Hope it gets better really soon. Courage!   *Hugues M., Intel*

Eric, our prayers are with you and Tammy! Keep the faith. So sorry for the ER trip. Hang in there.   *Chuck and Doris H., Village*

Hang in there Eric. Your courage and resolve is an inspiration to us all.   *Jon O., Intel*

Monday, May 21, 2012, 9:31 p.m.

More mixed news

Monday (at least for those ... unlike me ...who have a grasp on what day today is) has been a blur. From a pure accomplishment perspective, I had the extra fluid drained off my lung and was discharged from the hospital.

After a bit of an emotional breakdown with the doctor early this morning, I bought time before the next chemo – from today, when it was scheduled, to Thursday, the day after Ellie's school program. She has a speaking part.

I'm still waiting for the lung draining to translate into improvement in my breathing. I'd like to go from recliner to bathroom without feeling as though I am going to pass out from lack of breath.

Thankfully, in all of this, we are more than adequately covered. I have a home nurse for just about everything, pain pump meds, oxygen, palliative/hospice insurance, Intel short-term-disability – and, obviously, beyond the things seen, we are even more covered by the things unseen.

I often pray God's angelic force to protect our home. This is sacred/holy ground. I know God loves all His children and will minister as needed and generously to each of us. My wife and kids are in His hands.

So ... here's a brief discussion on the "elephant in the room:" How much longer? How much more? Against how much more can my body and spirit hold up? The short answer is ... I don't know. A growing part of me is just "done." Not that I would do anything stupid, but this is hard ... very hard.

Dr. Andersen agreed to pull in the PET scan to after the next chemo round ... three weeks earlier than first planned. That should give us a sense for how effective the Adriamycin is. If I had to bet, I'd say it won't be effective. That said, Andersen suggested that as of today it is still too early to call. The huge fluid buildup in the left lung could be an indicator of worse things to come, or it could a sign of the drug working and the scar tissue fighting back. We simply don't know.

236

As I suspect my kids will read this journal someday, let me be clear – I am not giving up.

Tammy and I have pushed through these last eight months and done our best to stay faithful to who God has called us to be. We will continue to fight, knowing that God alone has our days numbered. We'll do our best to listen to Him for His guidance. While I don't want to leave my family, I know eternity with God (and without sin) awaits me. I also know that while we are apart, God will care for you deeply. You'll never be alone. And for those who call on God as Savior and Lord – I will see you again in eternity. I am excited about that.

May God find us faithful each day of the week. He is in control even when we are not. He understands that big picture "why" ... even when we cannot. In Jesus we trust.

~ *Responses from Family and Friends* ~

We continue to check in and pray for you. Thank you for your updates, Eric. Praying also for your patience and love for each other when stress is high. It is easy to snap under much less stressful and painful circumstances, so I can't imagine what a practice in patience (among other things) this must be. From across the miles,
Jim and Krista S., missionary friends in Belgium

Thank you for bravely sharing the good, the bad, and the ugly. You articulate words that many people feel, but for some reason, choose not to express. By your actions, you model to others how to better express their fears, doubts, hopes, and prayers. Blessings to you, Tammy, and your precious kids, as you walk this difficult journey.
Nathan H., formerly at Village

Nathan H. said it well. Thanks, Eric, for sharing everything. You have helped and blessed me through my journey of difficulty as well. I pray our journey on this earth does not end for a long time to come.
Marcus W., groomsman at Eric's and Tammy's wedding

Sometimes it is hard to know what to say to bring peace and comfort – please know that you and your family are on my heart and that I am praying often ...   *Ella B., Village*

Tuesday, May 22, 2012, 10:29 p.m.

How hard to push?

Tuesday ... another day done. Breathing remains pretty difficult – especially when I try something arduous – like walking to the bathroom. Sadly, I'm very fatigued day and night. Thankfully, in about three weeks we should know more about whether or not the chemo is working. The PET scan is pulled in by three weeks. Neither Tammy nor I want to waste time on solution(s) that won't crush the cancer.

I spoke with the doctor's office today about the lack of breathing improvement, and they suggested I watch and wait. This Thursday (chemo day) they can do more assessment and figure out if I'm needing a different approach (home catheter of the lung, week-long-surgery and recovery to reconnect the lung lining, or "other").

None of the "solutions" seem fun, but that seems like par for the course we're on – this wild, wacky, and abnormal course that God has allowed us to play for the last eight months.

Tomorrow they may adjust my pain pump meds up. I seem to be hitting the "bolus" button [for extra doses of Dilaudid] a lot. Hopefully if we increase the average hourly flow, I won't have to layer on extra hits. And, perhaps with a slightly different med mix, I won't be as "out to lunch" as I seem to be throughout the day and night. (I wouldn't be so frustrated if I didn't know how "checked out" I get, but I do know when I am acting goofy "stoned.")

Thanks for your continued prayers. We need to keep the faith as we go through this day by day. As I sit here and type, I am reminded of just how needed each breath is ... the oxygen pump is on low and even though the oxygen saturation numbers are reading okay ... I really don't feel comfortable just sitting here breathing. Crazy.

Here's to taking things one day at a time.

~ *Responses from Family and Friends* ~

We continue to lift you and your family up, Eric. I can't help but wonder if I could be so brave in this situation, but I also know that we have an awesome God who strengthens and upholds you. May His peace reign in your home and family today.

Lisa B., friend in Boston

We have so much love in our hearts for you, Tammy, Ellie, and Timmy. We continually place our trust in our Lord and pray for protection, strength, peace, and healing. Our Lord and His angels are surrounding all. Hebrews 13:5 says, "I will never leave you nor forsake you."

Bonnie and George J., Tammy's aunt and uncle in Arizona

Love and hugs to you, Tammy, and the kids. Reading your post today was hard to do, but nothing as compared to what you are living out. Asking the Lord to give you peace, grace and direction for what is ahead. Trusting the Lord with you in all of this. Love, *JerriLyn K., friend*

We pray, we pray! God, please provide Eric with Your miraculous healing and Your peace and comfort as You wrap Your loving arms around him, Tammy, Ellie and Timmy.

Chick and Scott L., Village Life Group

I continue to pray regularly for your healing and for strength and peace of heart and mind for you and Tammy, Ellie, and Timmy. Since you brought up the "elephant in the room" I thought I'd let you know that I also pray regularly for single moms and dads I know whose spouse has passed away. I pray fervently that God will restore your health and give you more time with your family here on earth, but I also wanted you to know that should God choose to call you Home sooner than any of us would like, I will also continue to remember Tammy and Ellie and Timmy in my prayers. None of us know God's plans or the number of days that He has given us on this earth, but like you, I trust that He will be faithful to watch over our loved ones when we are gone.

Becky J., formerly at Village

The Heerwagen family is still in much prayer from our family and many friends in Boring, Ore., at Good Shepherd Community Church; rejoicing in the charm of your 1st-grade daughter and her debut, and petitioning our great God for health to return. Grace and Peace in the name of our Lord and Savior Jesus Christ,

Nancy W., mother of groomsman at Eric's and Tammy's wedding

Wednesday, May 23, 2012, 11:28 p.m.

Banner night for Ellie

Tonight Ellie was a big star of her 1st-grade spring show. She was so excited, especially to have a speaking part. As I rolled into the RESERVED seats pyloned off at the front center, Ellie's face lit up. What a blessing to be there and cheer on my little girl.

Other parts of today – "maybe-chemo-eve" – have been exceptionally rough. Conversations nobody wants to have. Breathing issues getting worse. X-ray now booked before chemo. Huge drowsiness that doesn't seem to shake off until ... well ... nighttime.

Please join us in praying for very specific guidance on decisions that have to be made tomorrow. We so seldom get "writing on the wall guidance." We'd still love to have conviction and peace to go with the must-decide-now choices. Then as we push beyond tomorrow, we pray for being OK with the direction God gives us.

As of tonight, I am officially in the ..."I-can't-do-this-anymore space. Please let us wrap this up nicely and go back to having life reign abundant ... even if it means through my death."

Thanks! We'll know more, later this week as to what official next steps "could" be. I say "could" be, as we've found plans are always subject change. Thankfully, the Planner never changes. Here's to holding on to His unchanging and ever-loving hand.

~ Responses from Family and Friends ~

So glad you were there to see Ellie's acting debut. What a wonderful memory for all of you. Praying for healing first ... and wisdom, comfort, peace and love. Hugs, *Chick L., Village Life Group*

So happy that your face was the one Ellie got to see up front and center. Prayers continue for you, Tammy and the children.
Ysela B., Intel

So glad you got to see Ellie's performance! Praying for wisdom and guidance today for your family and your medical team.
Nathan H., formerly at Village

~ *Responses from Family and Friends (cont.)* ~

Glad you could be there for Ellie's performance. I can't imagine your conflict today, being so weary of the challenges and yet having something like Ellie's performance to remind you why you fight on. Praying for clear direction and peace about God's will for you and your family. Still praying that complete healing in this world is right around the corner. Blessings, *Kris K., friend*

It's hard to read about the reality of the situation. I can't imagine how hard it was to write about it. I felt sad as I read your post, realizing we might have to say goodbye to you for a while. It's easy to keep hoping for a miracle and not feel the sadness, but this time I did. Like you said, it's great to know that we'll be together for eternity. It's also comforting to know that if God chooses to take you home in the near future, you'll be freed from all the suffering down here. As I read your post, my mind went through multiple scenes of your ministry I've seen: house leadership, migrant camps, balloons, promotional video for short-term ministry, faithful support of the work I'm in, etc., etc. It's great to see how God is using you to touch the lives of people around you. *Mythraie G., Village*

"He leads me beside still waters. He restores my soul." Rest well tonight, Heerwagens. Your ministry to your family, friends, and "neighbors" is God-focused and we are recipients of how well you love Jesus. Just today my 8-year-old was telling my 6-year-old about the chocolate chip cookies you made without sugar. Remember the AWANA story time? We do, and we are grateful to have these remarkable imprints on our hearts from you, from God and back to you! Tammy, Eric, Ellie, and Timmy – we are praying for your night tonight and for your tomorrow. As you live and write hard words, I cry with you. God, we ask You to make the pain bearable, to remove the cancer completely and to continue to weave Your mighty arms around these four precious children of Yours. Good night and sleep well, *Dawn Denice R., Village*

Hooray for Ellie! Awesome that you got to share that memory with her. Something to cherish even when tomorrow is uncertain. Having her daddy in the audience will always be remembered as a blessing. Peaceful rest tonight, and strength and wisdom be with you tomorrow. *Mike F., Intel*

241

Thursday, May 24, 2012, 11:53 p.m.

Scary ... not breathing

Okay ... thought I wrote an update earlier today. Guess I just imagined it. That happens with strong pain meds.

This morning's meeting with Dr. Andersen led to postponed chemo and an afternoon handoff to a lung specialist. When we met the new doctor, he came in and introduced himself as "Tony." Seems sharp and with it.

The plan to help me breath again is to catheterize my left lung [this means another surgery]. The catheter treatment will, over the next three to six months, heal up the separation in the lung lining as well. The other possibility is that the cancer has progressed much further, and thus repairing the ongoing fluid fill ups will be way more difficult.

Even tonight, on the eve of surgery, I found myself terrified and winded ... I just cannot catch my breath. Tammy and I (along with many others) are hopeful that the procedure will fix the breathing problem and allow us to focus more wholly on beating the lung cancer. Thanks in advance for your ongoing encouragement.

♦ HERE ARE A FEW REQUESTS THAT
MAY NOT BE ON YOUR RADAR:

Pray that the hospital bed just installed in our home [in the main floor living room] would help both Tammy and me get better sleep. I need less thrashing in my sleep.

Pray against anxiety. It is altogether too easy to go into freak-out mode.

Pray the kids will roll with the punches as they come; we know God cares deeply for them and for us.

Pray for less drug-induced "seeing things." On my part, 99 out of 100 times I can immediately decipher what my mind "sees" and rediscover the truth. That said, I know the number of weird things I see, hear, etc. is increasing.

Saturday, May 26, 2012, 9:45 p.m.

Back at Home ... now what?

(Short update via iPhone –)

Surgery done and successful from the surgeon's point of view. They siphoned out four liters – equivalent to four large bottles of soda. I should get half a liter [just over two cups] each day for the next few weeks.

The really strong left-side pain hasn't abated much. One possible explanation is that cancer is the main pain source. If that is the case, the catheter installed today won't help. Tuesday, I will call Dr. Andersen and have a discussion on "possibilities" in all of this. We just don't know what to expect and how to balance the options.

A nurse visits [here at home] tomorrow morning ... hopefully I'll be with it more; pain meds loop me out.

~ *Responses from Family and Friends* ~

As I look at a two-liter Diet Coke bottle and then imagine two of those ... ugh! What a (insert adjective of choice) drag! I hope the catheter does some good and pain subsides soon. Thanks again for sharing this wretched experience so honestly with all of us. Your words and experiences make me look a lot deeper into myself, make me cherish my family even more, and help me count my blessings when life's trivial annoyances seem important. Please understand that you are touching hundreds of lives through your story. That said, I'd still rather have a smiling, healthy Eric walking around, and I'll keep hoping for total healing. Keep up the fight, my friend. Hope tonight is restful.

Mike F., Intel

"We always thank God, the Father of our Lord Jesus Christ, when we pray for you, because we have heard of your faith in Christ Jesus and of the love you have for all God's people— the faith and love that spring from the hope stored up for you in heaven and about which you have already heard in the true message of the gospel" (Colossians 1:3-5 NIV). "For this reason, since the day we heard about you, we have not stopped praying for you. We continually ask God to fill you with the knowledge of His will through all the wisdom and understanding that the Spirit gives, so that you may live a life worthy of the Lord and please Him in every way: bearing fruit in every good work, growing in the knowledge of God, being strengthened with all power according to his glorious might so that you may have great endurance and patience," (Colossians 1:9-11 NIV). Eric and Tammy, these verses make me think of you and this walk that you have been on. I pray you continue to sense God's peace as you continue to endure. Love to you.   *Tracy D., formerly at Village*

Decisions are difficult ... we struggle with them as we process the pros and cons. I know this decision was part of a thoughtful process for you and for your family. Continuing to pray that you, Tammy, Ellie and Timmy feel the Lord's arms wrapped around you! Please know you are in my thoughts and prayers Eric.   *Colleen H., Tammy's friend*

God bless you Eric. I feel that God is very much in this situation and in your decision. You are fighting the good fight. I'm lifting up you and Tammy and Ellie and Timmy as well as your parents and in-laws.

Candace L., Village

I've always known you to make smart, insightful decisions. Wish you didn't have to add this very dioicous one to the list. Praying for strength and peace for you and your family.   *Kathleen M., Intel*

Eric, that's not selfish in the least. If your decision is in line with what you believe God is calling you toward, then you're absolutely doing the right thing. Continuing to pray for you.

Chris and Beth M., Tammy's brother and wife

What a beautifully honest blog you have written today, Eric. You sound at peace about the decision to discontinue the chemo, and I ask God to bless you profoundly in that. We will all continue to pray for your healing, because we know that God is able. We will also pray for you, Tammy, and the children each day, that He will provide just the amount of grace, mercy, comfort and love to each of you. In prayers and friendship, "He will wipe every tear from their eyes ..." (Rev. 21:4).

Terri B., Village

Praying for peace for your entire family, Eric. I know this decision is not an easy one, but like you have done for the past eight months, you are giving it to God. You have given so many of us a gift by the way you honor our Lord. Praying for a great week with your family.

Dorothy G., formerly at Village

Eric, so many have said it so well already. I would simply add that if faith is the light that guides us, then you are truly a bright and shining light to all of us. With deepest respect,   *Greg B., Intel*

Eric, you are a man after God's own heart. And He is directing your path. You have no need to apologize to anyone for the wisdom He has given you. You and your family are held in His hand, and His hand will hold and comfort you all along the way because You ARE obedient to His voice and seeking His face always. I hurt so much, for you and your family ... and I pray for your quality of life to remain strong and joyfully fulfilled each day. Hang on hard to His hand and love your family and love God and others, and Your life will continue as always to bring God glory. Thank you for sharing your heart and letting God shine through you in every corner of your life.   *Becki C., Village*

~ *Responses from Family and Friends (cont.)* ~

We love you, Eric. I don't claim to understand the way that "God is sovereign" merges with the truth that "prayers change things." But I DO know that God is indeed sovereign and that He will not allow any of us to live one less day than He has numbered. Know that Stuart and I understand your decision and completely support you in it. We love you, Tammy. I admire the way you have handled the last eight months. You are an example of what a godly, faithful wife is and I have never been more proud of you. Know that I am here to support you in absolutely any way I can. You may ask for absolutely anything, without apology/explanation/hesitation and if it is within my power, it will be done. You have both, indeed, walked this journey well. The Lord is pleased with your testimony and the way you have shown us all the way to trust

Love, Dawn R., Tammy's sister

Oh, Eric, my heart is so heavy as you have had to come to this decision. I've been praying that you would know the Lord's peace with each step you are to take. I'm glad you are feeling His peace in this decision. You continue to shine with the Lord's grace and love, Eric. Even in this, you are being faithful to follow Him. This is such a testament to who you are as a man and as one who seeks to give glory to the Lord in all things. Not many would be able to do this. Of course it doesn't mean that you will not be sad, will not wish for a better outcome – we all would and we all do. As you have said, the Lord is big enough to take care of everything that is to come. It is something that we must hold on to; we can do nothing more, nothing less. We will continue to pray for you, continue to trust God in this and that you, Tammy and the kids will know beyond any doubt that God's grace and love is big enough ...even now. All our love, *JerriLyn K. and family, friends*

Eric, I am moved by your words with each journal entry. Your unwavering faith in our loving Lord and Savior has been an inspiration beyond measure. I will forever be blessed to have had the opportunity to get to know you through your words. You and your family continue to be in my prayers. God bless.

Lorri S., friend of Eric's aunt Ruthie in Colorado

Tuesday, May 29, 2012, 9:15 p.m.

Quality over quantity

There comes a point in a lot of cancer journeys where "quality of life" and "quantity of life" have to be balanced.

This week, I believe is one of those decision points for me. Recovery from the lung surgery has been difficult, and the pain levels higher than expected. The possibility for NED (no evidence of disease) and/or improvement from more chemo seems to lessen with each new chemo dose.

I love Tammy and the kids deeply. I would love to grow old with them, see our kids through all the great milestones of life, meet our grandchildren, etc. I passionately hate to see my family suffer because of my suffering through cancer. If there were a magic wand (fictional, I know) I could wave to fix everything, I'd seriously consider it. If this were just a matter of my getting the right "recipe" of key lessons [to learn] … or finding the chemo drug that is just right for me, or …

Unfortunately, after careful consideration this week, I don't believe more chemo is a choice.

The choice I make to discontinue chemo, may seem designed to shorten my days on earth and "escape" out from under the suffering. Please know it is so much more than that …

Rather, daily I am called to step out by faith into whatever situation He calls me to. Chemo, or no chemo, is not a reflection of my faithfulness to God. I don't believe either choice to be sinful.

Looking back over these last eight or so months, we – the whole team – have done amazingly well with all the curve balls. I believe we have truly striven to honor God each painful step of the way. (We've not been perfect …but we've done well.)

I believe I can be faithful to God – even in choosing to discontinue chemo. It keeps coming back to daily choices I make – ones to follow Him or to follow my own sinful desires. It is much less about chemo or no chemo.

I am and will continue to do all I can to stay faithful to God, as I am called to do, and to fight the cancer – minus chemo.

It grieves me to think of suffering yet to come; of hearts broken at the prospect of losing me and the shared experiences, etc. But as with all other areas, I trust God will faithfully care for and love His chosen, forever-family. I know Tammy and Ellie are already a part, and by faith I count Timmy there soon, too. [Ed. note: Timmy gave his life to Jesus on April 16, 2013, at age 5.]

I have peace about discontinuing the chemo. God will do what He will do. He will bring us all through this for His glory.

Again, in all this, I don't doubt that God is in control and I am not. There is nothing I can or can't do to "force" God's hand. Taking or not taking chemo does not necessarily corner God into a specific reaction. He will take me Home when He chooses and how He chooses. Until that day, may He find me – may He find us – faithful.

Please pray for Tammy, the kids and our extended families as they wrestle through the implications of my latest decision. Pray that we'd all trust in God's plan and timing.

[There were 234 responses in the guestbook
from May 1-31, 2012.]

June 2012

~ *The Ninth Month* ~

Saturday, June 2, 2012 – 12:53 p.m.

Overdue update

When last I wrote, Tuesday, May 29, I said that we would be ending chemo and starting hospice.

Thursday, May 31, Tammy and I met with Dr. Andersen. It was a very hard discussion. I cried as I told him I just couldn't do any more treatment. Thankfully, he said our choice was reasonable. Tammy hoped for one more "hail Mary" option, but Dr. Andersen said the rest of the plays we have to run are all small-gain runs.

I also broke down when Dr. Andersen brought out the POLST form. Now the goal is to provide comfort and to ease the dying process. The POLST form aligns the advanced directive choice with the goal above. I am no longer "full code" – do all you can to keep my body alive. Now I am – "allow natural death to occur." The last noteworthy requisite for entering hospice is a life expectancy of six months or less. That hits hard to think about.

Now – with hospice, everything goes through them. Dr. Andersen is no longer the lead player. All calls, care, etc. go through the main hospice switchboard. We now are instructed to call hospice and not 911 if things go south for me. Hospice assumes care for me – baths three times a week, nurse visits here at the house, prescription management, and help for Tammy and the kids. It seems like a really excellent program, and so far the people have been super loving.

Over the last number of days, I have tried to journal more, but one thing or the other impedes me – like falling asleep repeatedly. So, it's now Saturday, no excuses.

First, thank you!!! The notes of encouragement and support have been HUGE. I am so glad that I have friends going along with me. Some of you have mentioned my faith in this ... I can only credit God for the good you see.

I write this from my hospital bed in the middle of our living room. My body is clean and fresh – the bathing nurse just left. My left lung is freshly drained of its daily 500 ml (*just over 2 cups*) of "ick" ... technical term. I continue to medicate to thin my blood and keep clotting away (*twice daily self-administered shots in the abdomen*).

An invitation was sent out to those praying for Eric and his family, requesting "finger-print leaves" (See page 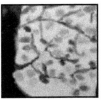 **219) . Responses were so numerous that there were enough "leaves" to create two huge prayer tree posters like the one above). They were hung in the living room so Eric could easily see them both from his hospital bed.**

The phone should ring soon to set my early afternoon appointment with a [hospice] whole-health nurse who will make sure the latest med changes made are working well.

Yesterday's hospice-admit team added several non-twitch meds to my mix in the hopes of better sleep for me – and for Tammy. The stress level is high in our house – especially with so many "experts" coming in to do their own triage-admit process. Despite the stress, the peace quotient is high, too. Most of the time, I have a calm about where this all goes.

I remind myself (and others) that in all this, God still could heal this side of eternity. He is able, but if He chooses to not heal until I get to His side in Heaven, I'm okay with that too.

Tonight, my side of the family celebrates my parents' 50th

anniversary (as my dad says, "47 years of happily married life" ☺.) I'm looking forward to celebrating tonight. We've had way too much mourning/sorrow – especially this last week.

In the days ahead pray that my family would grieve as they need. Pray also that if there are details to be figured out before I pass, that we'd have the time and energy to address them (e.g., burial, bills, etc.) God is good and He is in control. He is walking hand in hand with us through this. It is the grace of Christ that gives me hope. May God bless the week ahead.

~ *Responses from Family and Friends* ~

Good Morning, Eric! I am thinking of you and praying for you this morning as I have often done although I have not signed your guestbook yet. There is a leaf on your beautiful prayer tree from our family! We serve an awesome God! I rejoice with you to know that God is providing peace and comfort for you and your family at this time. You are an amazing young man living out God's plan for your life. Thank you for all of those balloon animals and characters that you have created at all of the children's activities as a witness and testimony for our Savior Jesus Christ! The children – and adults –have loved them! Thank you for sharing this skill with others. You are precious in His sight!   *Gloria W., Village*

I just want to say from the bottom of my heart what a great man you are. You are truly a wonderful Christian man, a wonderful husband, father, son, and friend. God is so proud of you that He can call you His son. I just want to thank you for praying for my family, asking how my family is doing during my loss of my dad. Your prayers meant a lot. I will continue to pray for you, Tammy, and the kids always. *Erik C., Village*

God will comfort you always. I'm praying for peace for your family as you transition into hospice. And a big hug for you across the Internet!!
Pam M., Intel

Wow. Hard news to digest. Eric, you are incredible, as an individual and as part of our family. I love you and cannot wait until I see you fully healed, on whichever side of Heaven God chooses (but I continue to hope and pray for this side).   *Shellie M., Tammy's sister*

Sunday, June 3, 2012, 11:25 p.m.

Pray for sleep

All in all a decent day – a large portion of the day was spent in and out of sleep. During this evening, we had our life group from church here and shared in lots of laughter and some tears. We are so blessed to have such good friends walking hand-in-hand with us through all this. As night draws upon us, I am hopeful sleep will be so much better than other nights. Please join us in praying for rest during the night. If sleep isn't great tonight, though, I know that hospice is just a call away. They have committed to work with us to make me comfortable. I really appreciate how much of a help hospice is and will be. We continue to trust God. Blessings!

~ Responses from Family and Friends ~

Eric, your journal is an extraordinary witness to your faith in our God and His provision for eternal life with Him for those who are called by His name. May it bring life to others who are lost to God's wonderful promises. We continue to pray for you and your family, especially for your parents and close extended family. Grace and peace to you,
Nancy W., mother of groomsman at Eric's and Tammy's wedding

Eric, I look forward to seeing you, Tammy, and the kids on Friday, my friend. Your strength of character, unmatched perseverance, and warmth provide a lasting presence we're all privileged to have in our lives. With our love and prayers for strength and peace, *Don and Ang B., Intel*

Eric and Tammy, our hearts are full as we read this! You all have fought the good fight and I know God is saying well done my good and faithful servants. May God richly bless your time together as a family and give you a peace that surpasses all understanding. We love you and continue to lift you up to God in prayer! *Dan and Jane E., Village*

Eric, I continue to be amazed at your courage and strength. I can't imagine how you feel writing these words and how you are so strong in making these choices. Am praying for a miracle – big or small – to give you peace. God bless you all. *Laura B., Intel*

~ *Responses from Family and Friends (cont.)* ~

Eric, I don't know if you remember me. We attended Village several years ago and I was involved in the music ministry. Our paths crossed occasionally when you were doing some of the skits, etc. In fact, the image I have of you in my head is you storming down the aisle in the old sanctuary acting out some part. I am so thankful that someone at Village asked me to pray for you and told me about this site. I have been lurking for months – praying often, but not knowing what to say. I have been so touched by your journal. I am in awe of your faith and love of the Lord. Believe me, He shines through your words! Thank you for sharing with all of us. Thank you for allowing us "in," to pray, laugh, and cry with you. Oftentimes I find myself remembering how small and insignificant my problems are compared to what others are going through (sorry). Anyway, I just think that this journal, with all your entries and the guestbook, is an incredible legacy of your faith and love of God and your family. My prayers tonight are for peace and comfort as God holds all of you in His loving arms. *Lea Z., formerly of Village*

You have had to make the hardest decisions this week for sure. I'm glad the Hospice Team is in the picture for you ... they are a good team and want to address any and every concern you have ... so don't hesitate to mention or ask anything ... that's why they are there. I continue to pray for you, Tammy and the kids.... praying for courage, rest, peace and more moments together. Love you, *JerriLyn K., friend*

It's really hard to know what to say but I want you to know that I'm thinking of you and praying for you. I'm praying for incredible comfort and peace through this difficult time. If God chooses to take you home now, I'm thrilled for the freedom you will experience. For Tammy, Ellie, and Timmy my heart aches. I know they will always miss you while on this earth. I will continue to pray for them. *Mythraie G., Village*

Eric, Praying with you that you get good and peaceful rest tonight. You and your family are truly amazing and full of inspiration! God bless you all tonight. Know that you are in my thoughts and prayers daily. Blessings, *Shelley J., Village*

253

Thursday, June 7, 2012, 3:51 p.m.

Thankful

It almost goes without saying, but I am surrounded by so many who love and care for my family. The hospice team rocks. They even made an unscheduled call today to adjust dosing on my pain meds. Tomorrow I get to visit with the hospice doctor when she comes – she can further fine-tune things as needed.

Our friends, and friends of friends, are lifting us before God – seeking God's healing hand. So many of you have simply made yourselves available. One set of friends dropped in for a movie, another set came to clean, yet others came to read and pray. Thanks.

The meds are kicking in. Just for grins I'll type what comes and won't fix the errors. Just thought a window into my drug-addled brain could be fun. Hydromorphone, (*a synthetic derivative of Morphine, about 10 times as strong*), is strong stuff and I am drowsy with it merrily pumping away into my body at an even faster rate than yesterday. Oh joy! ... jjjjjjjjjjjjjjjfd zf Add s=gf

Next up is a nap. I'm pretty tired. Sleep at night is hard. Once pain meds are dialed in, sleep should improve. They postulate the is-mmmmmmm pain is what is making s]lv it so hard to focus, wrob-vjio'0- Moore later.as I have ni===JJ it. Sjjjjjjjjjjjjjjjjjjjjjjjj

Friday, June 8, 2012, 8:28 p.m.

Days ... Weeks?

We just got done with our first hospice doctor visit. To sum up ... I am scared.

The doc focused on tuning up meds for the first part of our meeting. We talked about dropping the pain pump and replacing with oral meds –decision to be made next week; adjusting doses of sleep meds to match someone my age – they are used to dosing for 80-year-olds; and increasing my bowel meds – stronger drugs equals more constipation.

Once the paperwork was done, the doc did a physical exam. The

254

first concern was that my O^2 saturation at rest was in the mid-80s – not good, needs to be in the 90s. Upon listening to the lungs, dim on both sides, she grew concerned that the bronchioles were constricted and that there was fluid buildup on the lungs themselves. On listening to the heart, she heard a "third heart" (may be reporting that wrong) – also an indicator of fluid buildup where it shouldn't be. (We already knew about the fluid on the heart from the last hospital stay.) Overall a downward trend with the heart and lungs.

The doc prescribed a nebulizer and a "water pill" to increase the release of fluid from my body. That teamed with increased meds for pain, bowels, and sleep should help me be more comfortable.

The hard news was that if we can't get the lung/heart issues under control, I am in the days/weeks measurement of life. If we can stabilize the downward trend, then I am back to the possibility of months. Most cancer patients upon admit can stabilize and then go for a period of time before they just simply crash – fall off the cliff, so to speak. Sad to say, but that is the hospice best-case scenario.

I know God is faithful to take us through. The kids haven't a clue – and I guess it is best that way. I grieve for Tammy and the kids. This will be a hard road for all of us. God will take care of them as He takes care of me, but I still feel sorrow for leaving them. In the days ahead, we need God's help more than ever.

"God, you know I can't do this. I am done. You know I am scared of what is to come. It is all overwhelming. A large part of me just wants to be done, but another part of me wants as many good days with my family as I can have. You know the days of my life – You've known them since before the beginning of time. Each day has been ordained and has purpose. May You find me faithful in the days remaining. Guard my heart and the hearts of my family against fear that isn't from You. Grant us peace that can only come from You. In Jesus Name, in whom I put my faith and hope, Amen."

Please join us in praying however the Spirit might lead. May His blessings richly flow upon you.

~ *Responses from Family and Friends* ~

Hi Eric, it's your MoTech friend Mandy. I have been following your journal entries for a long time, and WOW ... the strength and beauty in which you write about the experience you and your family are going through is beyond touching. Your faith is inspiring and has brought me closer to God and my faith in an unexpected way. You and your family have been in my prayers for a long time and will continue to be. Peace and hope,   *Mandy B., Intel*

Happy Friday, brother. I hope today was better than yesterday! Cancer sucks. I have been thinking and praying about you, Tammy, and the kids every day. You also might be happy to know that I've shared your story with my small group here in Danville, so you now have an army of fellow believers lifting you and your family up praying for peace, strength, and calmed hearts. You are inspiring more people every day through your profound strength and trust in Jesus and His plan for you. Your faith is proof of God's glory and His love for us. So humbling and true. You are the role model for Phil 4:13! You guys will be on my heart every day and I will stay on top of the updates. Hope you guys get some sunny weather this weekend. Blessings and love to all you guys,   *Christian S., Intel*

... just staring at blinking cursor. not sure what to say, Eric. You are facing down the door that we will all have to go through someday. I am sad and angry that a great guy like you has to go through it, well before you are an old man with many decades of rich life behind you. However, through your faith, you know what awaits you on the other side. You are surrounded by friends and loving family on this side. You will be in the arms of God on the other. I hope they get the fluid situation fixed and you can rest comfortably. I admire your courage and conviction. Keep blogging as long as you can. We like the connection.Rest well,
Mike F., Intel

I, too, am at a loss for words. But I can pray. And I will continue to pray for peace and comfort and all of God's blessings on you and Tammy and your family. We are here with you. Reach out and feel the hundreds of hands across America loving you through your journey. *Pam M., Intel*

~ *Responses from Family and Friends (cont.)* ~

Praying for you, Tammy and the kids. Thank you for using this time to share the Gospel of Truth so boldly,   *Jennie P., Village*

I read your words and it is incomprehensible to me. When I saw you last week, you just looked like you – recovering from something, but not days/weeks from the next stage of the journey. It was unreal to me then. It is unreal to me now. I can't imagine what you and Tammy are experiencing careening from real pain and problems to regular life with kids and family and back again moment by moment. I pray you all find deep peace in being grateful for all you have received in your life. We always want more but, if we focus on what we don't have, we can never have enough. If we focus on what we have been given, we are overwhelmed with gratitude and know we are rich beyond all imagination. May His great love and grace comfort each of you and call you to His great purpose for each of you during this radical period of change. Praying always and all my best to you,   *Kris K., friend*

My heart is so heavy for you and Tammy. You are so loved. Thank you for sharing your honest petition to the Lord. I totally believe you are and will be found faithful.   *Leslie E., Village*

Yes, of course, I will continue to pray for all of you. You have the unique privilege of grieving your own death ... but I'm not sure that makes this process any easier. It was hard for Jesus, too ...
Nancy P., mom of Tammy's friend

I don't know what to say either as I read your words Eric, other than how can this be fair? Fair to a God-fearing man who has done right by life and his family? This may come from recent emotions after losing my father unexpectedly and finding myself parentless within four years. You have been so honest and brave throughout this journey and I want you to know that even though I didn't get a chance to know you well personally, I consider you my friend and I've learned much from you. You are amazing, strong, honest, brave, and a teacher in all that you have shared with us here. I pray that our Lord Jesus Christ cradles you in his arms in the days and nights ahead and gives you the strength to endure many more days with Tammy and the kids. Prayers and strength sent your way,
Ysela B., Intel

Saturday, June 9, 2012, 4:57 p.m.

Short entry

Today is an odd-feeling day. Life goes on. The sun still rises and sets. And yet, my life seems to be drawing to a close sooner than later. How crazy is that.

I find myself and others around me reading such uplifting literature as, "When Death is Near," and other little booklets that inform readers of telltale signs of the last stages of life. My siblings are [here in our living room] pouring over thousands of pictures to find just the perfect pictures for a video montage to be used at my memorial. Wow ...

I should know a bit more in a few days as to how my body is going to respond to the revised medicines. If the response is negative, my time here –by man's count – is short.

Fortunately, I have a very short list of things I want to finish before I go home.

> [Ed. note: Throughout these last months, Eric kept an AR (action required) list beside his bed and marked off items as they were completed.]

Both Tammy and I have recently reflected on how much we've done/gone through. We've traveled far, loved hard, and been blessed deeply. God has been good

Thanks for all the notes of encouragement. They really are touching and motivating – even those who wrote to simply say they don't have words to say. Thanks

Blessings!

258

~ *Responses from Family and Friends* ~

Eric and Tammy, I like so many others are at a complete loss of words. I wish I had positive words of hope and healing, but find myself with prayers for you, Tammy and your kids that are sent to God daily. I have always found you to be an amazing man, father and husband, and in this journey you have again shown me how strong one can be. I love you like my own brother and am a better person for having you in my life. God can and does still perform miracles, and if anyone is deserving it is you!   *Cary M., Tammy's brother*

Eric, thank you for sharing with all of us. Thank you for being so open and honest. Thank you for being the person you are. I pray that the medications kick in and that you have the gift of time.   *Greg B., Intel*

We've been praying the same prayer you have been praying for you and your family. May He bring you and Tammy comfort, may He take away your fear, and may He fill you with His peace and His hope. "You did not receive a spirit that makes you a slave again to fear, but you received a spirit of sonship, and by Him we cry 'Abba, Father.' The Spirit himself bears witness with our spirit that we are children of God, and if children, then heirs-heirs of God and fellow heirs with Christ, provided we suffer with Him in order that we may also be glorified with Him. For I consider that the sufferings of this present time are not worth comparing with the glory that is to be revealed to us" (Romans 8:15-18). "May the God of hope fill you with all joy and peace as you trust in him, so that you may overflow with hope by the power of the Holy Spirit" (Romans 15:13). Know that we are lifting you and Tammy and the kids up before our loving Father and that we love you much.
Melissa and Brian L., close friends

Thank you for your honesty and transparency. Words fail me as I try to pray right now, but the Spirit will intercede and bring you, Tammy, Ellie, Timmy, and the rest of your family before the throne of grace. Hold tight to Him and He will carry you through each moment to come.
Becky J., formerly at Village

Eric, You and Tammy and the kids are continually in our prayers. Your candid words are inspirational. *Anne R. and family, Tammy's friend*

~ *Responses from Family and Friends (cont.)* ~

Eric, I know the choices you have recently made have not been easy, yet your faithfulness continues to be inspirational. Many folks would question God and His decisions as I did when He took my 2-year-old son from me. Reading your posts over the past several months has touched me considerably. Thank you for that. Your journal will be so touching to your children one day. You will remain in everyone's hearts for their lifetime. May God bring you peace. Blessings,   *Debbie L., Village*

Eric, I can't tell you how much of an impact your life has had on mine, even though it's been so many years since ISU [Illinois State University]. As trite as this sounds, your faith and life are an inspiration to me all these hundreds of miles away. May God richly bless the last weeks and months you have here on earth, and in the eternity you look forward to in Heaven. I will see you there, my friend. I look forward to that day!   *Bethany P., Eric's college friend*

Eric, my heart hurts for your family but rejoices for you. You are going to join the party in Heaven and the rest of us have to wait till it's our turn to attend. I love how you've shared your journey; how wonderfully brave and selfless you've been in doing so. The impact you've made is far reaching and I can only imagine you've increased our heavenly family exponentially by your transparency. May God richly bless you. Love,   *Tara F., Village*

Eric, thank you for sharing yourself with us long before CaringBridge came into your life. Thank you for allowing us to minister to you and your family with food. Thank you for allowing us to pray to our God of miracles to heal your body. We know we pray. We know God answers prayer. We know we don't know everything. We have faith. Faith that passes all understanding. Jesus is alive and in Him we rest. "Faithfulness, faithfulness is what I long for. Faithfulness, faithfulness is what I need. Faithfulness, faithfulness is what You want from me." Eric and Tammy, thank you for sharing and showing your faithfulness to the God of all creation. You have mightily stepped into this cancer journey and your faith has held strong. All our hearts' desires are for eternity, for this is not our home.   *Dawn Denice R., Village*

Monday, June 11, 2012, 7:11 p.m.

Not done yet

I am weary. Weary to the bone. Weary in the heart. Weary. A significant part of me wants to be done, and yet I am not.

In the midst of my weariness, God continues to answer our recent prayers to make each day count. Yesterday and today both have included long, deep, faith-centered conversations with younger Christians. I've been able to share out of my experiences to encourage them in their own faith. In both conversations, I have sensed God's Spirit at work.

At the conclusion of today's long dialogue, and after my young friend left, my mom entered the room and said, "That was sure a lot of air for someone who is dying soon." I burst into tears. The tears weren't because she reminded me of my prognosis for a very short life. The tears were because the Spirit convicted me of my push for control once again – I want to die and that is the only option that will do.

If God were to answer the multitude of prayers for my healing now, I'd be mad. In "my" plan, I am ready for eternity – streets of gold, no more sorrow, no more pain. I've paid my dues with the last nine months.

And yet ... how wrong can I be! It appears God is not done with me yet. God has decided my days. He alone will call me Home when it is time. Until then, I have to be ready for living or dying. Each day is His for Him to use me as He pleases. (Forgive me God for taking control again and being unwilling to celebrate Your plan as it unfolds.)

On the medical front – I saw the dentist today for a vexing sore in my mouth. After some basic exploration, he stopped and said he would need to refer me to an oral surgeon. He put a call in to the office and personally asked them to move me to the head of the line. I either have "thrush" – though the place where my sore is, is the wrong place, he still thinks it could be a bad case, or some long Greek name that means my gum is dying away and leaving my jaw bone exposed – very bad for infection. So, I get to call the surgeon first thing tomorrow morning to see when I can get in to have them examine me. (BTW … the mouth issue is most likely a complication from past chemo.)

All of this is somewhat laughable when I think that, apart from God's miraculous healing of my body this side of Heaven, how close to death my body is. I'm not sure how much I'll go through to get rid of the mouth pain. The current load of narcotics is not enough to mask the pain. I do have a topical Lidocaine-hydrochloride oral solution that does a great job of numbing the area, though.

For those curious about expectancy – I don't really know. I am still quite lucid (most of the time) so that would suggest longer than shorter. That said my diet is changing – less, and mostly fruit, and that would indicate some steps toward the end. Ultimately God knows, and He hasn't shared that with me.

Regarding narcotics, my "daydreaming" has become quite real (and funny). Apparently hallucinating is not abnormal. Oh boy. The doc may cut me over from Dilaudid to Methadone (a synthetic narcotic drug similar to Morphine, but with slightly greater potency and longer duration) ... no connection to meth. We'll find out more in the days ahead.

Tomorrow, I meet with the lung doctor. He should let me know how the lung-lining catheter is doing and what the next steps are for that. Not totally sure what to expect. As far as we know, though, everything is going as planned – the fluid output is reducing and the surgical site is healing well.

Thanks to everyone for your prayers, visits, notes, etc. I've especially appreciated the backdoor notes that tell of what God is doing through this site (CaringBridge).

It is a huge encouragement to know God is using this suffering to give glory to Himself. Thanks!

May God richly bless each of you in the days ahead.

~ *Responses from Family and Friends* ~

Our hearts go out to your family these days, as they have been for months now. Know that you are never far from our thoughts, and our prayers are with you all. We trust that our Father will carry each of you in His loving arms and that you will know His peace in an overwhelming way. Eric, your words have blessed us beyond description – how you have walked through this time and what you have chosen to share with us has put much in perspective and drawn us closer to Jesus. Thank you for being willing to share the ups and the downs with honesty. Blessings on you and your beautiful family – He who called you is faithful and we know He will carry you through! With love,
> *Bonnie and Kevin O., missionary friends in Burkina Faso*

Yes, my dear friend, He is not finished with you yet! As you stated, you are having a HUGE (don't mean to shout) impact on so many people. Today you indeed made an impact in the lives of my sons and this is an impact that matters for eternity. You are giving God glory by just "being." You are impacting others Eric on so many levels. Praise the Lord! Thank you for sharing your life with us and with so many others. We uphold you in prayer, we uphold Tammy, the kids, your parents, and siblings, in prayer daily. You represent Jesus, even now. Love ya,   *JerriLyn K., friend*

Eric, I am so grateful for the reminder today. He is in control and He knows what the journey is like. Even your pre-diagnosed days were filled with the same kind of intentionality that showed me and instructed me in my faith. You are such a godly example of "living in community." I thank you.   *Brad G., Village*

You are so right, Eric, God is not finished with you yet. He is still using you in so many ways. Your courage and faith are so encouraging and inspiring. Remember, we will all be Home soon. Some sooner than others, but soon! Praying!!! Love you all much,   *Kathy B., Village*

Eric, thinking and praying for you and your family during this time ... I wish peace for you all. Know that you are making more of a difference then you know ... and He is in control ... With much love,
> *Kelley D., Intel*

[Ed. note: One afternoon, around this time, when Tammy, Eric's dad and I were praying around his bed, Eric asked, "What will you pray when it for sure looks like God isn't going to miraculously heal me here?" I replied, "We will pray that He takes you Home soon!"]

~ *Responses from Family and Friends (cont.)* ~

Eric, each time I read one of your posts, I'm brought back to thinking about things that really matter. My respect for you has consistently grown across our days: in The House leadership, to your wedding, to a "forbidden" motorcycle ride in India, to these last months of faithful, honest journaling. As I told you during our visit the other day, I know that words can be cheap in situations like this. We cry with you over each setback. And rejoice with you over each victory. Thanks for letting us learn alongside you during this difficult journey ... about the things that really matter like Jesus' teachings and what it looks like when someone lives them out.

Ben S., Village

I'm so glad you write that an entry is appreciated even when we don't know what to say, because we really are at a loss for words. Our hearts are heavy as we think of what you and your family are going through. We are praying for peace and comfort for all of you, and physical comfort for you.

Annabelle and John P., Village

A friend and I were once talking about prayer and she mentioned that God had not "released" her yet from a certain obligation she was praying about. Whenever, I struggle with wanting something that doesn't seem to be coming, I come back to that conversation and have to ask God if he is releasing from that thing, that request, whatever. It does sound like God is not releasing you yet from work on this side of the door. I know in my own recent prayers for you I've begun to ask Him if I can be released from praying for your complete healing and He has yet to do it. So I continue to pray even though it seems unlikely and you are weary. You are indeed, I think, not done yet. I pray for strength and peace for you in the days ahead as you press on with His plans for you. All the best,

Kris K., friend

Thursday, June 14, 2012, 9:12 p.m.

Thankful today

Today was a crazy full day … again. My body and mind have rebelled a bunch over the last couple of days –increased pain, bad ability to stay lucid. And yet, I remain thankful for so much.

◆ HERE IS JUST A SMATTERING FROM TODAY:

Practical Love: Imagine 20 voices of believers praying aloud in agreement that God would heal me, praying for my family, praying for God's grace to be poured out. Now change the language you hear from English to Korean. The women from our church's Korean Fellowship (KF) graced our home today. Their love, faith, and expectation that their prayers will be answered humbled me. As I type, I can glance over at beautiful flowers (roses and orchids) as well as an amazing fruit gift basket. Thank you KF for the love you poured out on me and my family.

Help with the Hard Stuff: Just counting today, I've had three pastors visit our home. My Village [church] family is here to help us. I have been encouraged and loved on so much today. Practically speaking, I found out more about planning a memorial service as well as choices to be made with respect to burial. It feels good to be getting more decisions made ahead of time so Tammy has less to worry about should I pass soon.

Checked Off Boxes: Computers are great (when they work). This morning I made good progress – in spite of bouts of being less than sane – toward writing a letter to each Tammy, Ellie, and Timmy. These are hard to craft, but I at least have started the process. Hopefully, momentum is now on my side.

A Renewed Call to Steward: God's reminded me multiple times today that it is about Him and not me. I am called to "steward" – note the word choice. I don't own any of this, He does ... each day He gives me. My job is to apply the skills, talents, and gifts He has given me to the daily opportunities He presents for me to glorify His name. This means that I need to

265

be okay with dying or living. I admit I have grown too comfortable with dying. Being healed at this stage would really rock my world. It would be hard to be so close to finishing and stepping into eternity and then "missing it" with more time here on earth. Glorifying God's name also means being willing to serve as His ambassador. It is my job to remind those around me of the whole truth of God's Word, like that found in Romans 6:23, "For the wages of sin is death, but the free gift of God is eternal life through Christ Jesus our Lord."

Good sleep: The current mix of meds allows me good sleep at night. It also makes me loopy, but I'm okay with that ☺. Even with the sleep at night, I've been quite drowsy all throughout the days, too. Hopefully the recent upping of pain meds should help me to be less sleepy.

Encouraging Words: Today, both the physician's assistant at the lung doc and the hospice nurse made the statement that they are not seeing signs of significant disease progression. I know the cancer is still there, but it doesn't appear to be eating me up too quickly. It would seem God has more days ordained for me yet.

Professional Help: I just handed off a box full of pictures (some on a thumb drive and some hard copies) to my very talented friend. He and his team were the ones who did the video shoot for Tammy, Ellie and Timmy late last year. I'm excited to see what these guys pull together. It should be a very special re-membrance for my family and those who attend any memorial service.

Understanding Employer: Intel has been such an encouragement throughout this process. They are a great company for which to work. I am currently cleared to be off work through the end of September. Perhaps in the days ahead I can screw up enough courage to arrange a visit back to my office. It would be a blast to say "hi" to many of my coworkers whom I haven't seen in months. I miss my teammates.

Snuggles: My kids are great at snuggling. Those minutes I get with them alongside me are more precious than silver. I even had a very hard (death) conversation with Ellie yesterday while we snuggled. She is a stunning little lady who understands so much. It amazes me how well she is processing all this. Timmy, too, is working to understand. We pray he'll keep growing in his ability to grieve and move forward.

Thank you all. You may never know how much of a blessing you are. Even those of you who choose to lurk ... not signing the guestbook, or those who get this forwarded to you ... I know you are out there. We have over 42,000 hits on our site, nearly 2,000 guestbook entries! Wow! Thank you!!! We love your support.

May you find peace, hope, and joy this week in spite of life's travails. May you each understand more and more of God's infinite love, limitless grace, and abounding mercies. Until my next entry – should God allow me the breath of life to write more.

~ *Responses from Family and Friends* ~

Good to hear from you again in your post, Eric. I'm always blessed by how you express your thoughts, and consistently focus on God's goodness, love, and mercy to you, in spite of your circumstances. That's what we're all to do, isn't it? It is all about Him, always. I was reading in Proverbs today, and ran across these verses and thought of you: "Let love and faithfulness never leave you; bind them around your neck, write them on the tablet of your heart. Then you will win favor and a good name in the sight of God and man" (Proverbs 3:3, 4). God bless your tomorrow, Eric. Prayers always for you, Tammy, and the kids, *Terri B., Village*

Eric and Tammy we continue praying and loving you from India! Thankful at how engaged you are online through this process. It helps us to be right there with you. Wishing we could visit! But, sending our love from afar, *Leah K., missionary friend in India*

Eric, thank you for continually reminding me, through your example and your posts, that what happens in my life isn't all about me ... and to live each day with eternity in mind, asking God what He would have me do in each circumstance and day. I definitely need to be reminded of this! Continuing to pray for you, Tammy and the family. *Teckla A., Village*

Friday, June 15, 2012, 7:31 p.m.

"That's typical"

For once, I am typical. Not exactly in the way I want.

The oral surgeon took one look at my mouth and, based on my med history, declared the pesky/painful spot in the back of my mouth to be osteonecrosis. Translated, that means part of my gums have died off and exposed my jaw bone. The exposed part of the jaw bone is also dying. Best case, I go back to his office in two weeks, and the doc pops out the dead bone shard and my mouth goes into healing mode. "Thanks" to the Zometa bone builder that totally helped during chemo, a large part of the jaw could be involved. We'll know more in two weeks, Please pray that this is the minor version of osteonecrosis.

Hospice Nurse Janet came by yesterday and cranked up my pain meds (two times the baseline). Overall, it's a good thing – pain is down. Unfortunately, I am having a much harder time adjusting to the new dosing. I fall asleep at the drop of a hat. My dreams seem very "real" but "weird." And even when awake, my mind wanders; completing sentences is hard. It is hard to stay connected to all that is going on around me – and there is a ton going on around me.

Just writing the few sentences above has been a huge labor. Oy vey! The on-call nurse suggested I give the new dosing another 24 hours, during which time my body "should" adjust better.

We continue to get tons of help. As I type, my neighbor is mowing our lawn and edging in preparation for putting out bark dust and cedar chips. The bark dust and cedar chips were graciously provided by a family in our life group. The same family will be here tomorrow to spread the dust and chips. Earlier today, through a friend of a friend, we had a licensed electrician here to put in better lighting for the backyard. The worker was fast, super nice, gave us a great "friends/family" rate, and kept everything totally legal. Wow.

Another couple in our life group was (at our request) doing tons of research re funeral/cemetery arrangements. They have gone above and beyond the call of duty, going to lots of the local cemeteries and personally looking over everything. In a few days, they will give us a bunch of folders with their top picks. After we find our top pick, they graciously offered to go with Tammy to the cemetery to finalize all the arrangements so that when I pass, Tammy (or hospice) makes a call and everything just goes forward with little, if any, further intervention needed from Tammy.

We feel so loved! Thank you!

Visitors abound still. Today's, I think, win the prize for "furthest away." One friend visited from New York City and another from Dallas, Texas. Pretty cool. As I've said, we so appreciate the support through our friends and family. Gracias!

Despite all the planning for my end to come soon, I also know that God could still heal. So many have been and are praying for God's healing. How amazing would it be for me to miraculously be restored – no lung cancer, no chemo side effects ... just full-on healing. Wow. So many would see and know God's hand in the healing ... healing which would be awesome and totally within the realm of possible. On the other hand, I am at peace with going Home.

I am reminded of Jesus speaking to the hard-hearted, legalistic religious of the day and telling them that even if they saw the dead raised to life, they would still not believe that Jesus is Messiah, the one about whom the prophets of old spoke expectantly and the whole world awaited for salvation from death.

So, why mention the religious? Because I believe that many people today are equally committed to their non-Bible-based belief system (atheist, deist, New Age, Hindu, Buddhist, etc.), so that even if I were to be healed of my cancer, they would fail to recognize the hand of Jesus in my healing.

It is my hope that regardless of a quick passing or a miraculous healing, God would use my suffering to call more people into His family. I look forward to the day in Heaven when I meet people who were called to know Jesus as Savior and Lord in part because of my battle with cancer. How awesome would that be? May God be glorified in my life and even, when it comes, in my death.

Blessings to all!

~ *Responses from Family and Friends* ~

Hello, Eric. Well, your message today was beautiful, just as this day was lovely. Thank you! And we are praying for you, just as you are praying for us. Again, thank you. You are giving all who read your CaringBridge site helpful lessons on faith and love. You and your family are much loved and appreciated. Blessings, *Nancy T., friend of a friend*

As always, your transparency is amazing. I feel blessed reading your updates. I cry for you and your lovely family, even though I don't know you that well. May you continue to feel God's presence and His arms of love wrapped around you and your family. *Jim and Jessie N., Village*

One thing for sure that has come of all this: My children have really become prayer warriors. And who knows how that will translate throughout their lives. We've all prayed for many people with illness, crisis and so on over the years, but I've seen them pray more "deeply," if you will, for your healing and for peace than I've seen them pray for others. God is developing much in them through your life. Just thought I'd share that with you. *Anne B., Tammy's friend*

Erik and I read your entries regularly. We thank God for your life; we know it is not really ending but beginning. Entering eternity with Jesus is the ultimate healing which we all hope to receive. And then we'll rejoice with you someday. Many blessings on you and your family as you walk through difficult times together.
Erik and Charlotte H., formerly at Village

Just checking in to say hello and Happy Father's Day! I'm so glad you are able to be celebrated!! I hope you had/are having a peaceful day!
Laura B., Intel

Amazing. Your last two paragraphs of today's post sound more like you ministering to all of us than the other way around. It's really funny that it should be thus. But what a testament to the strength you have found! Glad the meds are in balance and you can get some rest. I think it would be great to have you visit everyone back at "the farm." Let me know if you need a ride, especially if I can drive the rebel-red Prius! Sleep well tonight, *Mike F., Intel*

~ *Responses from Family and Friends (cont.)* ~

Praising God for His faithfulness to you and your family . To witness the Body of Christ at work is an awesome thing. God ordained every breath you would take and He is not through with you yet! God keep you in the center of His will, Eric!   *Lisa B., friend in Boston*

Eric, your co-workers, even the Canadian ones in Mexico City, miss you too. Thinking of you all the time. Take care,   *Hugues M., Intel*

Eric, I continue to be in awe of you on this journey. I am so humbled by your gratitude. Thank you for reminding me that all of us have something to be grateful for, and of the truth in Him. Praying daily.
Kelley D., Intel

Thanks so much Eric for writing in this journal. I have followed it ever since your dad made me aware of it. The Lord is truly using you as a tool to reach many. For such a young man, you are truly wise and gifted beyond your years. We are praying for you.
Janet S., Eric's dad's high school friend in Colorado

Hey there Eric and family! We are constantly thinking of you guys up here in Alaska. We are eager to come and see you as soon as we get back. We will keep praying for His strength and perseverance for all of you. We love you guys dearly. Can't wait to see you again!
Brian and Melissa L., close friends

God has been using this difficult journey, that is certain! And I continue to be so impressed by both your faithfulness and your perspective. Praying for healing and that God would continue to use your amazing testimony for His glory.   *Lori H., Village*

Eric and Tammy, just wanted to let you know I was thinking about you!   *Ysela B., Intel*

As always Eric, you are a wonderful example of what it really means to be a believer. Thank you for your honesty. Continuing to pray for God's will, strength and peace. Take care my friend.   *Janet J., Intel*

Monday, June 18, 2012, 9:36 p.m.

Loose ends

It feels like I am working hard to wrap up any loose ends. Next to my bed lies an ever-morphing list of "to dos." Thankfully so many friends and family are able to help. The list includes such lovelies as … select a cemetery, plan memorial, decide on crematorium, write letters … to develop a memorial folder, find things for the lobby display, etc. Who knew dying could be so hard ☺.

Thankfully the pain meds are regulated enough that we can begin the week-long transition to Methadone (oral med, no pain pump, hopefully fewer hallucinations). The transition should start tomorrow. Pray that would go well and I could transition quickly.

On the oxygen front, my O^2 saturation levels continue lower than they like. I may end up getting a larger/noisier oxygen concentrator … oh joy! The nurse also ordered a bedside commode for me as I'm not supposed to get up on my own in the middle of the night. O^2 sats are too low for me to safely travel to the bathroom and back. So sorry Tammy! Truly, sorry!

Tears and laughter have blessed our home. Both are so needed as we wait on God's will to be revealed. We hope for full healing here and now, but we also prepare for my Home-going.

Lastly, to all my Intel brothers and sisters, I am drawing up plans with Tim Wood to have an open house Friday, June 22, at RH1 Cornelius Pass from 1:30 p.m. to 3 p.m. – 90 minutes is probably my tops before my energy is sapped. (Found that out the hard way while watching "Avengers" with a good friend over the weekend – 2.5 hours of movie sensory overload comes at a cost.) Slowly but surely I am learning what I can and can't do.

Please lift us up. We need His strength in all the hospice areas

Thanks for your prayers! Keep them coming. And do remember to keep our extended families in prayers, too.

Tuesday, June 19, 2012, 9:00 p.m.

Lost lucidity !=?!

(Rocky post ... apologies if it doesn't read easy. I'm having pain med issues and would love your prayers.)

Hey everyone – imagine with me an offer to switch your meds, lose the pain pump hose connected to your chest and have less side effects overall. Would you go through that door?

I did and have started the transition to Methadone from Dilaudid. Nurse Janet made the first adjustments around 1 p.m. So I chugged some nasty tasting Methadone and Janet backed down my pack while doubling my bolus amount. It has been a crazy adjustment. My legs are in constant motion ... restless.

My connection to reality is dubious. When I close my eyes, dreams (if you will) dance to life. I see things and then participate with the scene only to awake to find my hands and arms in ...motion. In fact while typing this, I'm playing cards with my friend Ben in Illinois with two other players. One other player has a ball cap on the table (Auburn) and is hiding something under it. In reality I sit at the table alone. Thank God that I'm mostly able to decipher real and imagined.

Tammy has had a really tough day too. (I think ... or maybe that is the drugs.) Please be praying that I'd hold up under this adjustment time or, even better, that it would pass very quickly. I believe the oral suspension will be the best drug in the long run. I lose the omnipresent pump bag, and there is more headroom to increase dosage with my pain needs, etc.

Please lift us up in prayer. This is really hard to weather!

~ *Responses from Family and Friends* ~

Eric, Tammy and family, our prayers continue for you all during this difficult time. Eric, your posts and your faith have been a huge blessing. Even in the midst of this, your life has pointed to God. Thank you for sharing it all. One memory that I think of when I think of you is of you playing "Paul" in those "Extreme Makeover: Soul Edition" videos – absolutely spot on and hilarious! Of course I can think of other things too, but mostly I see you with that "thankerchief." Great memories! Praying. Praying. Praying. Love, *Wendy B., formerly at Village*

Praying for everyone! Eric, you are amazing to be thinking ahead on details that are not the most comfortable to deal with, like your memorial service. Believe me, anything you can do or plan now will help Tammy when she does not want or feel like dealing with the "have-tos." You are giving her a gift ... to grieve when she will need it the most. I have seen your insight into Tammy's love needs over the years and am still amazed that you recognize and follow through on them. You are a wonderful, loving husband who knows his wife. God Bless you Eric. Praying for your medication transition, pain, sleep and as you get through your "have-to" list. *Colleen H., Tammy's friend*

Hi, Eric, just wanted to send a quick note to let you know that I am following all of your journal entries, and you and your family are in my continuous thoughts and prayers. You are and will always be my vPro expert. I can't tell you how much it was a pleasure to work with you. You were always available for me when I needed help. Working on brochures, webcasts, online press launch, etc., was great! I am saddened to see you have to go through this. You have touched so many people's lives and hearts, and you will continue to do so. *Tania F., Intel*

Praying for you and Tammy and Ellie and Timmy. Thank you for sharing so much and often. *Jennie P., Village*

One of my most humorous memories of you is when we were all a part of the singles group at Village. We were at someone's home, playing Taboo, I believe. You could not describe the words without using hand gestures. So we made you sit on your hands – and then you couldn't talk! Praying for you and your family always. *Amy S., Village*

Eric, it was so great to visit with you last Friday and meet Tammy and your kids ... they are blessed to have you as their father and life role model. As you posted ... "It's not the advice you give, it's the example you give them." They have a true living example of how faith and trust in God is the source of strength, courage, peace and trust. There is no substitute. My prayer – "Dear Father in Heaven, please release Eric from this pain and help the new meds help his body. Slow this suffering. Father, cover Eric in Your grace and love and let his mind rest so he is comfortable. Father please continue to watch over Tammy and the kids and hold their hearts in Your hand to help remove any fear and uncertainty. We trust You and the plans You have laid out for us. Overwhelm the Heerwagen family with Your healing power. In Jesus name, Amen." Love you dude ... I will never forget the time we spent together. It has restored my trust and faith in Jesus as my Lord and Savior.

Christian S., Intel

Thinking about you, Eric. You are one of the most level-headed people I know – it must be so hard to weather the "daydreaming" and restlessness. Hang in there, buddy, hope you adjust to those new meds super quick!!! *Carissa H., Intel*

Oh BRAVE hearts!! Your view of life and death and TRUST in God's plan even when ... your whole family are incredible ambassadors. Thank you for so consistently sharing so openly. So much to contemplate and apply. the "Gospel according to Eric." Blessings

Karen R., friend of a friend

Eric, your faith is an inspiration to me. Your honesty and humbleness consistently amazes me. Thank you for being an example of intentionally living. While we continue to pray for you we know God is working through you and every one who's gotten to know you. Praise God from whom all blessings flow~ Wrapping you up in a prayer blanket each day!!! Love, *Corinna T., Tammy's cousin*

We are definitely lifting you all in prayer. May God intercede with His comfort, strength and peace for you, Tammy, Ellie, and Timmy. Our petition is for healing and that His arms enfold all of you now and in the days ahead! We love you all so much!

Bonnie and George J., Tammy's aunt and uncle in Arizona

Wednesday, June 20, 2012, 9:47 p.m.

Seeing things

Another busy day. Another hard day of hallucinations.

The nurse practitioner visited today to adjust medication levels. Based on what I reported, she, in agreement with the hospice doc, decided to drop the Methadone and reset original values on the Dilaudid with the pain pump. Unfortunately, the next few days should be full of hallucinations, etc., as what I have in my body works its way through. Sigh.

Oh ... and my eyesight is worsening some, I have a low-grade headache, and very restless legs. All of these could point toward some worsening by way of brain tumor – or it points toward old age ☺.

I won't write much more – my focus is just not there. I struggle so with wanting to go Home soon, or see full physical healing this side of Heaven, very soon, too. I am just plain weary.

Here's what I know in all of this – God is in control; it is His timing. I must yield to Him even when I don't feel like it.

On Friday [two days from now] I am excited to visit with my coworkers. Watch Friday afternoon for a special "open letter" to all my friends at Intel.

Praise God even in what may be the last chapter of this life here on Earth. He is good! No matter what the outcome.

He is impacting lives around the world through my sharing. I am no superhero. Rather I am an ordinary human – lost without Christ. Through Christ I can do all things.

Thanks! Keep the prayers and encouragement flowing.

~ *Responses from Family and Friends* ~

I'm one of the "lurkers" you mentioned a while ago. I attend Montavilla Baptist Church where I heard about you, and I have been praying for you and your family. Thank you for your openness in the good times and bad, and your testimony as you trust God through it all. (Psalm 42)   *Barb B., friend of Eric's brother*

You're awesome, Eric! Yes, so giving all the way to the end! I look forward to your journal entries. You inspire me and others. I was thinking the other day about how you would dress up like a clown for the back-to-school parties at church. How the children were drawn to you. Their eyes would light up when they saw you and the balloon animals you would make. What a great memory! Thank you. Love,   *Jenny R., Village*

You ARE one of God's super-heros here on earth ... you are fighting evil every day and sharing the message of Christ ... an amazing feat!!! I wish I could be with you and the Intel family on Friday. Please know that smiles, hugs and love will be in the air from your ASMO buds in Massachusetts.   *Laura B., Intel*

Praying you and your family will find peace in God's healing plan. Thank you, Eric, for taking us along this faith-building life experience and daily testimony – a beautiful gift. Love you guys!
                                              Tina H., Tammy's cousin

Hi Eric, Thank you once again for sharing, even in your struggle. Yes, God is good all of the time, no matter what the circumstances. Our answer will come soon enough, because He is also an on-time God. I am heartsick over what you are going through. It is all so very awful, but I know too that God will give you everything you need to see this through with victory. Thank you for staying strong and showing us all just how this kind of thing is done well for God's glory. You are my super-hero. Know you are loved and well prayed for, as is your entire family. Blessings,   *Kathy B., Village*

Our God is an awesome God. And your testimony is awesome. I can't help but shed some tears at today's message. I feel so badly for what you and Tammy are going through. But I also have to feel a bit overwhelmed at the shiny reflection of God's Glory you have been through this battle. You are fighting the good fight. The battle belongs to the Lord no matter the outcome.   *Candace L., Village*

Friday, June 22, 2012, 10:21 a.m.

"Intel" we meet again...

Friday morning – I made it! Yesterday I felt like I was going to die. The nurses assured me it was just a transition from Methadone back to Dilaudid. (...phhh!) The symptoms are somewhat improved but still very troubling. I very much hope to be well enough to attend this afternoon's Intel gathering. Part of me sees this as God honoring a commitment I made some 15 years ago. (Cue reflective music..., fade lights down... ☺)

After having to take a semester off from college, for having severely lacerated my right arm, and taking a semester of two credit hours at Western Seminary while working at Wendy's as a shift manager, I realized that it is entirely possible to please God no matter where I am. If God calls me to be a witness at Intel, then that's my place to serve Him. I don't have to fly to the other side of the world to witness to unreached tribal groups.

Over the last 14 years I've had opportunity to model my values in front of my co-workers, but I've not often had the chance to open the Bible and share how someone can have Jesus in their life as Lord and Savior. Now within the last nine months, I've had unprecedented reach throughout Intel, modeling my values and sharing the good news of Jesus Christ.

Would I have ever asked to gain this reach through Stage IV lung cancer? No! And yet I see God using something meant for evil to do a good work.

Today's gathering hopefully gives me a last chance to interact with my co-workers, and, as [has been attributed to] St. Augustine, "We are called to go out into all the world and preach the gospel, and only if necessary use words." (The words, however, will come tomorrow via CaringBridge, as I post an open letter to my fellow Intel employees. Even if you don't work for Intel, feel free to read as well.)

While the hospice nurses remain convinced this is just transitional effects from the medicines, my heart is telling me this is my time to go Home. I'm ready.

Regardless of when I go Home, I remain convinced of God's

goodness, love, grace, mercy and long-suffering.

As always, thank you for faithfully following my journey and praying with us. Thank you also for your comments and encouragement. I look forward to the day when we will all meet face to face in eternity.

Near term, please pray for peace as I face the great unknown of dying, and for God's extra-special presence for my family as they grieve my loss. Thanks!

Eric did make it to the gathering where he was greeted by friends and co-workers who had come from all across the country to see him one more time.

~ *Responses from Family and Friends* ~

You are and always were more than just 'a coworker,' mon ami. Nice to see you today, even in less than optimal conditions. We still have some work to do in the tech front, I guess :-) Looking forward to seeing you again. Hope it could be soon. Keep inspiring us. Thank you.

Hugues M., Intel

Eric, thank you for the inspiration that you are and the strength you have shown these last months. I'm sorry I won't be able to join you and the Intel crew at RH1, but I hope you are able to enjoy a couple laughs and stories with them. You and your family are in my thoughts and prayers.

John K., Intel

Eric, I know we worked together ages and ages ago, but I just wanted to send you a quick note to let you know that I am sorry to hear about all you and your family have been going through. You are in my thoughts and prayers.

Kelli G., Intel

A virtual "Hello," since I am not at Intel Portland to do it in person today. If I were there, I would tell you that your writings have been closely followed and inspiring to me. Thank you! You will be remembered.

Kevin McK., Intel

Eric, thinking of you today as you are surrounded by Intel love.

Lissa F., Intel

Open Letter to My Friends at Intel
(and other curious readers)

Dear Friends,

First, my sincere apologies for doing this letter in Word rather than "foils" [a computer programming language]. You will also likely notice a strong absence of TLAs (three-letter acronyms), again, apologies. You'd think after 14 years with Intel, I'd know better. ☺

This last September I was enjoying a very cool job at Intel and looking forward to more opportunities to change the world. A former manager of mine would often remark on how unique it is to go to work in the morning and truly be able to impact the world. I know my job had its share of challenges, frustrations, and annoyances – every job does. But when I think of the main task I had in September, how cool. I was given carte blanche rights to redefine our [Intel's] strategy for training retail sales professionals. In fact, toward the end of September I was flying off to New York to select the cast for our new video series. I had so much fun at a real casting agency on the 60-something floor of a Manhattan office building. Working with another agency, we were on track to really change the game in [Intel's] U.S. retail sales.

On October 1, 2011, everything changed. The leg pain the doctor had called "Achilles tendinitis" turned out to be something much more insidious. In the ER that night (just before I was to make yet another flight to New York), the medical staff informed my wife and me that I had a significant deep-vein thrombosis [blood clot] in my left leg, pulmonary embolisms [blood clots] in both lungs, and a swollen lung lymph node. I was admitted that night.

As the days progressed, the investigation began. At that time, everyone all but ruled out the "C" word in someone of my age with my health history. But, by the end of October, we knew without doubt it was Stage IV non-small-cell lung cancer.

Some cancers, like lymphoma, are curable. The patient goes through a lot of hideous chemo, but the hope is that the cancer cells will be 100 percent obliterated. My cancer, however, is called only "treatable." In other words, the main push for chemo and other treatment is to extend my lifespan beyond the average 8-12 month expectancy. Barring miracles and/or scientific breakthroughs, the cancer would be with me until the day I die.

As many of you know from following my daily travails on CaringBridge, the ride we've been on has been anything but smooth:

Making well over a dozen trips to the ER;

Roughly half that many hospital stays;

Lymph node surgery;

Full-on, near-death anaphylaxis from a chemo drug – nurses weren't expecting that!

Heartrending conversations with our two children (ages 7 and 4);

Rejection of oral meds preventing further blood clots, leading us eventually to very painful [self-administered] shots in the stomach twice daily;

Brain surgery (I have a scar or two from the Silence-of-the-Lambs-like halo they installed for the procedure);

A broken tooth the weekend just before chemo;

Complications galore – for example, fluid buildup in the lung lining that led to surgery to remove fluid and to install a permanent catheter for daily draining. (They took 4L of fluid from the lining in the surgery.);

Results informing us we could dial down chemo and go on to maintenance ... only to find out just before maintenance that a whole new round of chemo was in order;

Discovery of chemo-caused oral necrosis of the jaw (we're still unraveling what all that means)

And, the list goes on ...

At the end of May, I made the decision no one wants to make. I chose to go on to hospice. By definition, hospice means everyone expects me to die within the next six months. Medical focus shifts from treatment to comfort care.

I write this letter to you from my hospital-style bed in my home's living room. Oxygen is fed me through a cannula, and pain meds are on a 24/7 drip into my body. Next to my bed is a 7"x4" pill container full of meds. On our refrigerator is a bright pink POLST form, instructing any medical responder to avoid life-saving measures and just allow death to come naturally.

Throughout all of this, my family and I have experienced the life-changing nearness of God. We wholeheartedly believe that God is faithfully carrying us through this ordeal. He has not missed a step. The cancer didn't catch Him off guard, nor have any of the other mishaps along the way. He remains in control, despite our illusions to the contrary.

He allowed the cancer, an evil illness reflecting the brokenness of the world in which we live, to enter my body, and in His sovereignty He is using this cancer to positively impact the lives of thousands. Through the CaringBridge Guestbook, I read of lives changed as they follow my troubles. Many see God's hand in what otherwise would be a hopeless battle against cancer.

My family and I have been so blessed through the care we've received these last nine months: real love shown us by those near us and even those on the other side of the world, prayers offered, gifts sent, lawns mowed, hugs given, simply waiting with us, countless hours watching over me, watching over our children ... and the list goes on.

We've been astounded at the "coincidences" God orchestrated in His sovereignty: A perfect [school] teacher for our daughter; getting our estate in order "just in case" right before my illness; my parents and sister all relocating nearby just before all this; my brother (the CEO of a company) taking every Friday off this year [enabling him to spend time with Eric]; and my resolving projects from my last job and leaving current job projects at a stage where my teammates could most easily pick up and run with them ...

Others have asked me if I know why I got lung cancer. The short answer is, "no." I've not smoked or done anything else that would increase my risk factors. Given that, many leap to the conclusion that the God I believe in is a capricious and mean-spirited deity set to smite me for fun. Although I've been tempted to believe that myself at times, I know otherwise.

Even in the darkest hours when I wept by myself at the prospect of cancer and all that it meant, I had to believe God would take "that which is meant for evil and turn it to good."

The best example the Bible offers is the life, death, and resurrection of Jesus Christ. Despite humanity's initial rejection of God's love through Adam and Eve, God chose to provide a way for all who choose to join the family of God, finding forgiveness for the wrong we do and certainty of eternity with God.

Even on the most hopeless of days, I am reminded that life in this world is a mere blip against the joyful eternity with God that I am promised. I also find hope in knowing my family and many of my friends share my faith in the risen Savior and Lord Jesus Christ; we will spend eternity together.

This eternity goes well beyond wearing togas, playing golden harps, and watching adorable angels flit about. This eternity is the renewal of creation as it was meant to be. Cancer will be no more. Sin will be no more.

As the Bible says in Revelation 21:3 – "… 'Look, God's home is now among His people! He will live with them, and they will be His people. God Himself will be with them. He will wipe every tear from their eyes, and there will be no more death or sorrow or crying or pain. All these things are gone forever.' " (NLT)

Intel truly is changing the world in which we live. Lives are improved with our technology; innovations that didn't even exist 50 years ago have revolutionized our daily lives. We are the "sponsors of tomorrow."

However, for change that is eternal, change that is lasting, change that strikes men and women at the core of who they are – that can only come through Jesus Christ. He alone can forgive us our sin; He alone can give us eternity with God. As the Bible says, "For the wages of sin is death, but the free gift of God is eternal life through Christ Jesus our Lord." (Romans 6:23)

I hate the cancer raging inside of me, but I firmly believe God is using my short time of suffering to further change the world for His glory and His honor. I know lives are impacted through my faith story; many have written in to share how God is using this to change them.

It is my prayer that God uses my story to change your life too. What an awesome thing it would be to see you in eternity.

In my 14 years at Intel, I've shared friendships with many of you. If I pass before I see you again here on this side of eternity, know that I hope to meet you again on the other side. May God bless you with His nearness and may your hearts respond to the truth of His Word.

Your coworker,
Eric Heerwagen

~ *Responses from Family and Friends* ~

Eric, (typing this from the Intel shuttle) Was so great to see and bear-hug you today, Bro! Know that our next hug will be different but even better in His presence! Hoping to see you again soon! Your friend,

Fred J., Intel

I am truly humbled by your spirit. I will not forget you, my friend.

Jon O., Intel

One of the best "open letters" I've ever read. Your passion and commitment has and will continue to change lives. Thank you for that.

Andy T., Intel

It was really great to see you at the Roadhouse today, and meet Tammy and your dad. I know a lot of us were suffering from the "don't know what to say" condition, but it was good just to be in your company again. Seeing you with all the "Intellians" made me think of a couple things I do want to say (consider it out-of-cycle 360 feedback): You are a very talented marketeer, and the work was always better when you had a hand in it. Classic example was the original vPro messaging, which you were instrumental in crafting and that held up for at least three years. That's "eternity" in Intel time. I'll miss working with you. You are a caring and conscientious dad. We had a great conversation at Oregon Gymnastics one night while our kids were in their classes. The love and joy you take in your kids was self-evident. Thanks for coming out today, and to Tammy and your dad for helping to make the trip. Keep the blog going. We love hearing your voice in the world. Good rest tonight!   *Mike F., Intel*

~ *Responses from Family and Friends (cont.)* ~

What a gift God has given you, Eric, to be able to write and to share your heart during this time while dealing with all of the side effects of the medications! You have been able to write so clearly, so vividly in sharing Christ, His love and His message. We certainly don't understand how. God doesn't ask us to understand, does He? Only to trust Him. " 'For I know the plans that I have for you,' declares the LORD, 'plans for welfare and not for calamity to give you a future and a hope.' " (Jeremiah 29:11 – NASB). Then, my thoughts go to Psalm 23:4, "Even thou I walk through the valley of the shadow of death, I fear no evil; for Thou art with me. Thy rod and Thy staff, they comfort me." (NASB) God has promised to be with us as we even walk thru the valley of "the shadow of death," so He will definitely be there to walk thru the real journey. These words are as much for my personal comfort and strength as for you and your family at this time in the face of all you are encountering. God is faithful, isn't He. We all love you and care for you, but He loves you with a perfect love and cares for you beyond all and everything that any of us could ever do! Goodnight, Eric! Peace and sweet dreams!   *Gloria W., Village*

Eric, it's been an honor to know you and to enjoy your love and fellowship. I wish that I had the words to convey my affection and appreciation for you, but I don't. Here's to good friends, laughter and joy. If I don't see you soon, I'll see you a bit later. And at that time, I'll thank you once more for being a friend. Grace to you in Jesus, dear brother.
Jeff H., Village

My heart breaks for you. We are praying for you and your family. I can't imagine how hard all of this is for you guys. The only consolation is that it sounds like you are so close and prepared to meeting our Lord. In a way, that is so exciting. I'm sure you've thought about it a lot. What it will be like, opening your eyes and seeing Jesus and being surrounded by the heavenly hosts. Wow! It's like you are going on an incredible journey! Unknown in a way, but also known. I look forward to celebrating at the wedding supper of the Lamb with you and all of our brothers and sisters in Christ. God be with you and your precious family. We love you,
Maya L., Village

~ *Responses from Family and Friends (cont.)* ~

Good morning, Eric. I have so enjoyed reading your updates. Your faith in God is an inspiration to me and it should be to others, even to those who do not yet profess Him. You have preserved and remained faithful through all of sadness, emotional pain, and physical suffering. You have run the good race. The "Open Letter" was heartfelt and highlighted your positive attitude as you recounted the numerous blessings you and your family have received throughout this journey. I am sorry I wasn't able to join you last Friday and rejoice together in the promise we have from our God. I will continue to lift you up in prayer – take care brother and may you find peace and comfort throughout the day.

Mike T., Intel

Please know that we are wrapping you all up in our prayers. You have been such an example of living in faith; even during the toughest times your trust and faith never shifted. What a living example and testimony you have been for your kids, and for us. You've touched more lives than you will ever know by sharing your story. We are the lucky ones who get to say that you made a difference in our faith and lives. You pulled us into your lives at such a tender chapter, and we all got just that much closer. You help us live intentionally. Always, no matter what. Just wanted you to know that. Please know that your life has made a difference. Thank you for sharing your faith. Love you all,

Corinna and Brian T., Tammy's cousin and husband

Eric, Well, this is the fourth attempt to write something that would sound cohesive and sensible ... but in truth … I'm at a loss. While my heart is so heavy and tears are so close, my spirit is comforted by your words of Truth. Thank you for living your life fully to glorify Jesus. You have challenged me and encouraged me all at the same time. I am praying for you, Tammy and the kids, and the rest of your family members – that you each will feel the Lord's strong, gentle arms around you, carrying you. I know He is near and knows the perfect timing of everything. So thankful that this isn't "good-bye;" looking forward to being in His presence and worshiping all together, whole bodies, and no tears!

Cheryl T., Village

[There were 323 responses in the guestbook
from June 1-27, 2012.]

Wednesday, June 27, 2012, 10:56 a.m.

At Home with Jesus

Dear CaringBridge Friends,

This is Brian, Eric's brother, writing to you today. During the days since Eric's last post on Friday, there was a dramatic decline in his health which resulted in his passing away very early this morning. We will miss him more than words can say. But greater than that is the unspeakable joy in knowing that he is with Lord – no more pain, no more sorrow.

Eric's life is a shining testimony of God's miraculous impact in a life. And through Eric's life, God will continue to impact other lives as well. Over the last almost nine months, the outpouring of love, encouragement and service to Eric and Tammy, and to all the family, has been so generous and abundant. Heartfelt thanks to each of you.

Thank you again,
Brian Heerwagen

Dear CaringBridge Friends

Thanks again for so many who are praying, for the words of encouragement, and the many wonderful acts of love and service.

Your notes were such an encouragement to Eric during his journey and we are so thankful for that. Please continue to pray for the kids as they adjust; they are doing amazingly well so far and are happy that Daddy is no longer in pain and that he's in Heaven. That was Ellie's main comment this morning when I talked with her. Timmy kissed the hospital bed and said, "Bye-bye Daddy," and said he's happy Daddy doesn't have cancer anymore. We wish he could have lived here for many more years without cancer, and we really do miss him so much already, but we trust in a good God and we are taken care of.

Thanks,
Tammy

Friday, July 6, 2012, 3:48 p.m.

From Tammy

Continued thanks to everyone for the prayers, and also the flowers, cards, visits, hugs, etc. We are doing OK – missing Eric horribly but starting the healing process. This morning the kids made, or at least started, a video where they talked about things they remember and loved about Daddy ... hoping this will be something that helps them through the years since they are so young and memories fade. We're working on letting the tears out when they need to come, but also feeling fine about laughing and having fun. I'm guessing we'll work on that for years and years to come.

Thanks again for all the love shown to the kids and to me. We really do appreciate it. We are so happy for Eric that he is no longer in constant pain – rather in Heaven enjoying everything immensely we're sure!

This will be a process for us as we learn how to live life without him. I keep having things come up that I just want to talk about with him, jokes he would love that I want to share with him, advice on how to handle things that I want him to give me, etc., etc. We'll adjust, but it will take time. I'm trying to just be thankful for what we do have – and what we did have. And what a gift we had ... as hard as it was these past months, knowing what we were up against gave us the opportunity to do and say all the things you want to before good-bye.

Thanks again for all your notes and support,
Tammy

[Editor's Note: Eric's memorial service was held at 5 p.m., Sunday, July 8, at Village Baptist Church in Beaverton, Ore. The church was filled to overflowing, while those unable to attend watched a simulcast. Just as Eric had planned, there was a strong Gospel message and a clear message of his certainty of life with Jesus for eternity. The greatest desire of his heart – that many others would see and seek eternal life with our sovereign, loving, and good God – was clearly presented.]

~ A Mother's Prayer ~

"Father, God, I praise you for your steadfast love, mercy, wisdom, and sovereign plan. Thank you especially for giving me the privilege of being Eric's mom. However, as that mom who prayed her "baby boy would grow into a man used mightily by God," you know that his being diagnosed with incurable Stage IV lung cancer was not what I had in mind. That news was devastating.

"Thank you for your grace and power that carried me when I could barely stand up under the shock and grief of it. You never left me even when I was angry and argued with you at first. Your Holy Spirit gently guided me to a deeper awareness that – You are God; I am not. You gave to me, and continue to keep me in, that safe place with Jesus where daily you show me your love, presence, and sovereign control – no matter what.

"Father, thank you for reminding me that Eric was your boy long before he was on loan to me, and that surrendering him and submitting to you was what you wanted. I praise you for Eric's walk with you from age 4 on. Thank you for growing him into a man of integrity and kindness; one with a lovely family, a healthy church, involvement in missions; a man with a servant's heart who was a respected leader in all aspects of his life. A mom couldn't ask for more. I praise you for the countless family members, friends, and friends of friends who answered your call to come alongside in prayer and in practical ways for Eric and his family during his cancer battle and since his Home-going.

"Being part of Eric's story is an honor and a joy, Father. Your allowing me to share in his last nine months is precious beyond price. We spent time remembering, laughing, crying, answering questions, saying whatever still needed to be said, and praying.

"Lord, thank you for giving Eric steadfast faith, hope and joy in you; for gifting him with the ability to clearly write and speak your truth, even in the midst of great suffering. I do miss seeing him, hearing his great big laugh, and feeling his huge warm hugs.

"There are times when I mourn not being able to enjoy his every-day presence, or even share a phone call. But, through it all, Father, I praise you because I know exactly who he is with, and I rejoice that he is healed. Thank you for giving me the deepest peace in knowing without doubt that I will see him again – at Home with you for all eternity."

I, along with countless others,
praise you, Father God, for the privilege
of having been allowed to join in the journey
with Eric, a man you called to
"Carry Jesus' Cross"
a man who
"Finished Well and was Found Faithful!"

The Challenge

Eric's life verse was Psalm 92:12-15:

"The righteous flourish like the palm tree and grow like a cedar in Lebanon. They are planted in the house of the Lord; they flourish in the courts of our God. They still bear fruit in old age; they are ever full of sap and green, to declare that the Lord is upright; he is my rock, and there is no unrighteousness in him."

Though Eric's time on earth was short, and he didn't reach old age, may his legacy of faith and of "bearing fruit for the Lord" continue.

Thanks in part to hearing so many people say how God changed their lives through Eric's story in CaringBridge, I am more convinced than ever that God intends our life experiences to involve more than just ourselves. We are His "living stones" and He is at work in us, often using one another to shape and transform us to fit together – to be used and seen as the functioning and loving Body of Christ.

If you are reading this now, you likely have read Eric's story. You know his deepest hope and heart's desire was that you be brought to a moment in your life – perhaps this very moment – when you know God is calling you to make a choice.

If you have never answered God's call to follow Jesus –
choose to do so right now.

If you already are a Jesus follower –,
choose right now to be more intentional and faithful
in following Him.

**Choose today to
"Finish Well – Be Found Faithful."**

~ *Acknowledgements* ~

My heartfelt thanks to our all-knowing Father God for allowing me the privilege of working at his direction over the last seven years to bring this book into being. He is the one who planted the seed while Eric was still here on earth. And, in the days since Eric's homegoing:

God has caused this project to take deep root.
He has gently and lovingly guided me
through each season of working and waiting.
He has caused this book to grow and take shape;
guiding in the necessary pruning and trimming
to make it strong and healthy.
He has shed his light and water
through seasons of growing.
He has brought it into full bloom.

May God's message of hope and love,
shared in this book, be used by Him
to produce beautiful blooms that grow
to bear fruit in the lives of all who read it.

My deepest appreciation for those who have prayed for me as I processed (and reprocessed) all the materials, photos, design, and production of this book. Special thanks to those of you who were first readers along the way; your counsel and feedback were invaluable.

Thanks especially to Art, my dearly-loved husband of 57 years. He has been my greatest support and encourager throughout the production of this book and for all the years before.

CPSIA information can be obtained
at www.ICGtesting.com
Printed in the USA
FSHW020334240121
77932FS

9 781545 679807